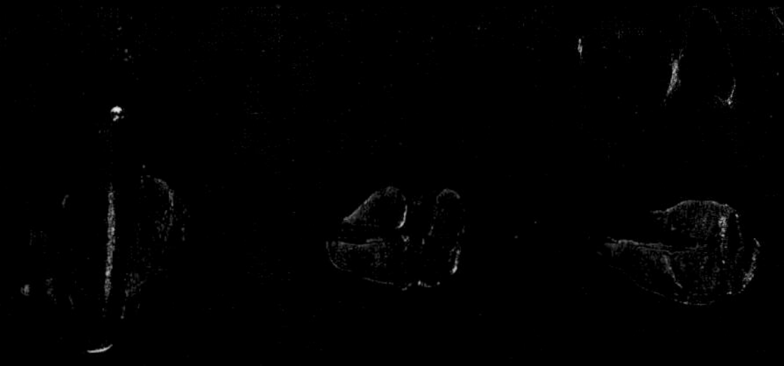

MARK WAID · PETER KRAUSE

IRREDEEMABLE

VOLUME 5

Ross Richie - Chief Executive Officer

Mark Waid - Chief Creative Officer

Matt Gagnon - Editor-in-Chief

Adam Fortier - VP-New Business

Wes Harris - VP-Publishing

Lance Kreiter - VP-Licensing & Merchandising

Chip Mosher - Marketing Director

Bryce Carlson - Managing Editor

Ian Brill - Editor

Dafna Pleban - Editor

Christopher Burns - Editor

Christopher Meyer - Editor

Shannon Watters - Assistant Editor

Eric Harburn - Assistant Editor

Neil Loughrie - Publishing Coordinator

Travis Beaty - Traffic Coordinator

Ivan Salazar - Marketing Assistant

Kate Hayden - Executive Assistant

Brian Latimer - Lead Graphic Designer

Erika Terriquez - Graphic Designer

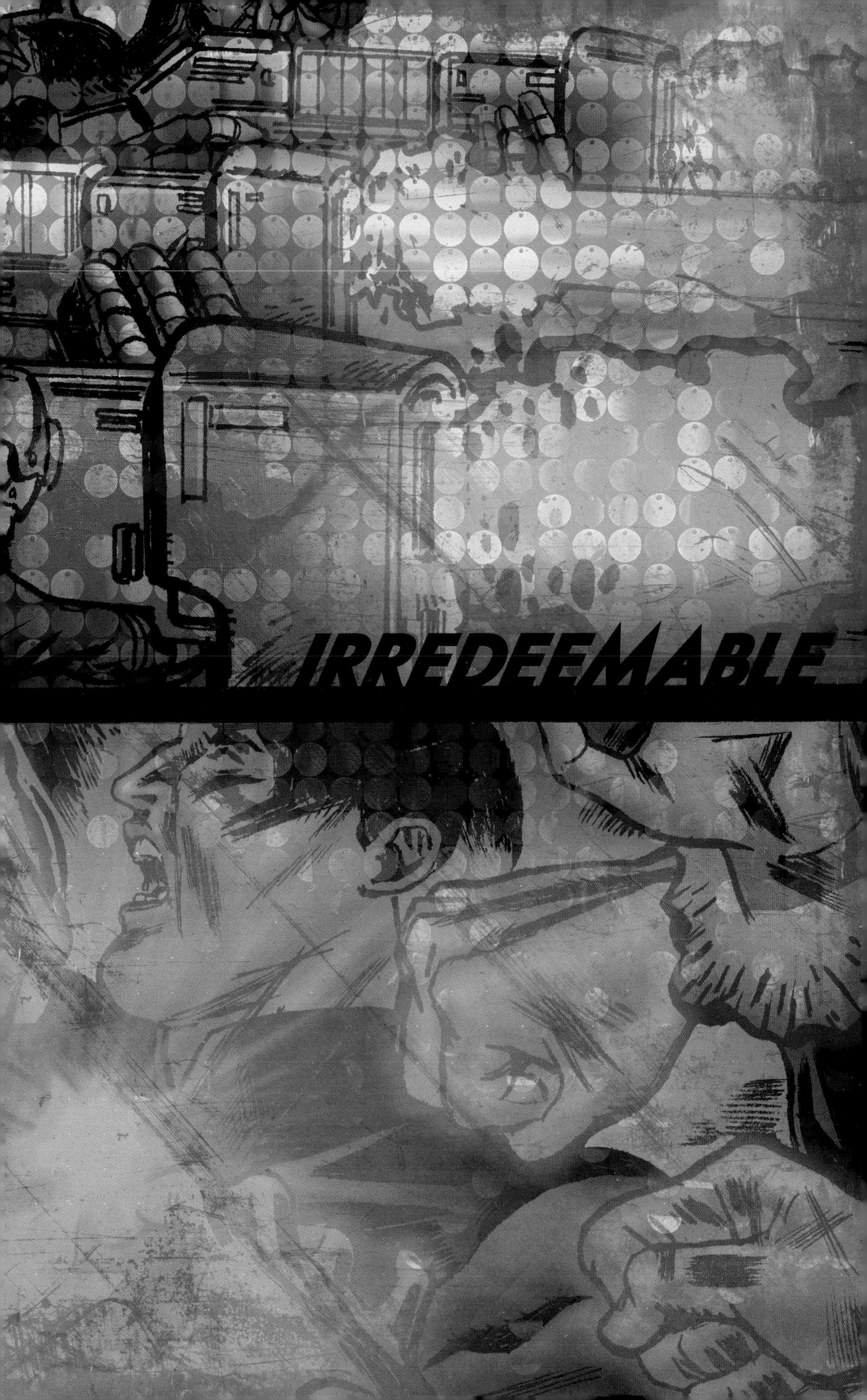
IRREDEEMABLE

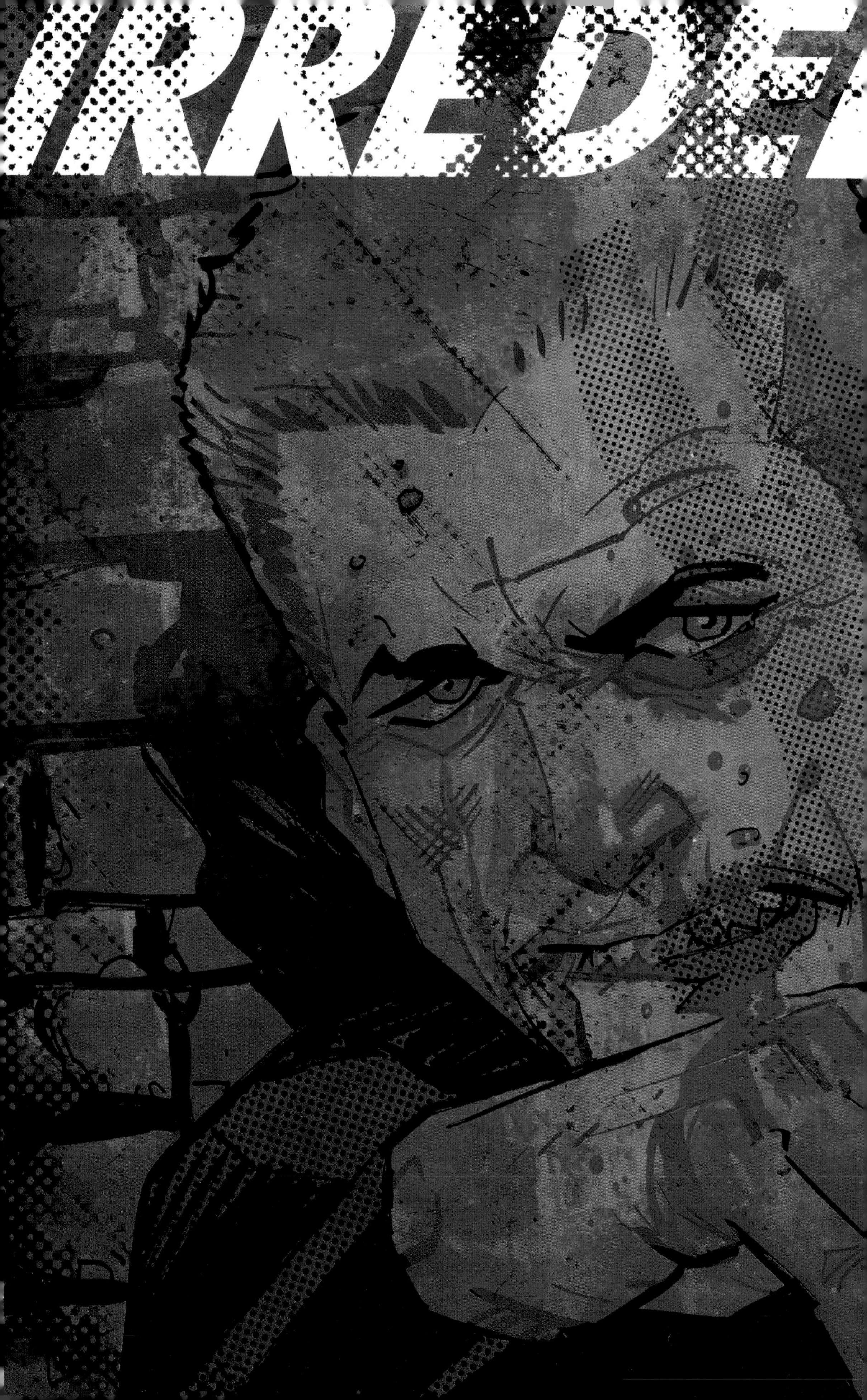

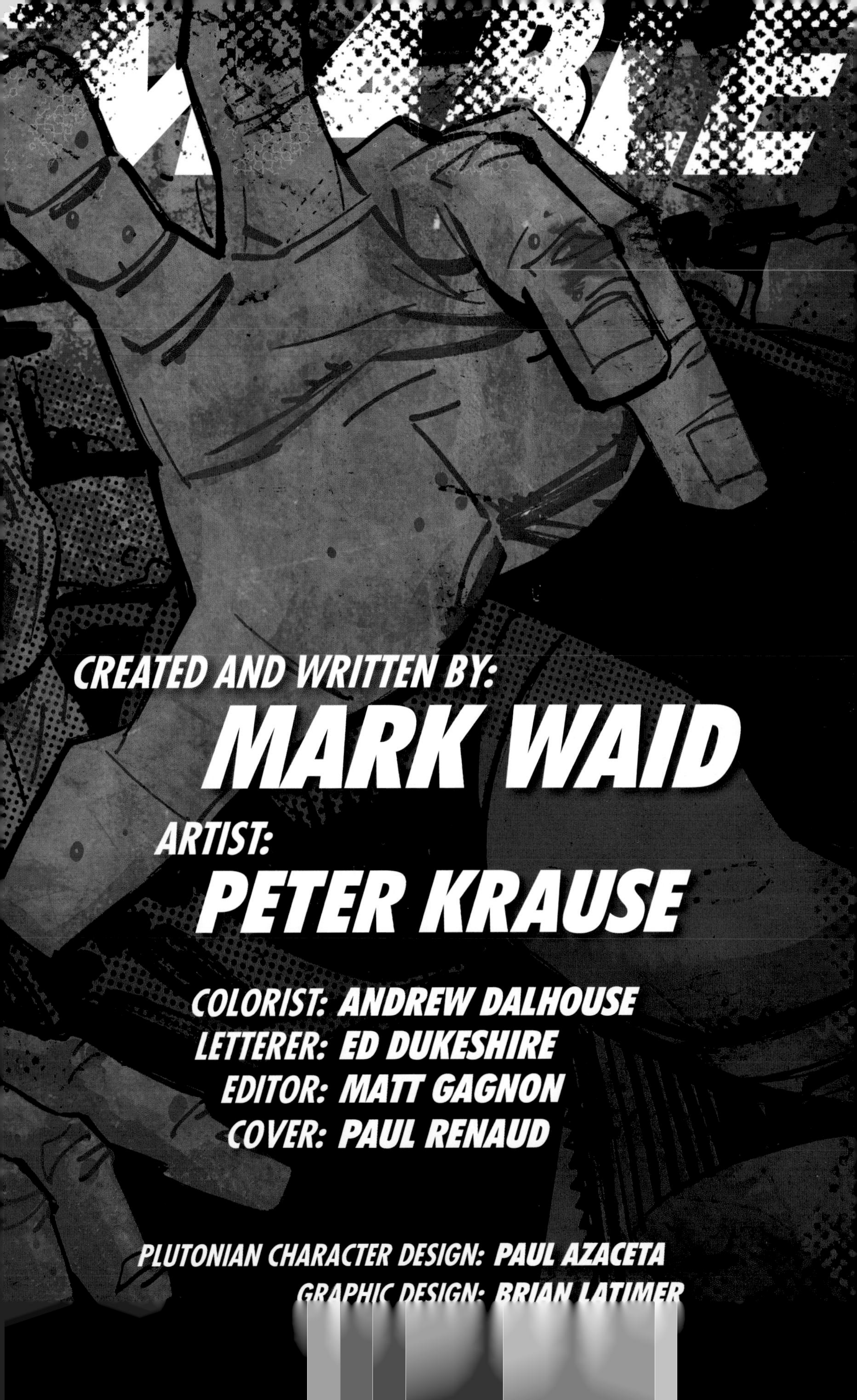

CREATED AND WRITTEN BY:
MARK WAID

ARTIST:
PETER KRAUSE

COLORIST: ANDREW DALHOUSE
LETTERER: ED DUKESHIRE
EDITOR: MATT GAGNON
COVER: PAUL RENAUD

PLUTONIAN CHARACTER DESIGN: PAUL AZACETA
GRAPHIC DESIGN: BRIAN LATIMER

CHAPTER 16

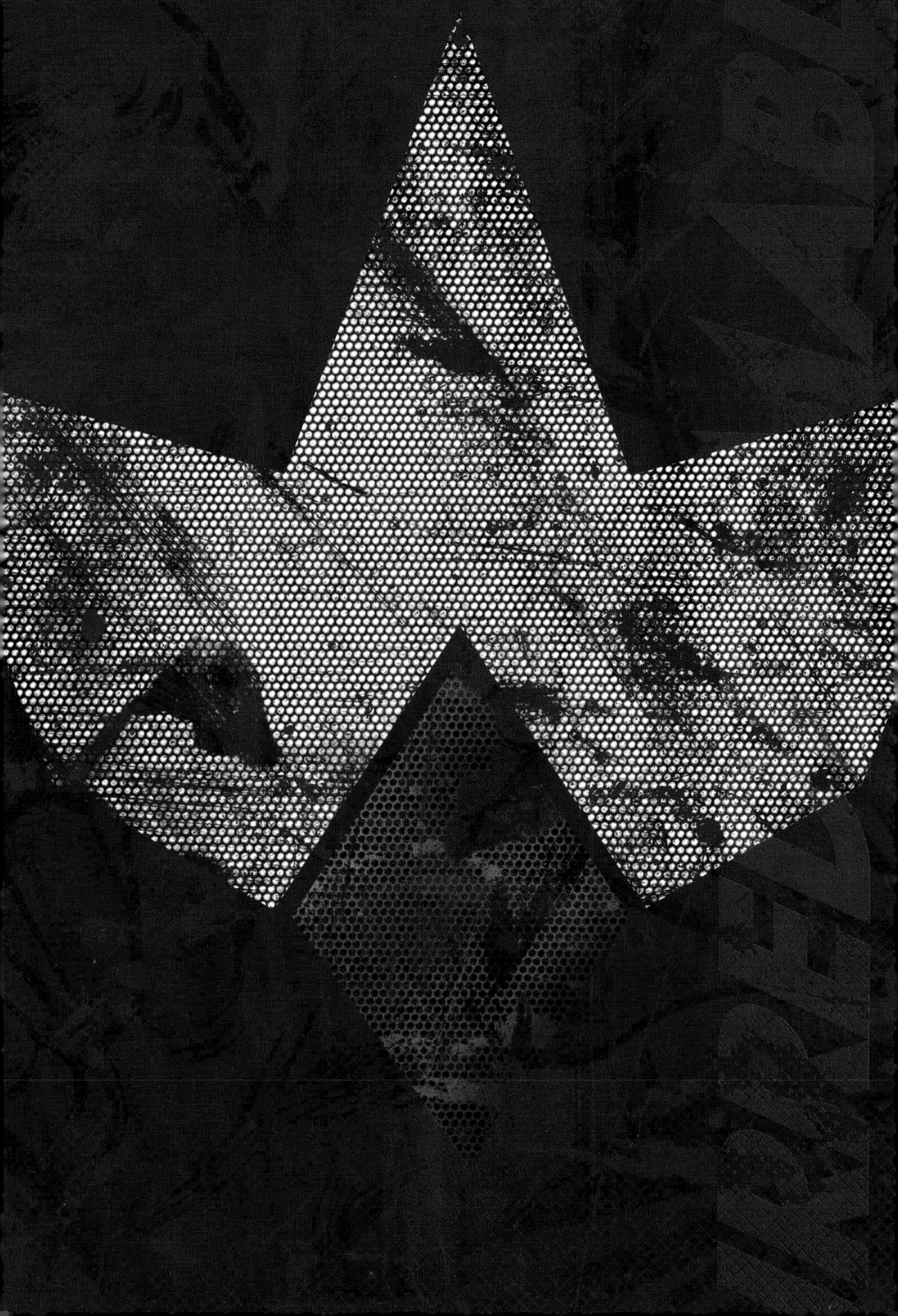

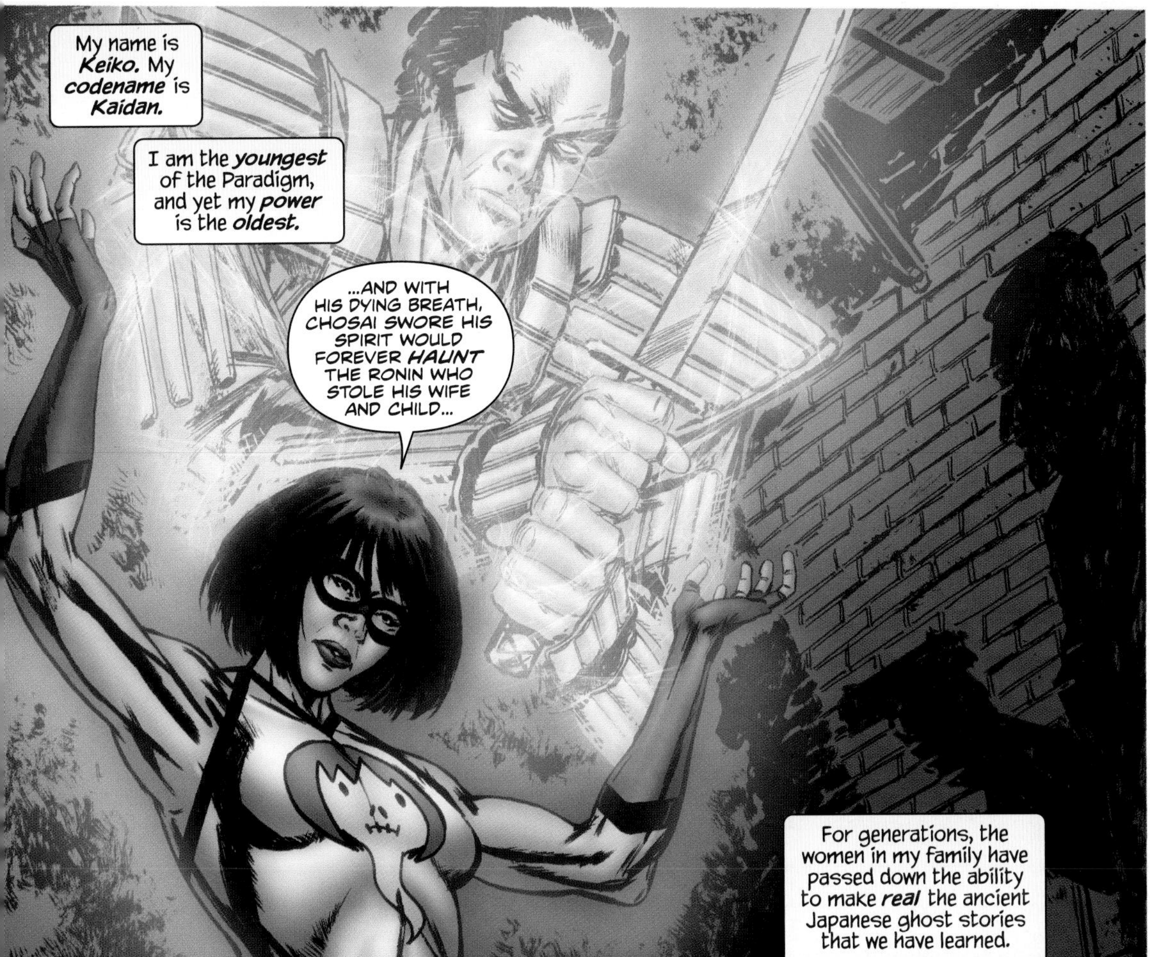
My name is *Keiko.* My *codename* is *Kaidan.*
I am the *youngest* of the Paradigm, and yet my *power* is the *oldest.*
...AND WITH HIS DYING BREATH, CHOSAI SWORE HIS SPIRIT WOULD FOREVER *HAUNT* THE RONIN WHO STOLE HIS WIFE AND CHILD...
For generations, the women in my family have passed down the ability to make *real* the ancient Japanese ghost stories that we have learned.

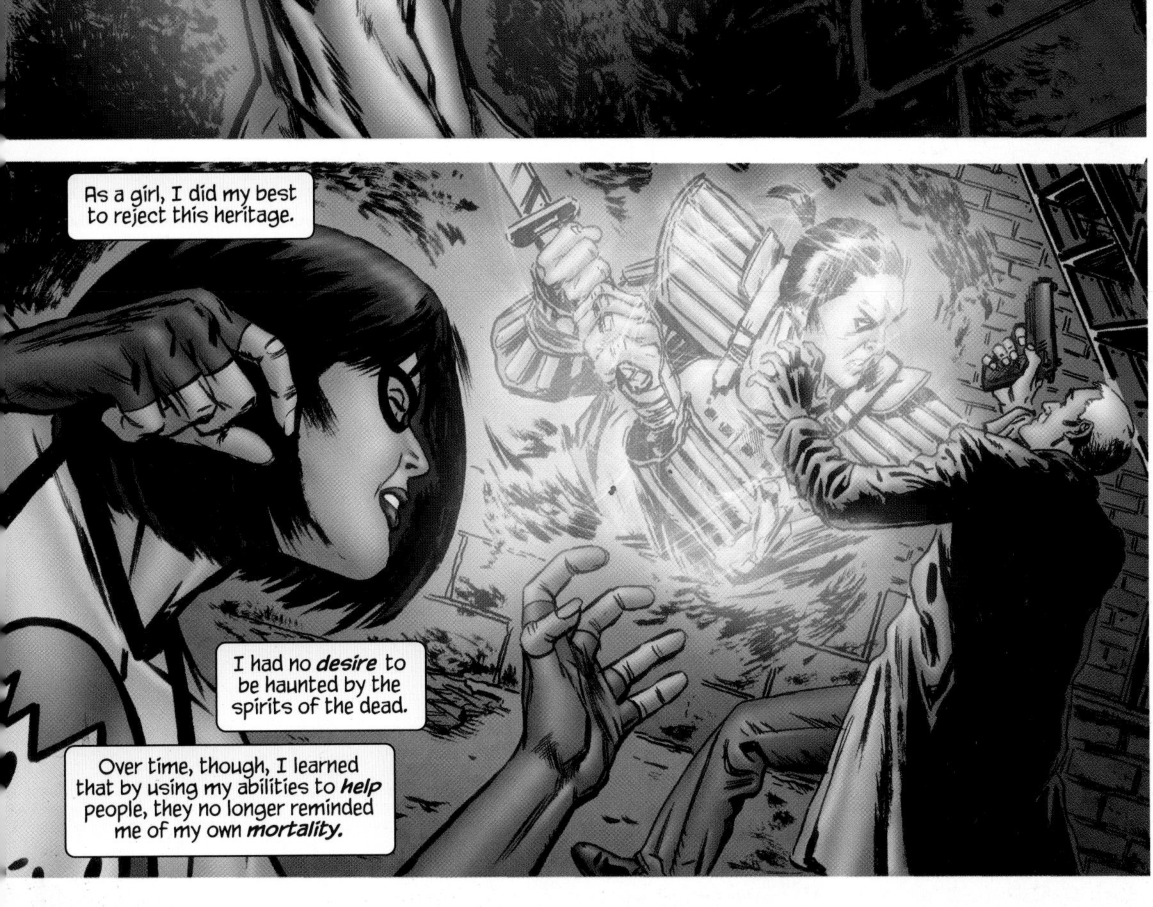
As a girl, I did my best to reject this heritage.
I had no *desire* to be haunted by the spirits of the dead.
Over time, though, I learned that by using my abilities to *help* people, they no longer reminded me of my own *mortality.*

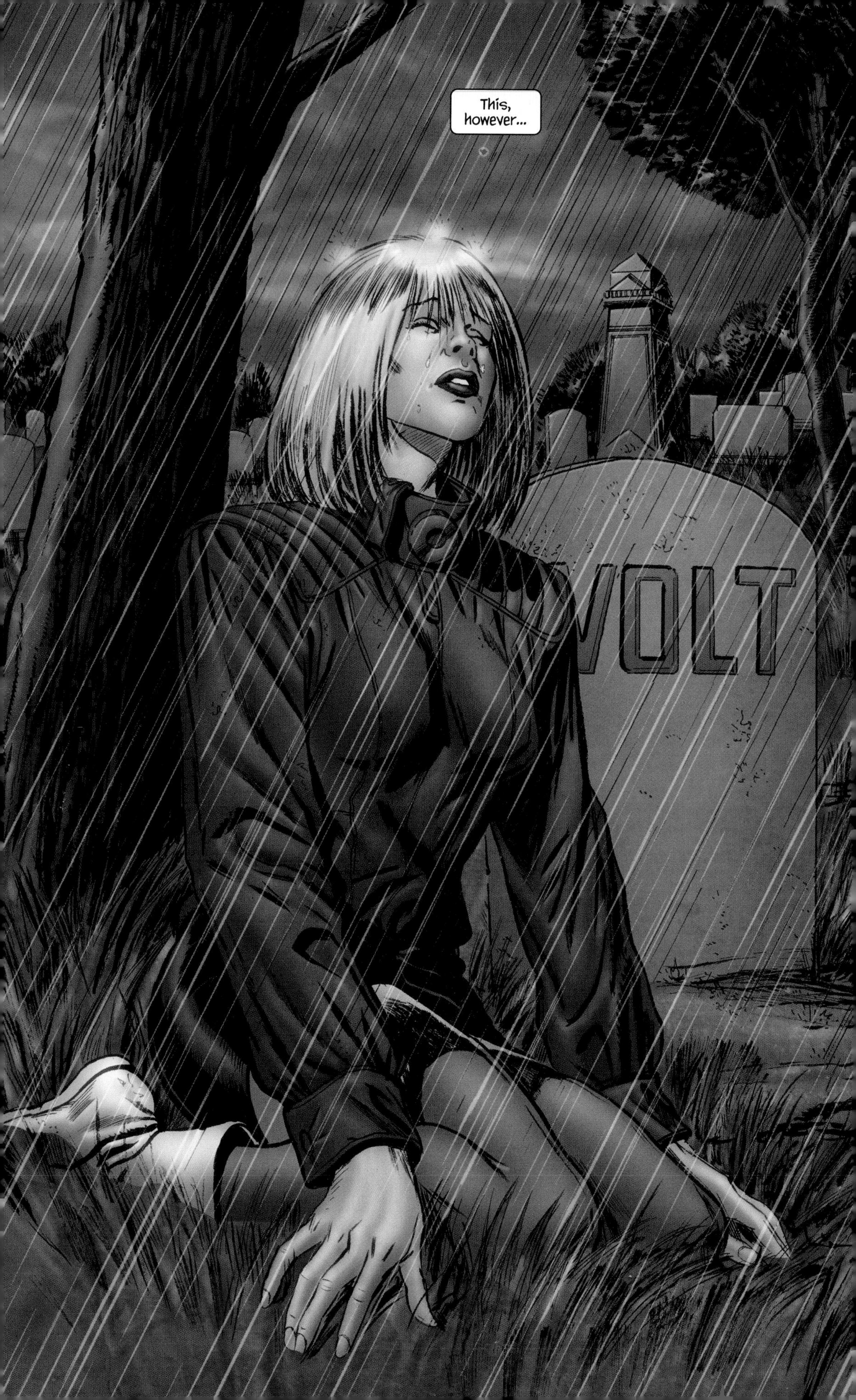
This, however...
VOLT

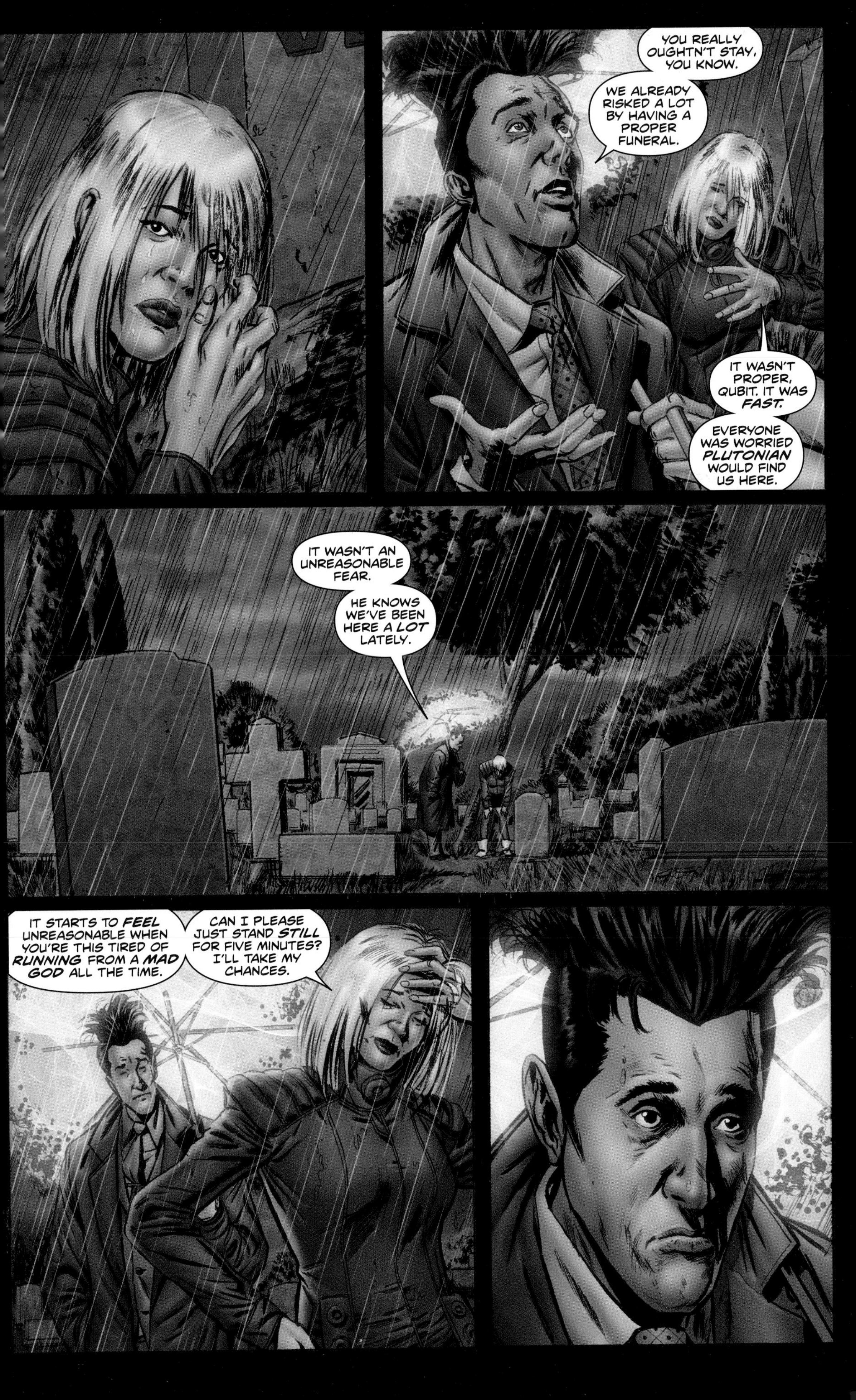
YOU REALLY OUGHTN'T STAY, YOU KNOW.
WE ALREADY RISKED A LOT BY HAVING A PROPER FUNERAL.
IT WASN'T PROPER, QUBIT. IT WAS *FAST.*
EVERYONE WAS WORRIED *PLUTONIAN* WOULD FIND US HERE.
IT WASN'T AN UNREASONABLE FEAR.
HE KNOWS WE'VE BEEN HERE A *LOT* LATELY.
IT STARTS TO *FEEL* UNREASONABLE WHEN YOU'RE THIS TIRED OF *RUNNING* FROM A *MAD GOD* ALL THE TIME.
CAN I PLEASE JUST STAND *STILL* FOR FIVE MINUTES? I'LL TAKE MY CHANCES.

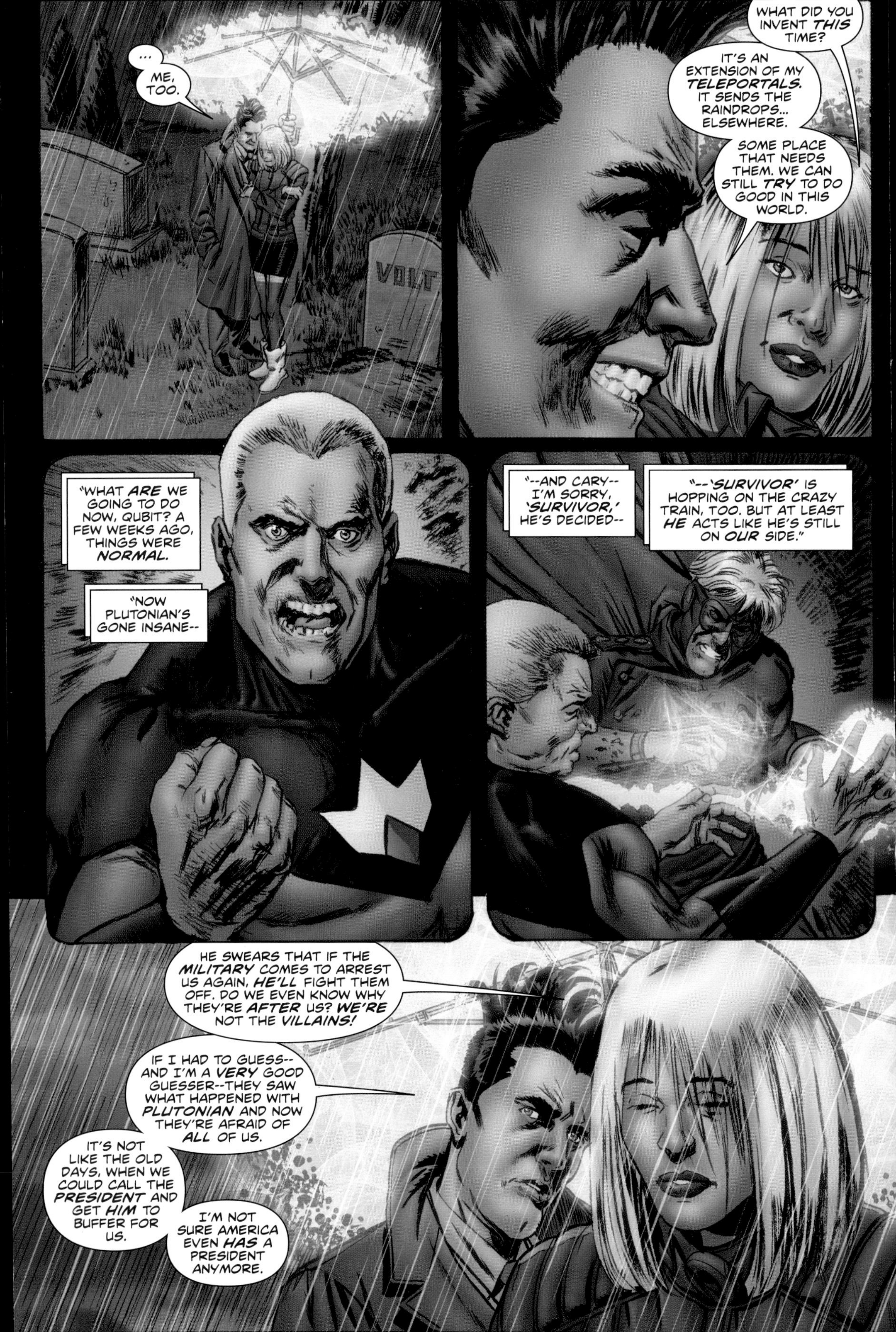
...
ME, TOO.
WHAT DID YOU INVENT THIS TIME?
IT'S AN EXTENSION OF MY TELEPORTALS. IT SENDS THE RAINDROPS... ELSEWHERE.
SOME PLACE THAT NEEDS THEM. WE CAN STILL TRY TO DO GOOD IN THIS WORLD.
VOLT
"WHAT ARE WE GOING TO DO NOW, QUBIT? A FEW WEEKS AGO, THINGS WERE NORMAL.
"NOW PLUTONIAN'S GONE INSANE--
"--AND CARY-- I'M SORRY, 'SURVIVOR,' HE'S DECIDED--
"--'SURVIVOR' IS HOPPING ON THE CRAZY TRAIN, TOO. BUT AT LEAST HE ACTS LIKE HE'S STILL ON OUR SIDE."
HE SWEARS THAT IF THE MILITARY COMES TO ARREST US AGAIN, HE'LL FIGHT THEM OFF. DO WE EVEN KNOW WHY THEY'RE AFTER US? WE'RE NOT THE VILLAINS!
IF I HAD TO GUESS-- AND I'M A VERY GOOD GUESSER--THEY SAW WHAT HAPPENED WITH PLUTONIAN AND NOW THEY'RE AFRAID OF ALL OF US.
IT'S NOT LIKE THE OLD DAYS, WHEN WE COULD CALL THE PRESIDENT AND GET HIM TO BUFFER FOR US.
I'M NOT SURE AMERICA EVEN HAS A PRESIDENT ANYMORE.

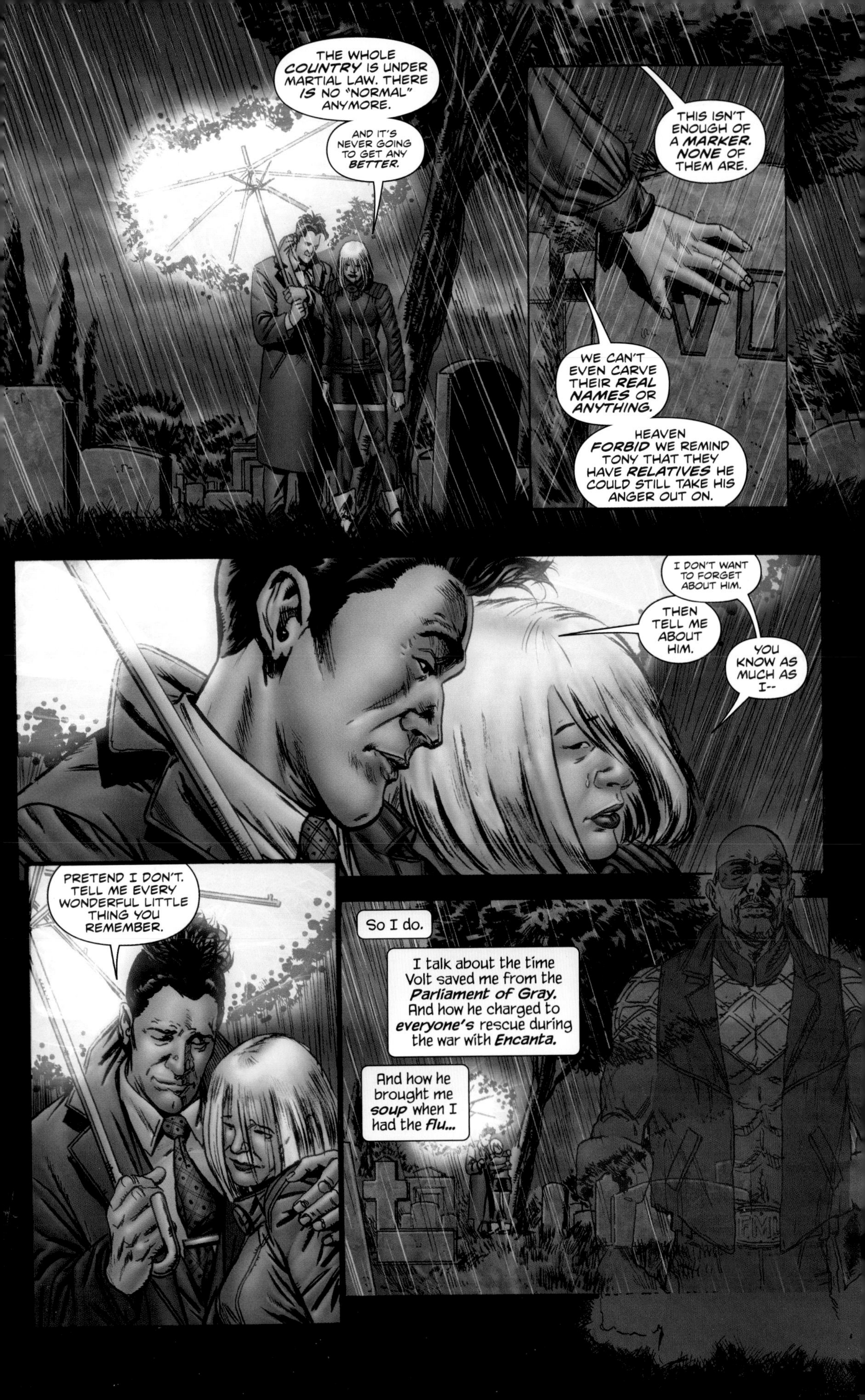
THE WHOLE COUNTRY IS UNDER MARTIAL LAW. THERE IS NO "NORMAL" ANYMORE.
AND IT'S NEVER GOING TO GET ANY BETTER.
THIS ISN'T ENOUGH OF A MARKER. NONE OF THEM ARE.
WE CAN'T EVEN CARVE THEIR REAL NAMES OR ANYTHING.
HEAVEN FORBID WE REMIND TONY THAT THEY HAVE RELATIVES HE COULD STILL TAKE HIS ANGER OUT ON.
I DON'T WANT TO FORGET ABOUT HIM.
THEN TELL ME ABOUT HIM.
YOU KNOW AS MUCH AS I--
PRETEND I DON'T. TELL ME EVERY WONDERFUL LITTLE THING YOU REMEMBER.
So I do.
I talk about the time Volt saved me from the Parliament of Gray. And how he charged to everyone's rescue during the war with Encanta.
And how he brought me soup when I had the flu...

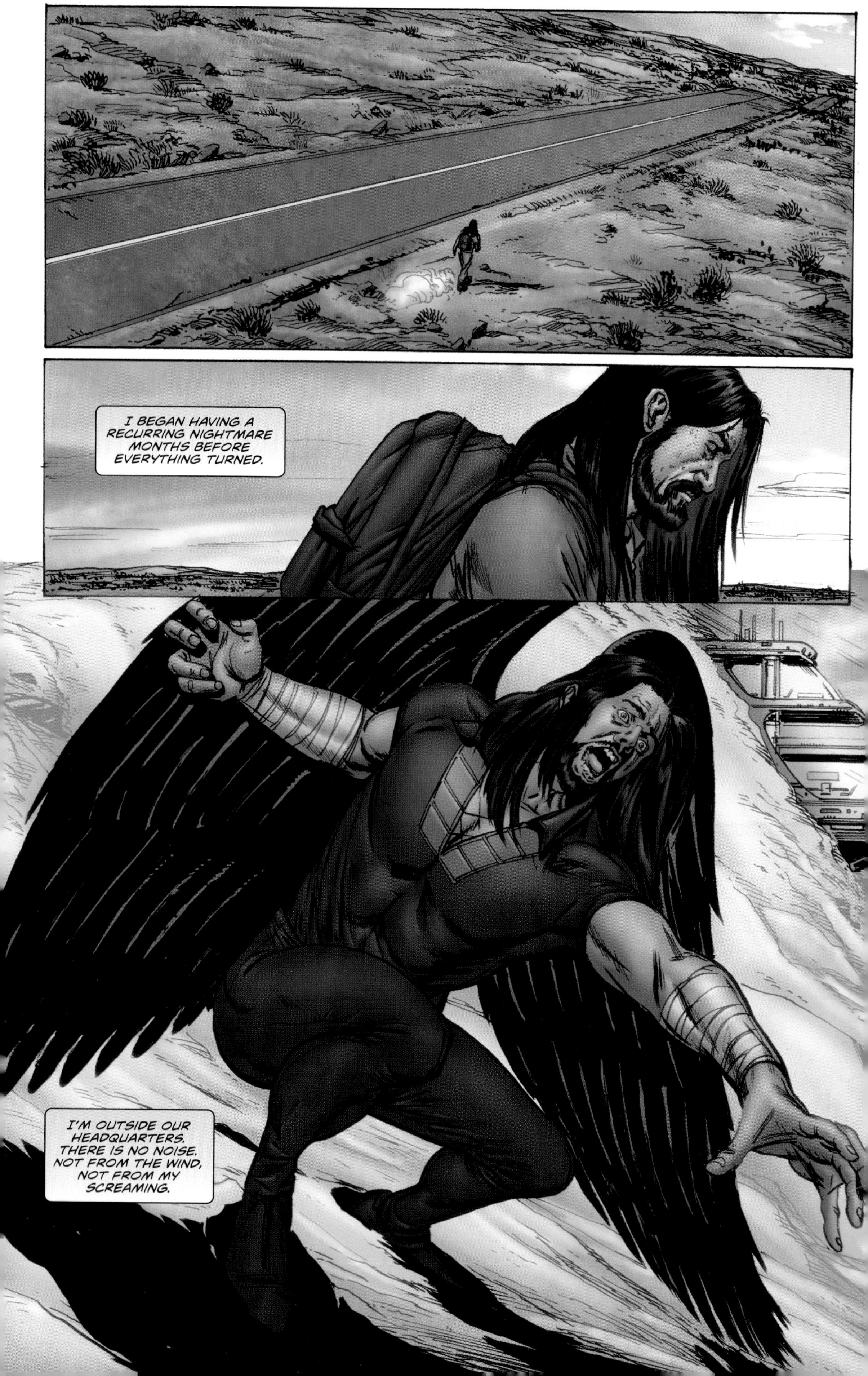
I BEGAN HAVING A RECURRING NIGHTMARE MONTHS BEFORE EVERYTHING TURNED.
I'M OUTSIDE OUR HEADQUARTERS. THERE IS NO NOISE. NOT FROM THE WIND, NOT FROM MY SCREAMING.

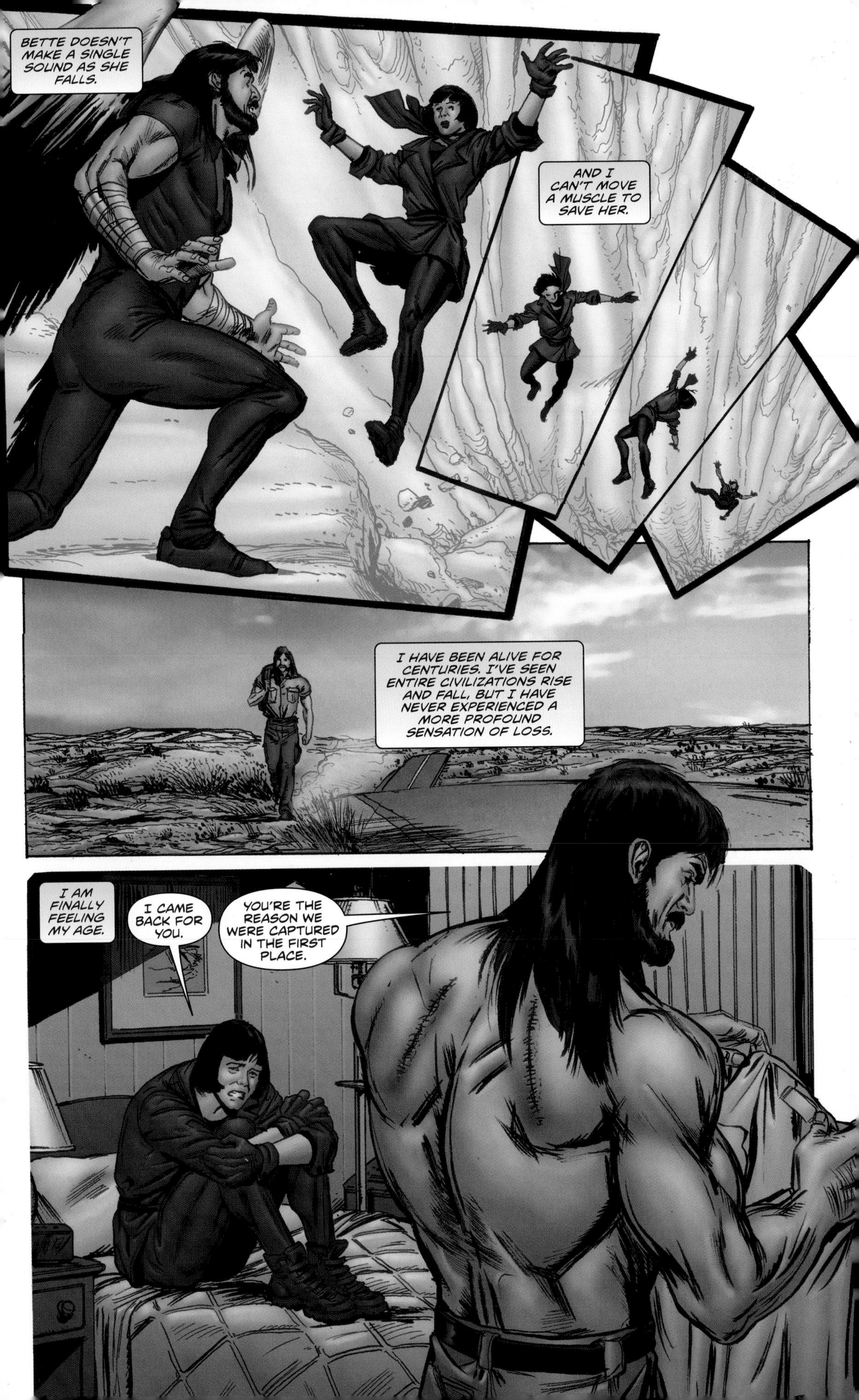
BETTE DOESN'T MAKE A SINGLE SOUND AS SHE FALLS.
AND I CAN'T MOVE A MUSCLE TO SAVE HER.
I HAVE BEEN ALIVE FOR CENTURIES. I'VE SEEN ENTIRE CIVILIZATIONS RISE AND FALL, BUT I HAVE NEVER EXPERIENCED A MORE PROFOUND SENSATION OF LOSS.
I AM FINALLY FEELING MY AGE.
I CAME BACK FOR YOU.
YOU'RE THE REASON WE WERE CAPTURED IN THE FIRST PLACE.

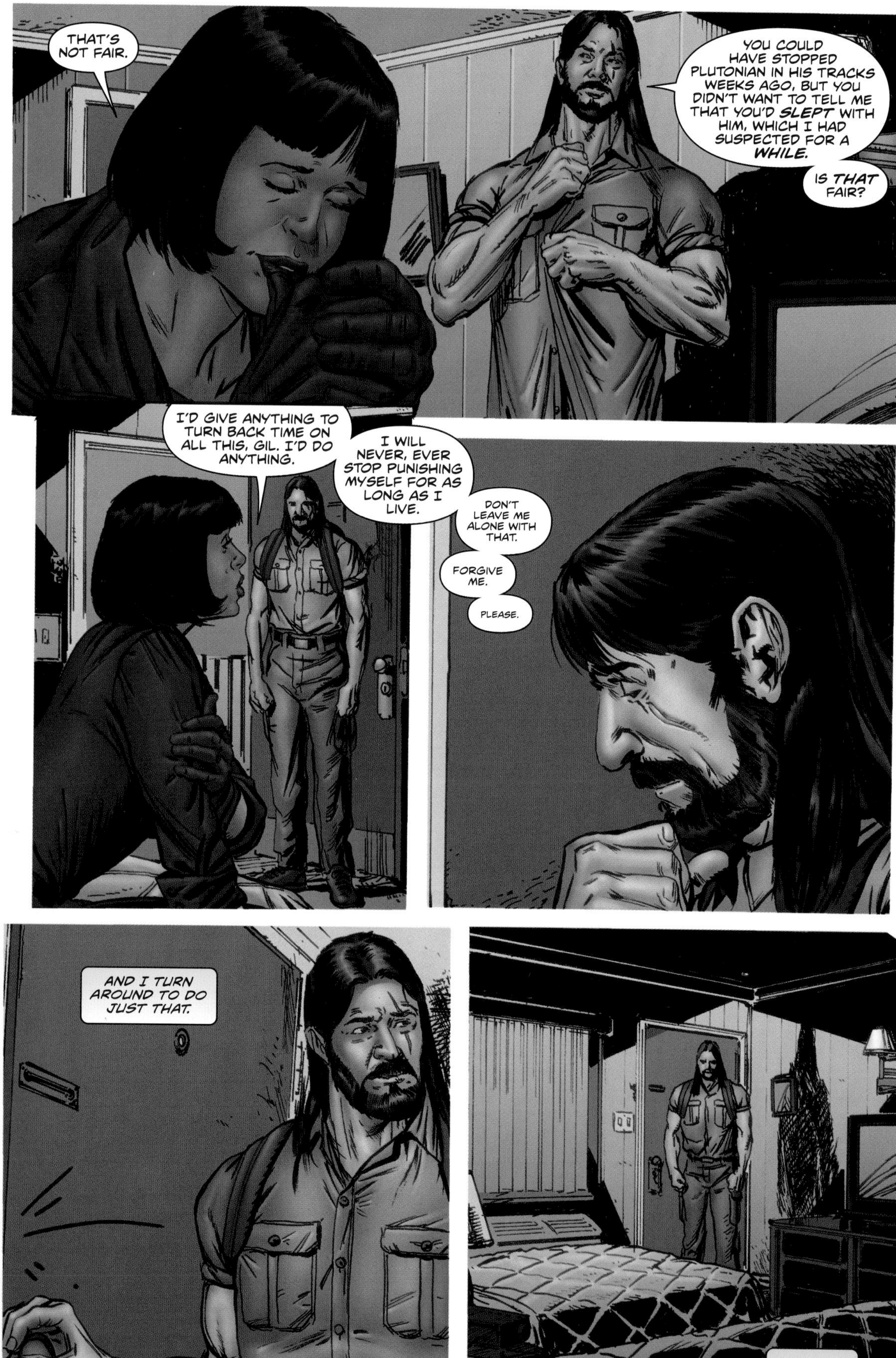
THAT'S NOT FAIR.
YOU COULD HAVE STOPPED PLUTONIAN IN HIS TRACKS WEEKS AGO, BUT YOU DIDN'T WANT TO TELL ME THAT YOU'D *SLEPT* WITH HIM, WHICH I HAD SUSPECTED FOR A ***WHILE.***
IS *THAT* FAIR?
I'D GIVE ANYTHING TO TURN BACK TIME ON ALL THIS, GIL. I'D DO ANYTHING.
I WILL NEVER, EVER STOP PUNISHING MYSELF FOR AS LONG AS I LIVE.
DON'T LEAVE ME ALONE WITH THAT.
FORGIVE ME.
PLEASE.
AND I TURN AROUND TO DO JUST THAT.
BUT THIS, TOO, IS A DREAM.

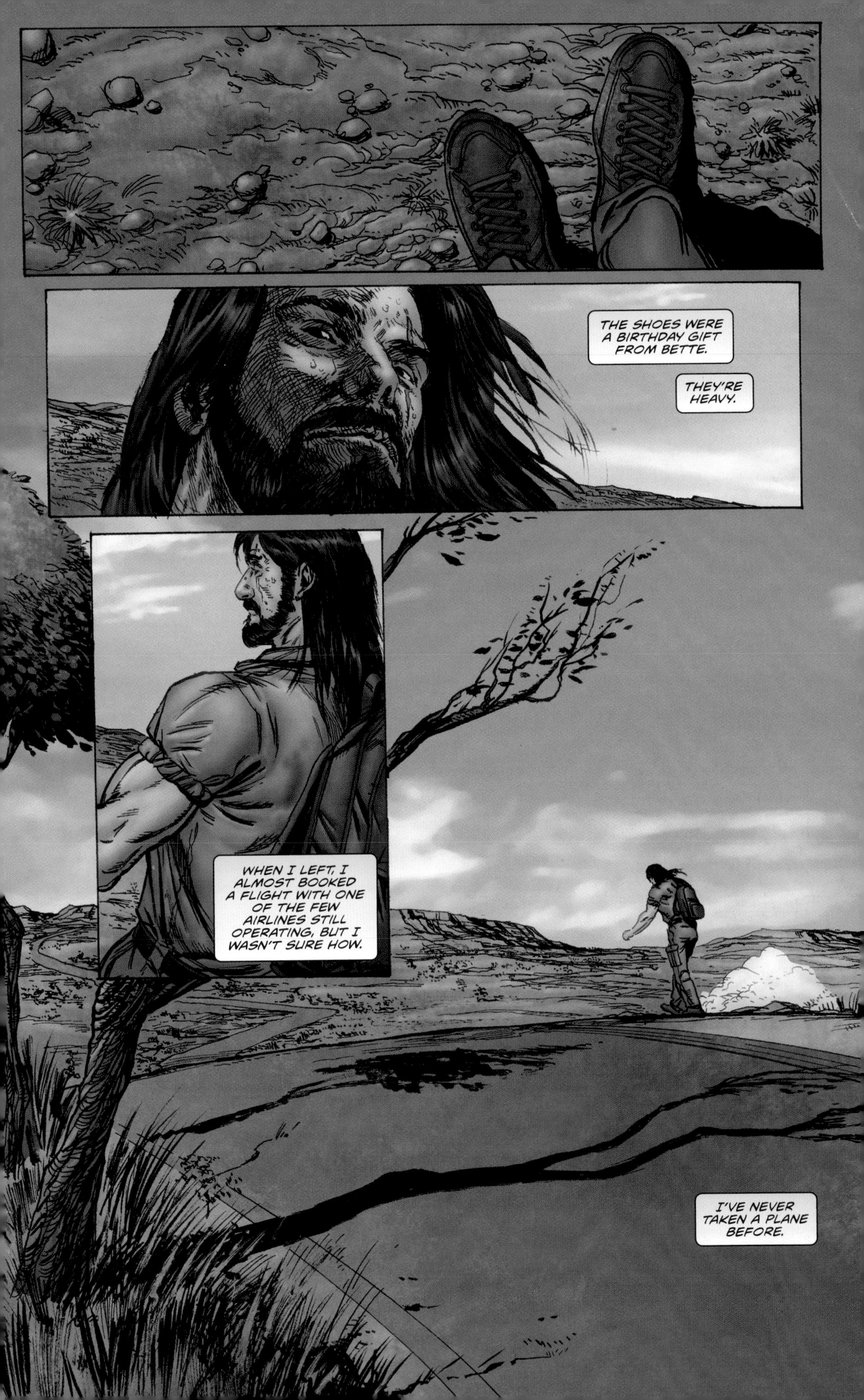
THE SHOES WERE A BIRTHDAY GIFT FROM BETTE.
THEY'RE HEAVY.
WHEN I LEFT, I ALMOST BOOKED A FLIGHT WITH ONE OF THE FEW AIRLINES STILL OPERATING, BUT I WASN'T SURE HOW.
I'VE NEVER TAKEN A PLANE BEFORE.

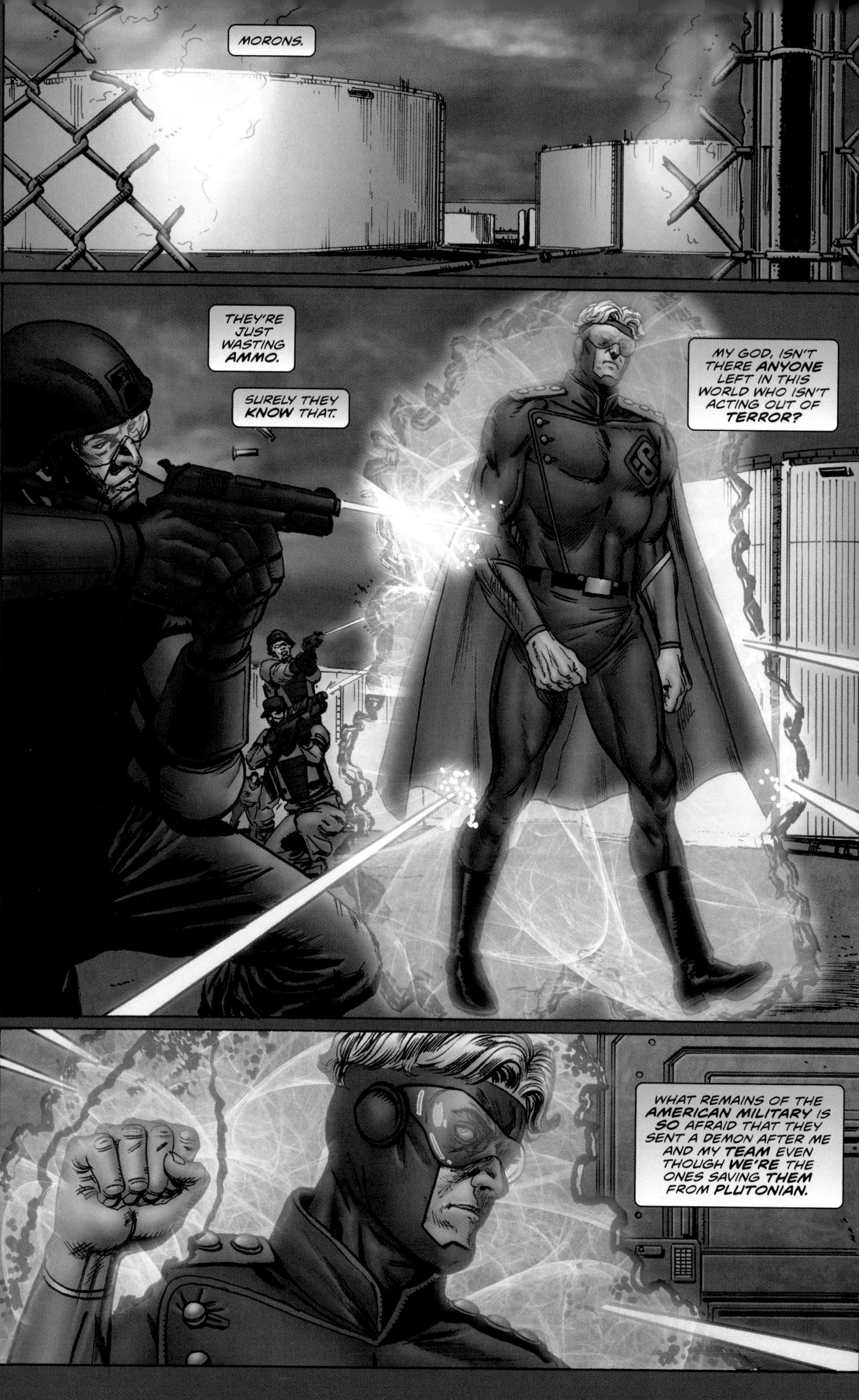
MORONS.
THEY'RE JUST WASTING AMMO.
SURELY THEY KNOW THAT.
MY GOD, ISN'T THERE ANYONE LEFT IN THIS WORLD WHO ISN'T ACTING OUT OF TERROR?
WHAT REMAINS OF THE AMERICAN MILITARY IS SO AFRAID THAT THEY SENT A DEMON AFTER ME AND MY TEAM EVEN THOUGH WE'RE THE ONES SAVING THEM FROM PLUTONIAN.

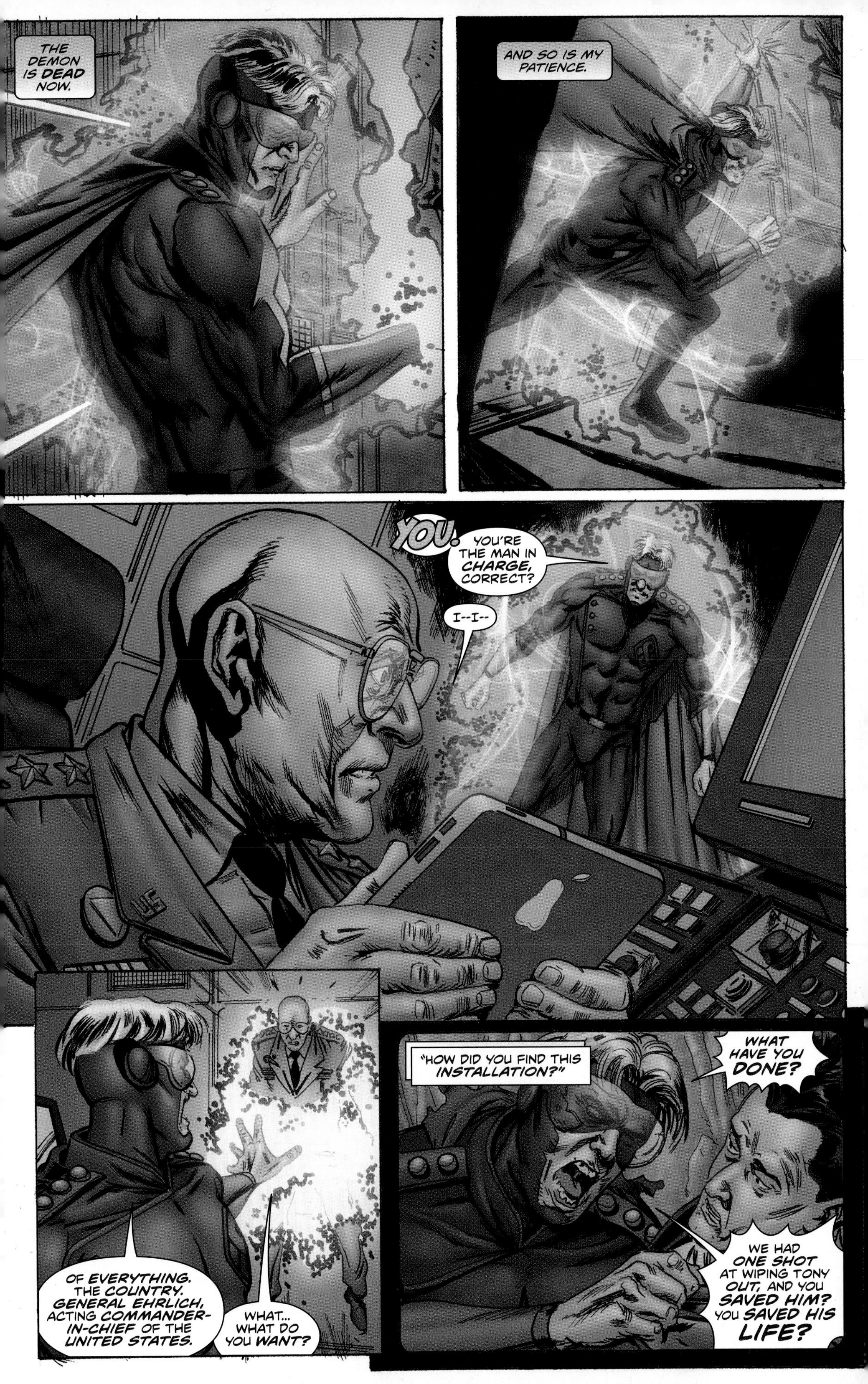
THE DEMON IS DEAD NOW.
AND SO IS MY PATIENCE.
YOU!
YOU'RE THE MAN IN CHARGE, CORRECT?
I--I--
OF EVERYTHING. THE COUNTRY. GENERAL EHRLICH, ACTING COMMANDER-IN-CHIEF OF THE UNITED STATES.
WHAT... WHAT DO YOU WANT?
"HOW DID YOU FIND THIS INSTALLATION?"
WHAT HAVE YOU DONE?
WE HAD ONE SHOT AT WIPING TONY OUT, AND YOU SAVED HIM? YOU SAVED HIS LIFE?

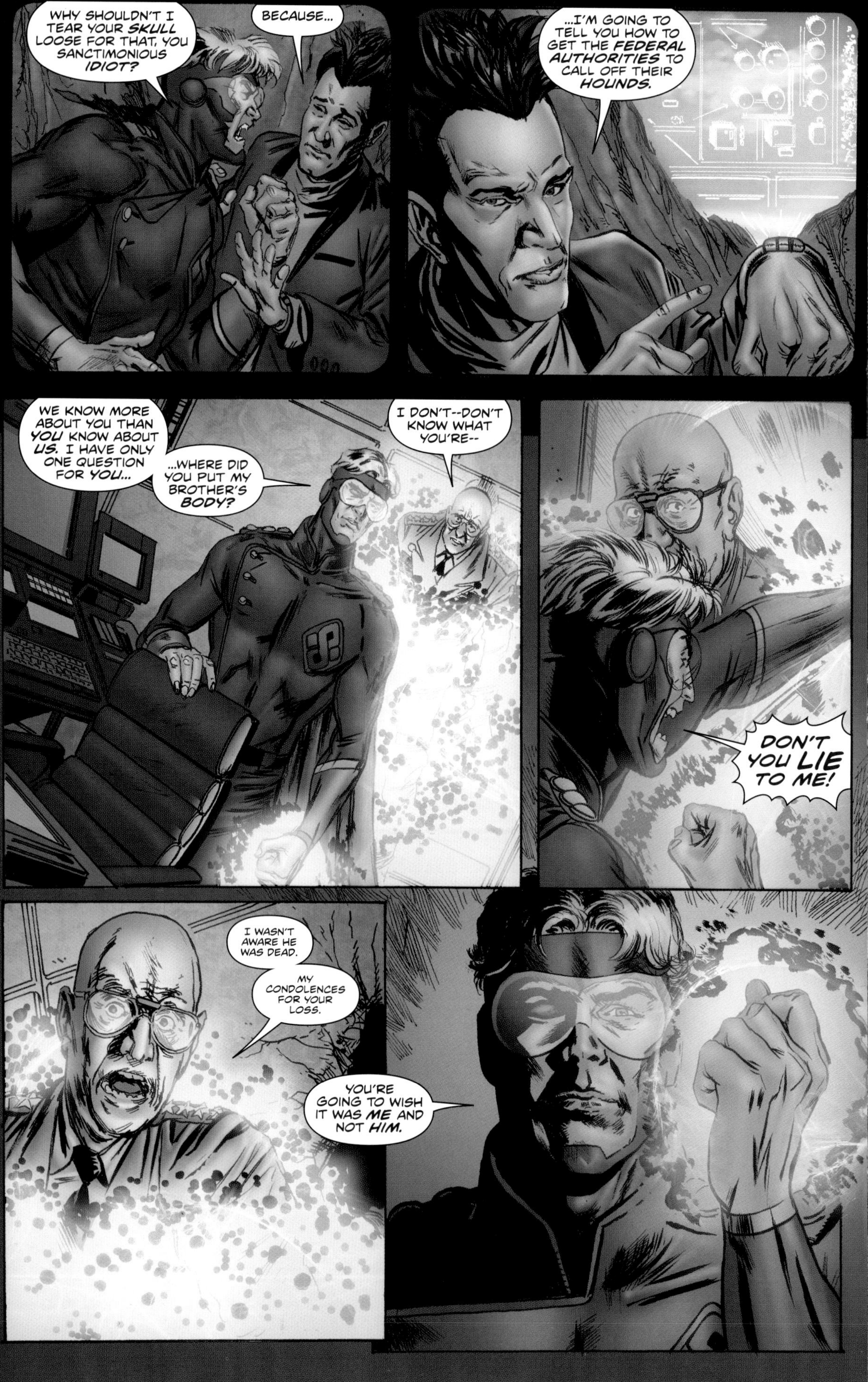
WHY SHOULDN'T I TEAR YOUR SKULL LOOSE FOR THAT, YOU SANCTIMONIOUS IDIOT?
BECAUSE...
...I'M GOING TO TELL YOU HOW TO GET THE FEDERAL AUTHORITIES TO CALL OFF THEIR HOUNDS.
WE KNOW MORE ABOUT YOU THAN YOU KNOW ABOUT US. I HAVE ONLY ONE QUESTION FOR YOU...
...WHERE DID YOU PUT MY BROTHER'S BODY?
I DON'T--DON'T KNOW WHAT YOU'RE--
DON'T YOU LIE TO ME!
I WASN'T AWARE HE WAS DEAD.
MY CONDOLENCES FOR YOUR LOSS.
YOU'RE GOING TO WISH IT WAS ME AND NOT HIM.

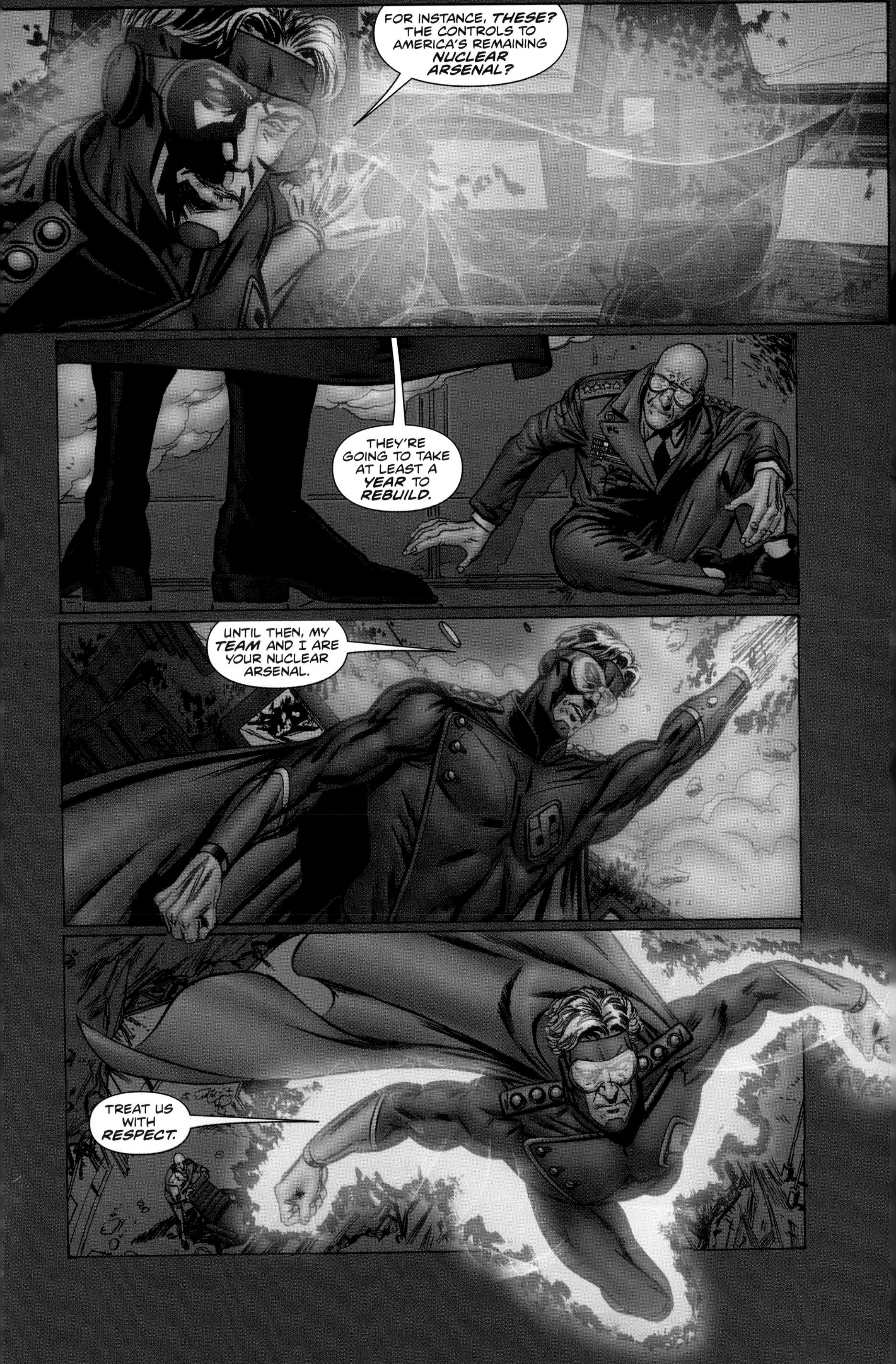
FOR INSTANCE, THESE? THE CONTROLS TO AMERICA'S REMAINING NUCLEAR ARSENAL?
THEY'RE GOING TO TAKE AT LEAST A YEAR TO REBUILD.
UNTIL THEN, MY TEAM AND I ARE YOUR NUCLEAR ARSENAL.
TREAT US WITH RESPECT.

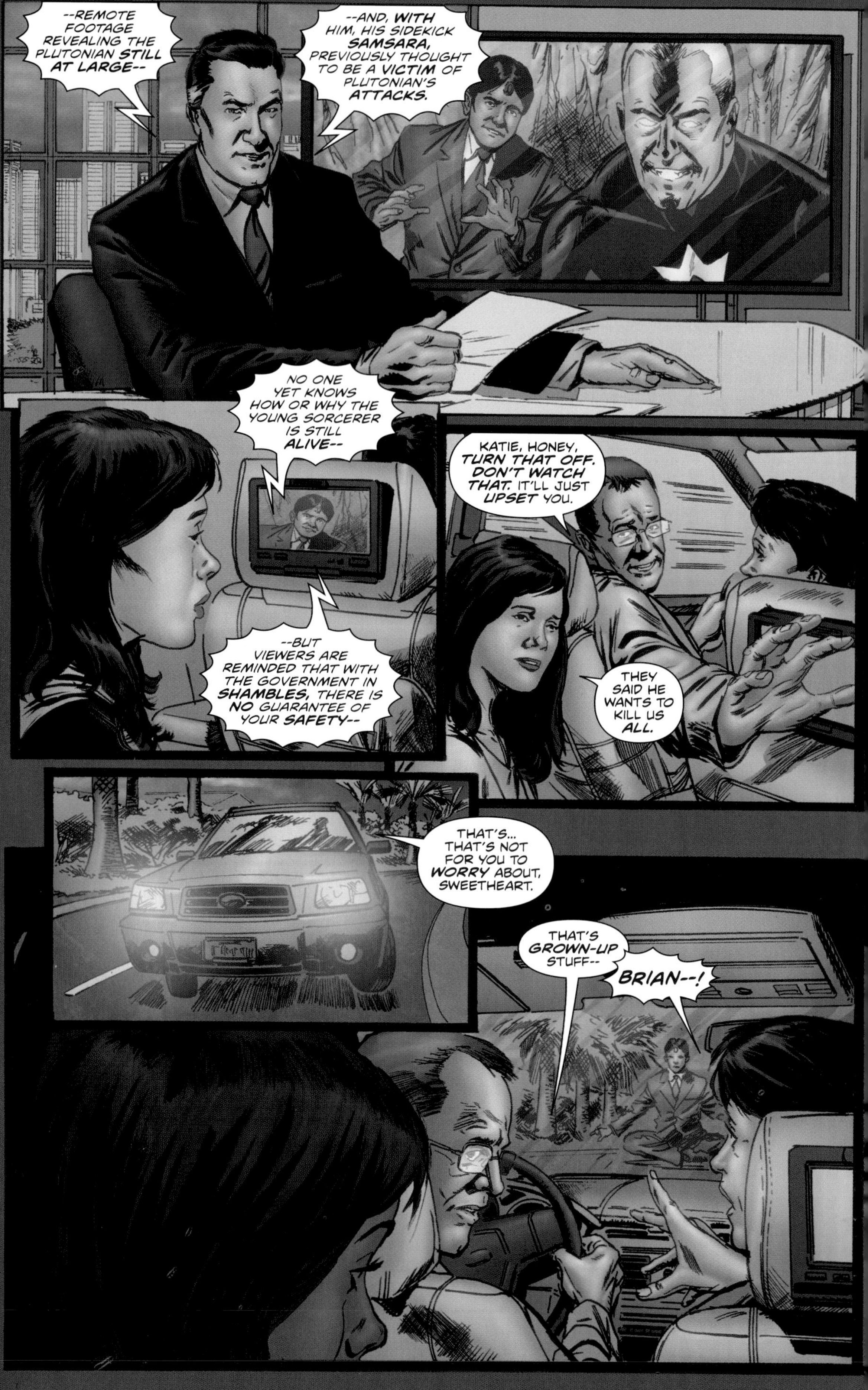
--REMOTE FOOTAGE REVEALING THE PLUTONIAN STILL AT LARGE--
--AND, WITH HIM, HIS SIDEKICK SAMSARA, PREVIOUSLY THOUGHT TO BE A VICTIM OF PLUTONIAN'S ATTACKS.
NO ONE YET KNOWS HOW OR WHY THE YOUNG SORCERER IS STILL ALIVE--
--BUT VIEWERS ARE REMINDED THAT WITH THE GOVERNMENT IN SHAMBLES, THERE IS NO GUARANTEE OF YOUR SAFETY--
KATIE, HONEY, TURN THAT OFF. DON'T WATCH THAT. IT'LL JUST UPSET YOU.
THEY SAID HE WANTS TO KILL US ALL.
THAT'S... THAT'S NOT FOR YOU TO WORRY ABOUT, SWEETHEART.
THAT'S GROWN-UP STUFF--
BRIAN--!

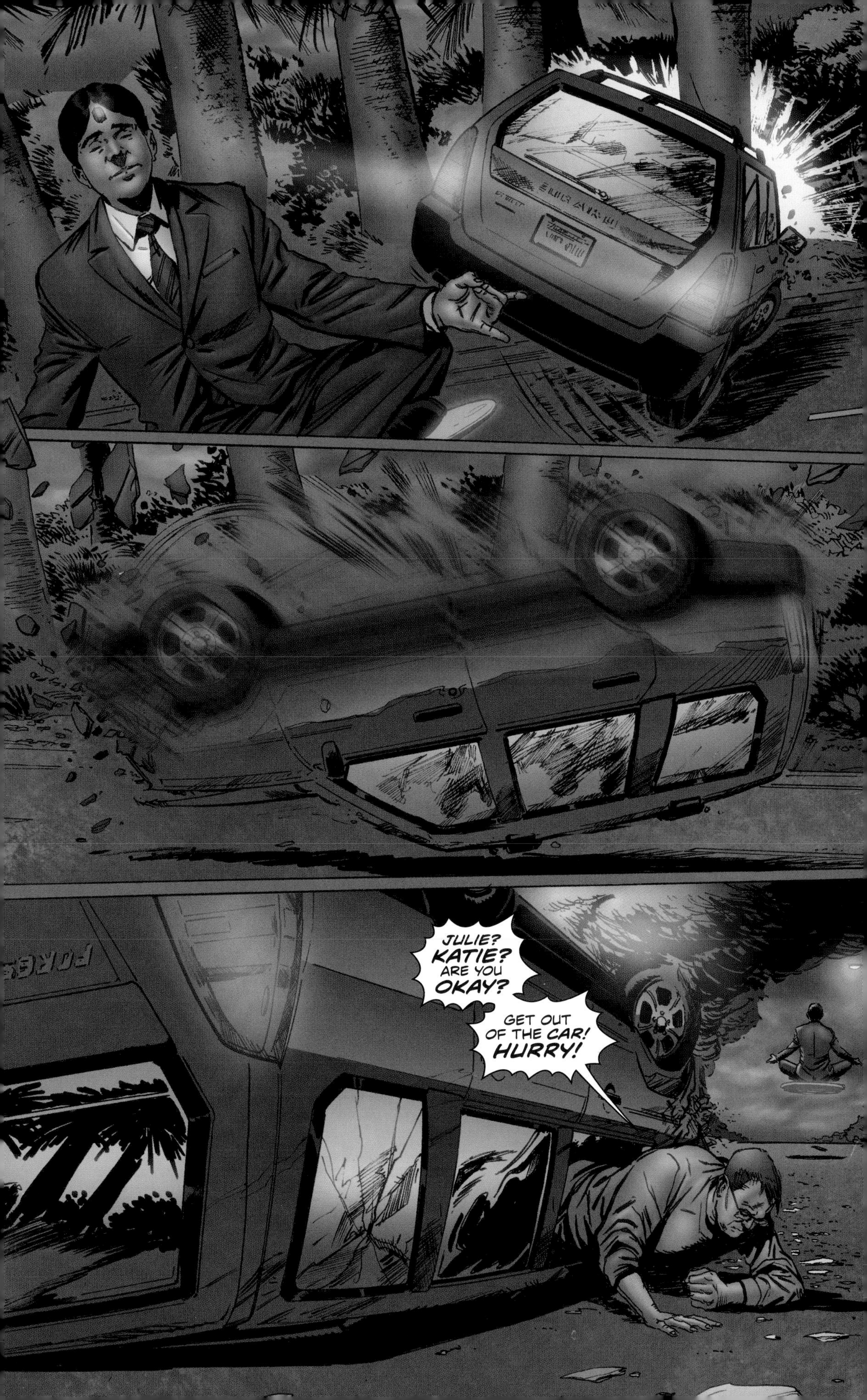
JULIE? KATIE? ARE YOU OKAY?
GET OUT OF THE CAR! HURRY!

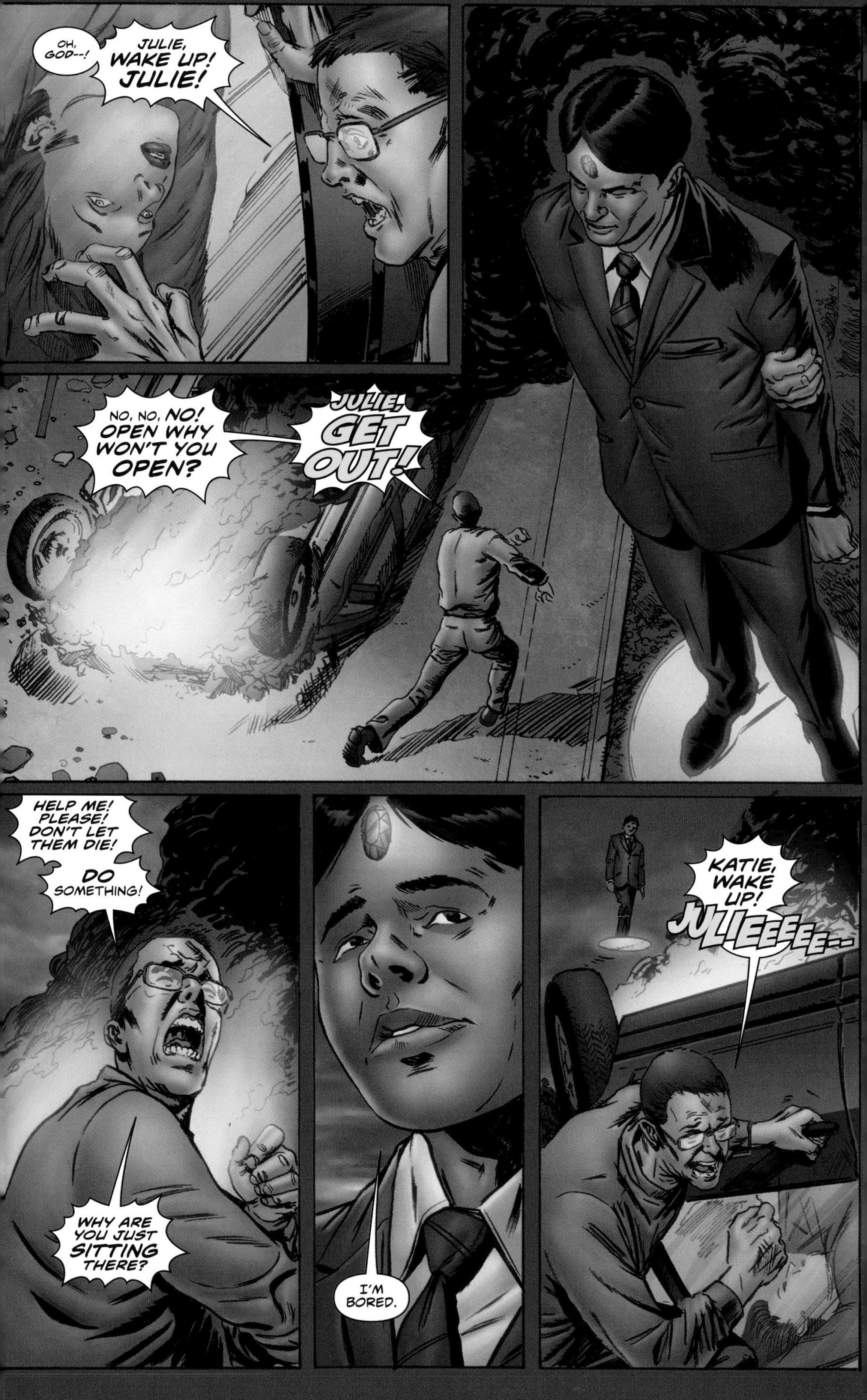
OH, GOD--!
JULIE, WAKE UP! JULIE!
NO, NO, NO! OPEN WHY WON'T YOU OPEN?
JULIE, GET OUT!
HELP ME! PLEASE! DON'T LET THEM DIE!
DO SOMETHING!
WHY ARE YOU JUST SITTING THERE?
I'M BORED.
KATIE, WAKE UP!
JULIEEEEEE--

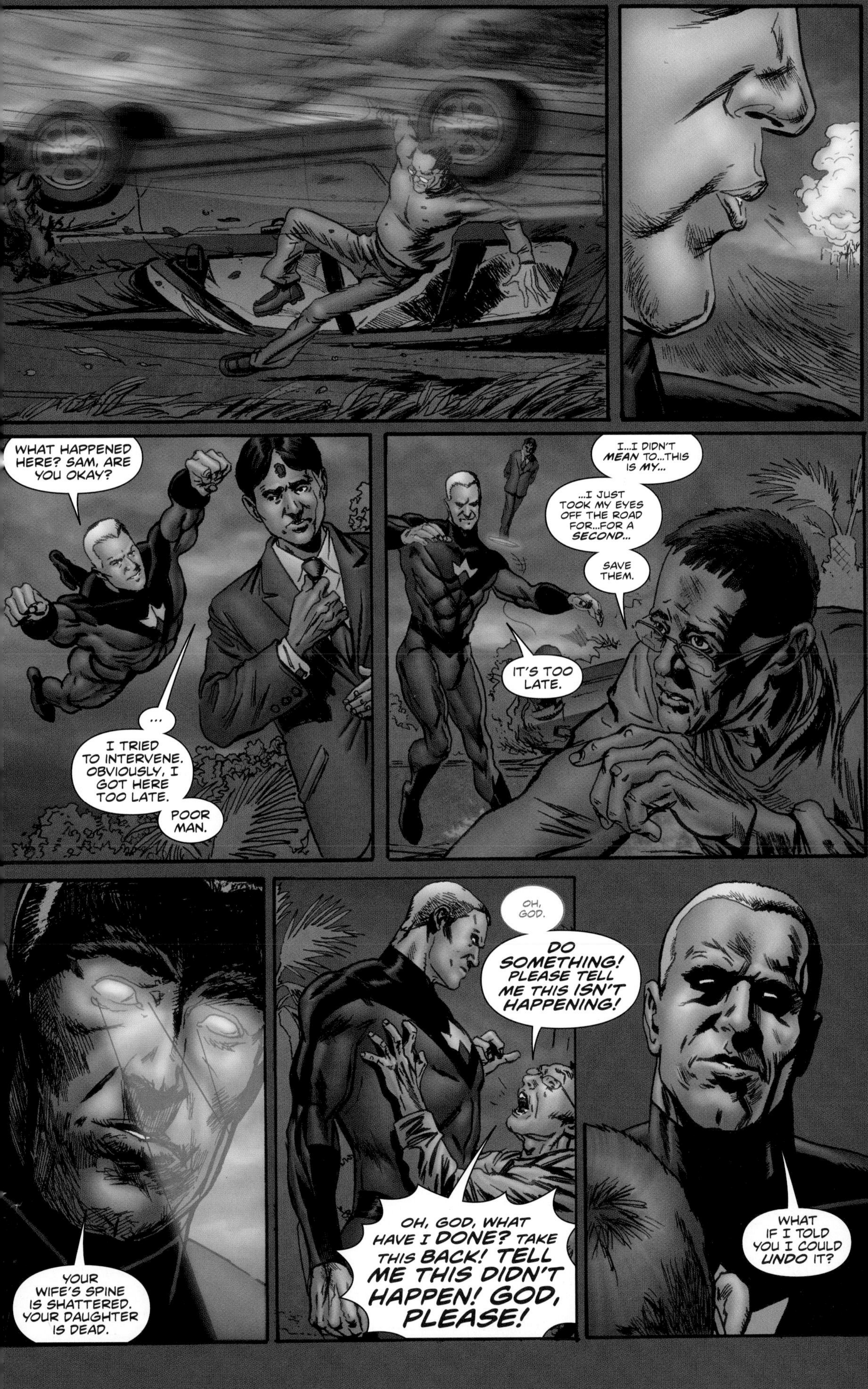
WHAT HAPPENED HERE? SAM, ARE YOU OKAY?
...
I TRIED TO INTERVENE. OBVIOUSLY, I GOT HERE TOO LATE.
POOR MAN.
I...I DIDN'T MEAN TO...THIS IS MY...
...I JUST TOOK MY EYES OFF THE ROAD FOR...FOR A SECOND...
SAVE THEM.
IT'S TOO LATE.
YOUR WIFE'S SPINE IS SHATTERED. YOUR DAUGHTER IS DEAD.
OH, GOD.
DO SOMETHING! PLEASE TELL ME THIS ISN'T HAPPENING!
OH, GOD, WHAT HAVE I DONE? TAKE THIS BACK! TELL ME THIS DIDN'T HAPPEN! GOD, PLEASE!
WHAT IF I TOLD YOU I COULD UNDO IT?

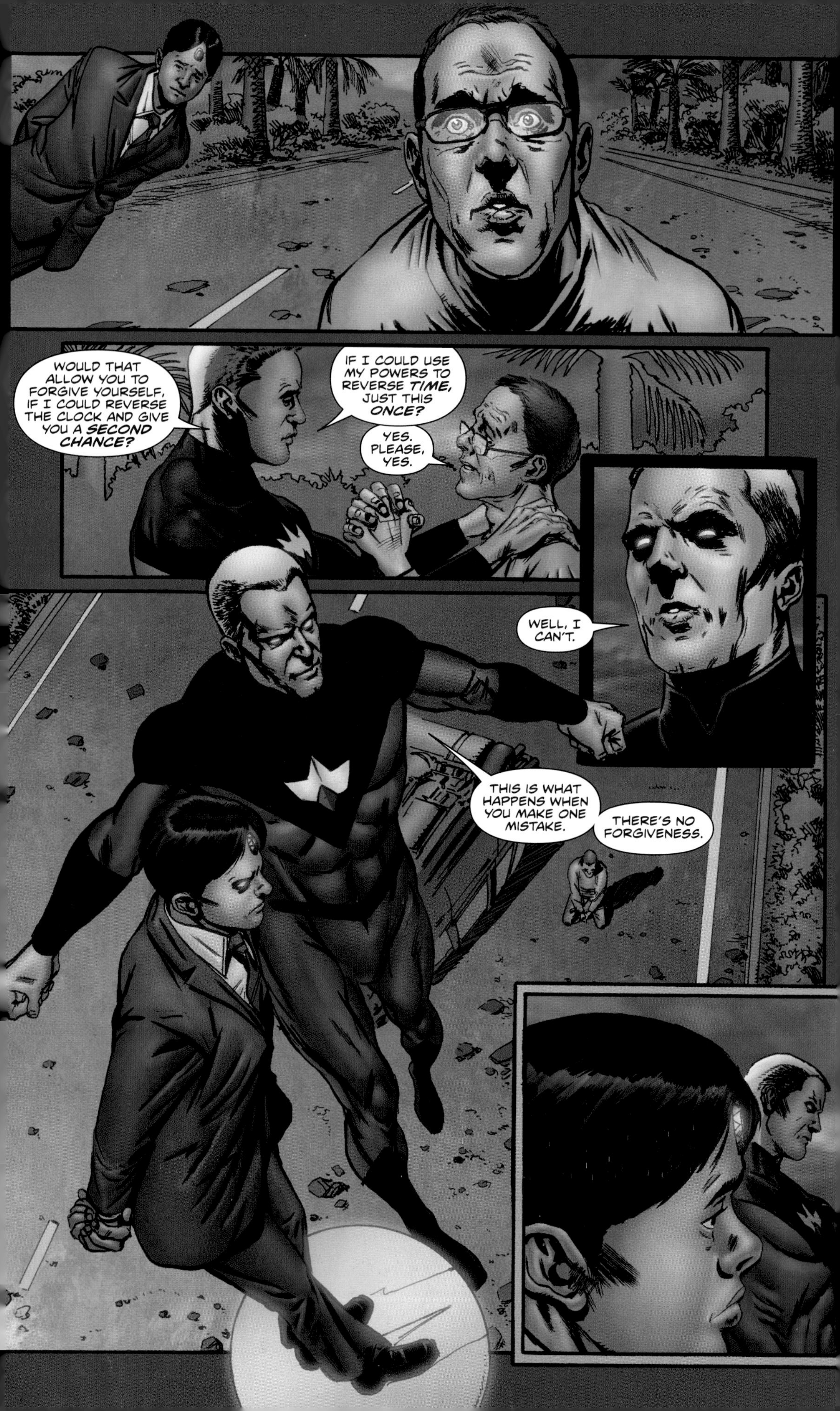
WOULD THAT ALLOW YOU TO FORGIVE YOURSELF, IF I COULD REVERSE THE CLOCK AND GIVE YOU A *SECOND CHANCE?*
IF I COULD USE MY POWERS TO REVERSE *TIME,* JUST THIS *ONCE?*
YES. PLEASE, YES.
WELL, I CAN'T.
THIS IS WHAT HAPPENS WHEN YOU MAKE ONE MISTAKE.
THERE'S NO FORGIVENESS.

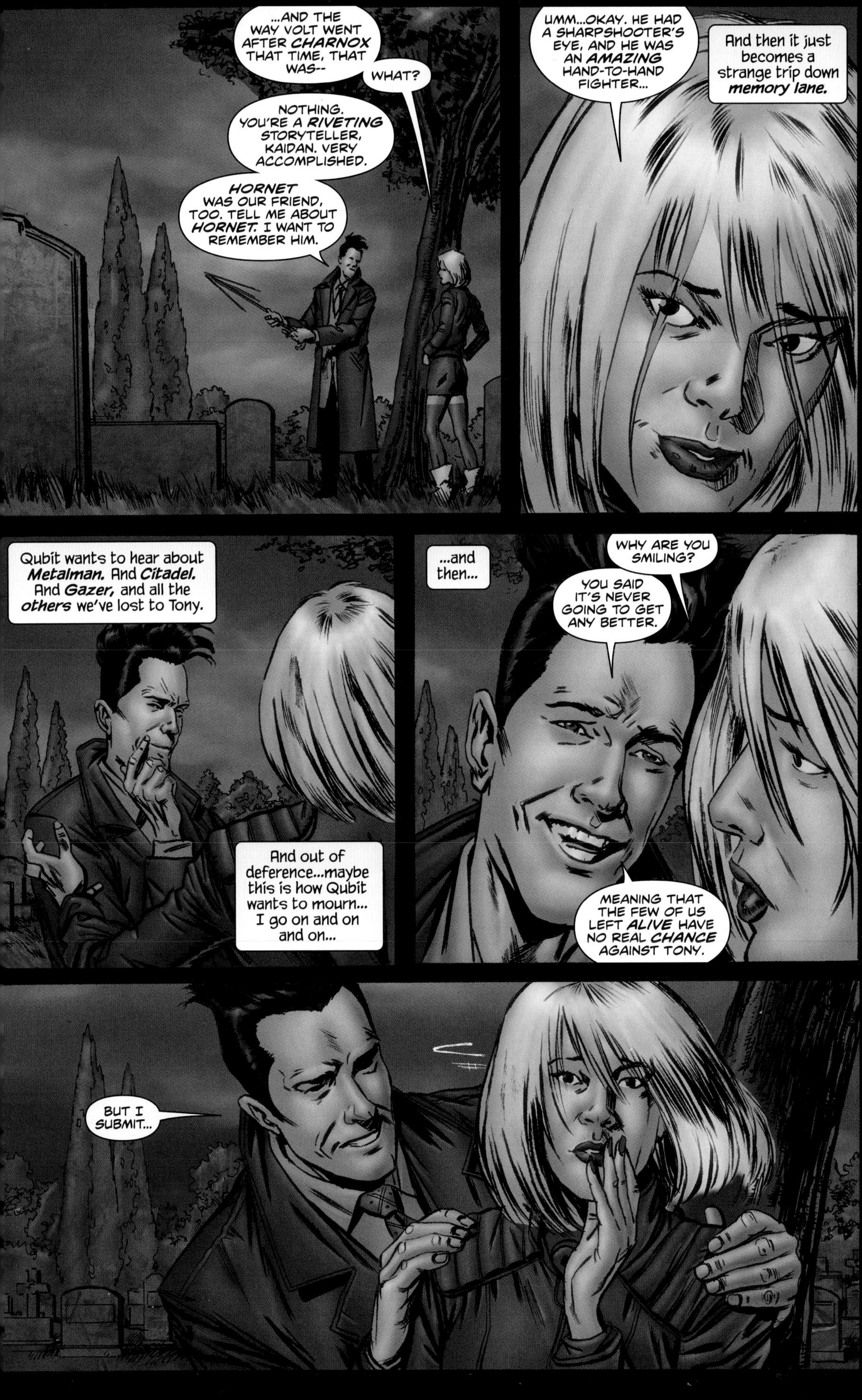
...AND THE WAY VOLT WENT AFTER CHARNOX THAT TIME, THAT WAS--
WHAT?
NOTHING. YOU'RE A RIVETING STORYTELLER, KAIDAN. VERY ACCOMPLISHED.
HORNET WAS OUR FRIEND, TOO. TELL ME ABOUT HORNET. I WANT TO REMEMBER HIM.
UMM...OKAY. HE HAD A SHARPSHOOTER'S EYE, AND HE WAS AN AMAZING HAND-TO-HAND FIGHTER...
And then it just becomes a strange trip down memory lane.
Qubit wants to hear about Metalman. And Citadel. And Gazer, and all the others we've lost to Tony.
And out of deference...maybe this is how Qubit wants to mourn... I go on and on and on...
...and then...
WHY ARE YOU SMILING?
YOU SAID IT'S NEVER GOING TO GET ANY BETTER.
MEANING THAT THE FEW OF US LEFT ALIVE HAVE NO REAL CHANCE AGAINST TONY.
BUT I SUBMIT...

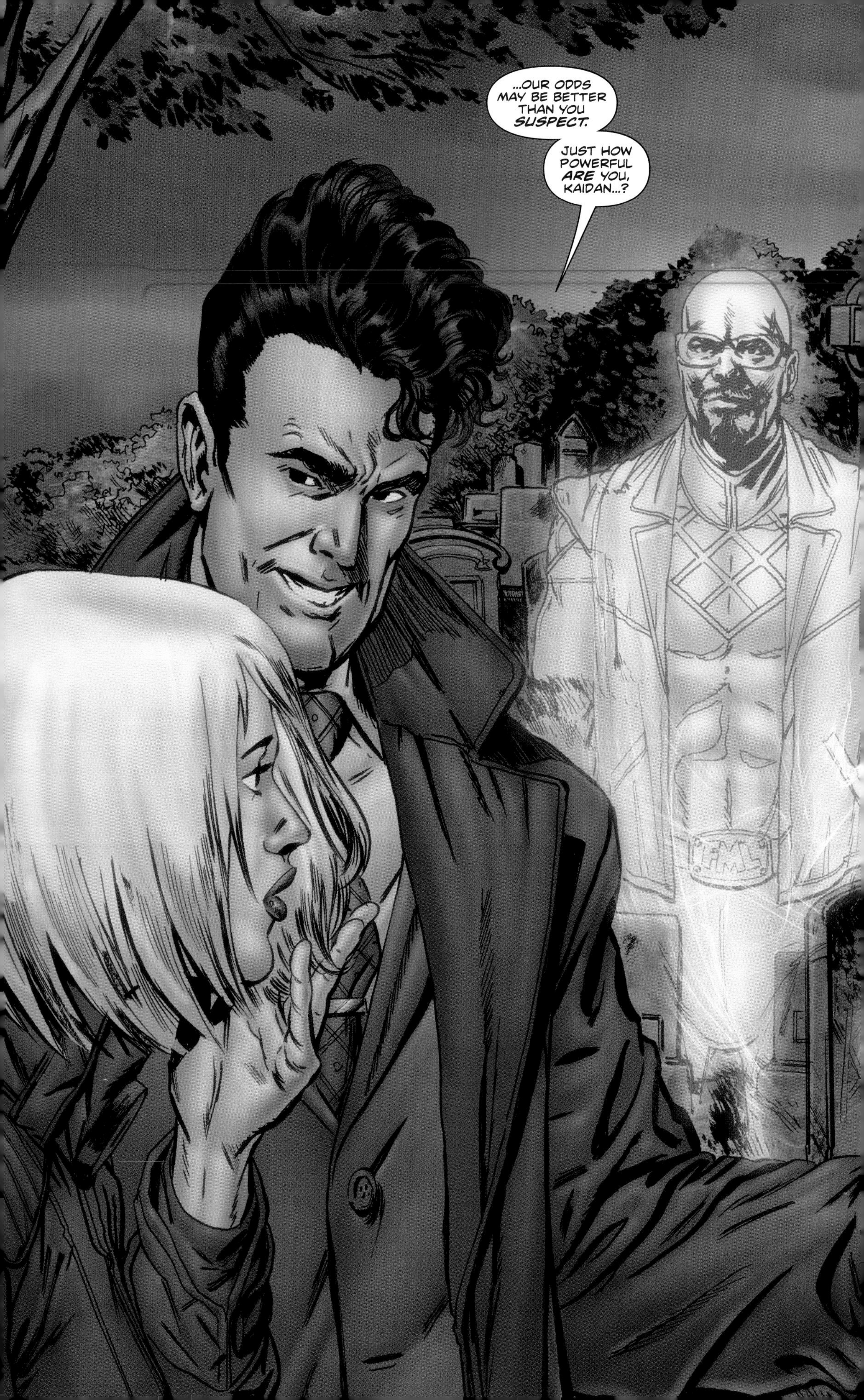
...OUR ODDS MAY BE BETTER THAN YOU SUSPECT.
JUST HOW POWERFUL ARE YOU, KAIDAN...?

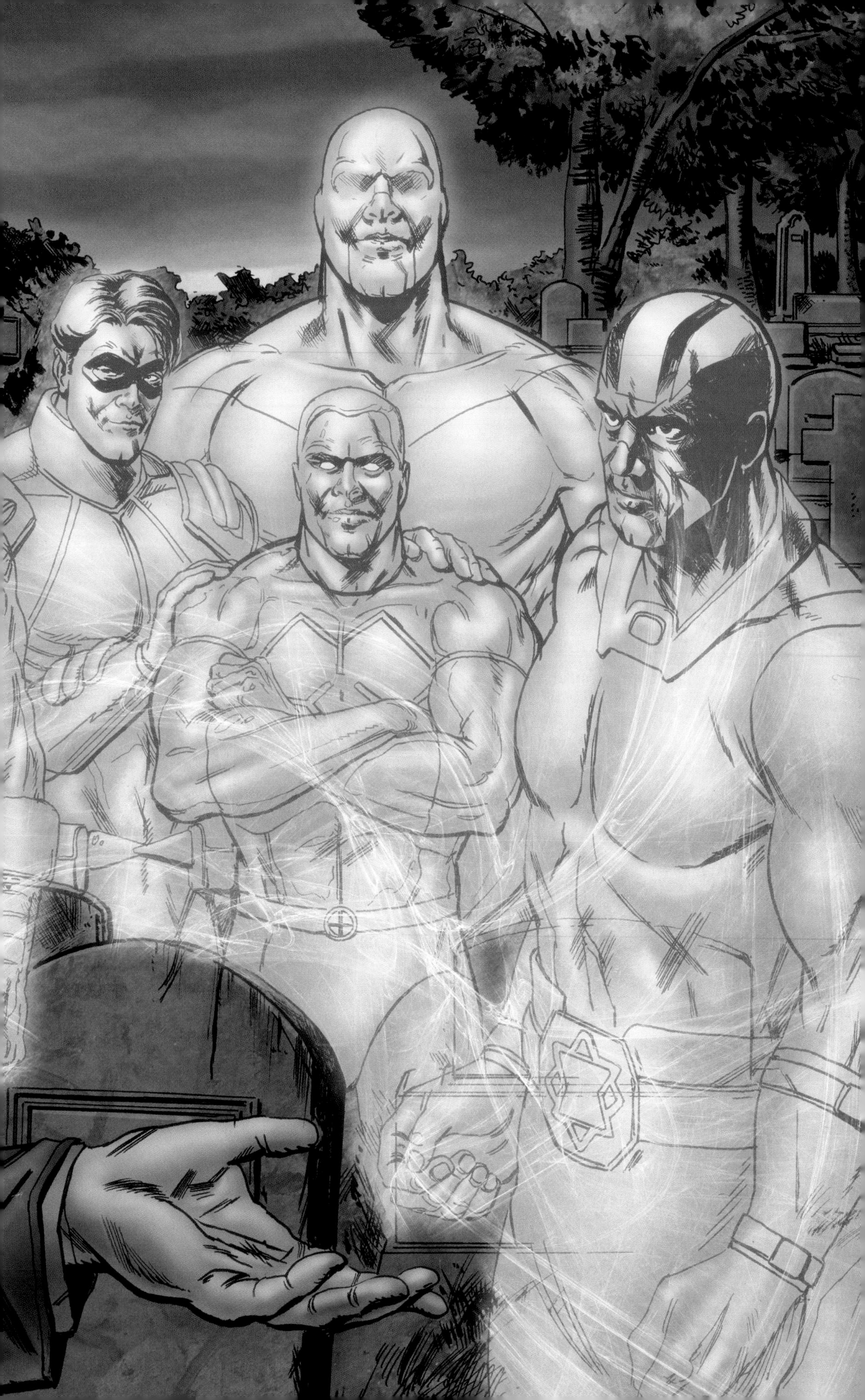

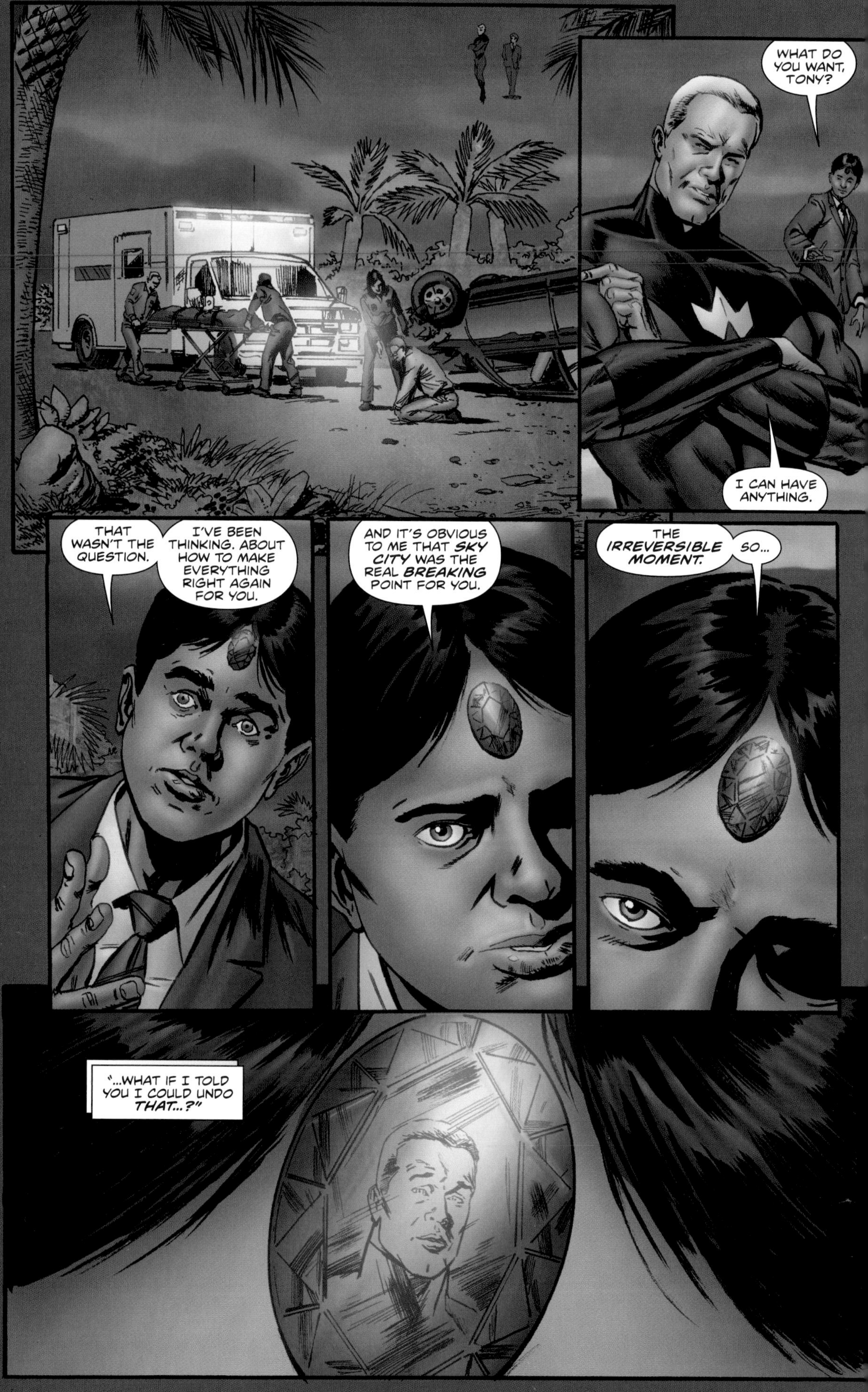
WHAT DO YOU WANT, TONY?
I CAN HAVE ANYTHING.
THAT WASN'T THE QUESTION.
I'VE BEEN THINKING. ABOUT HOW TO MAKE EVERYTHING RIGHT AGAIN FOR YOU.
AND IT'S OBVIOUS TO ME THAT *SKY CITY* WAS THE REAL *BREAKING* POINT FOR YOU.
THE *IRREVERSIBLE MOMENT.*
SO...
"...WHAT IF I TOLD YOU I COULD UNDO *THAT*...?"

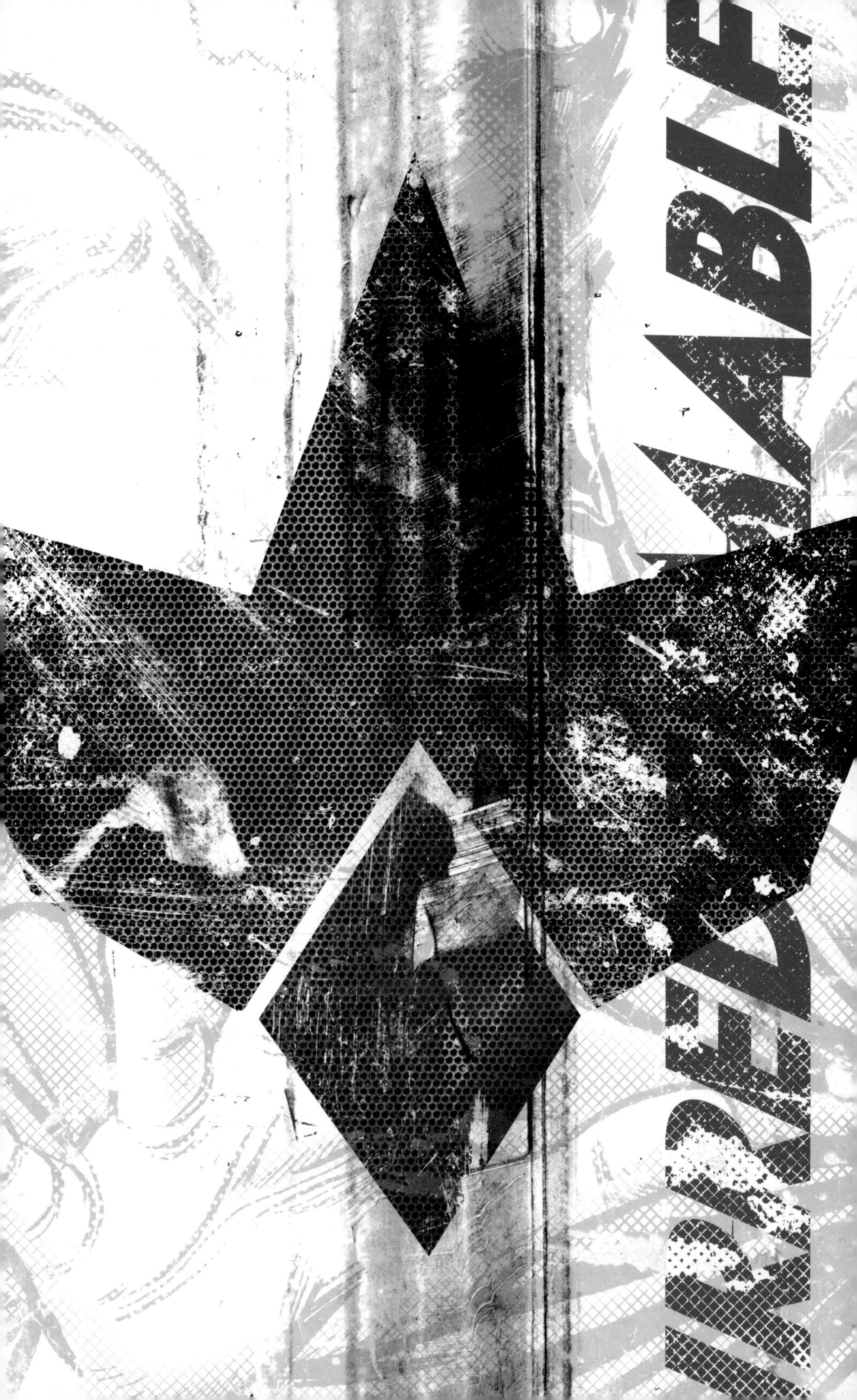

CHAPTER 17

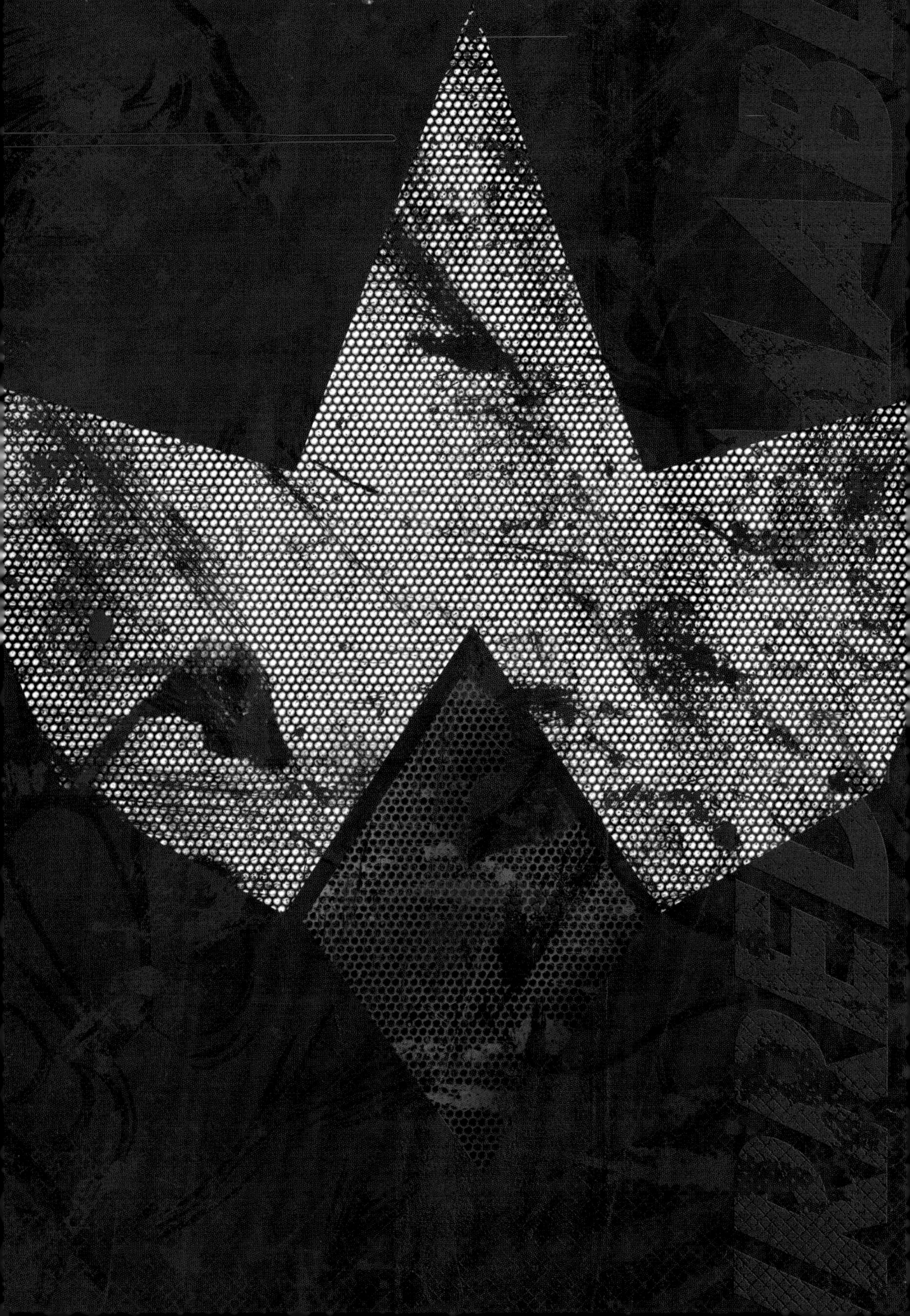

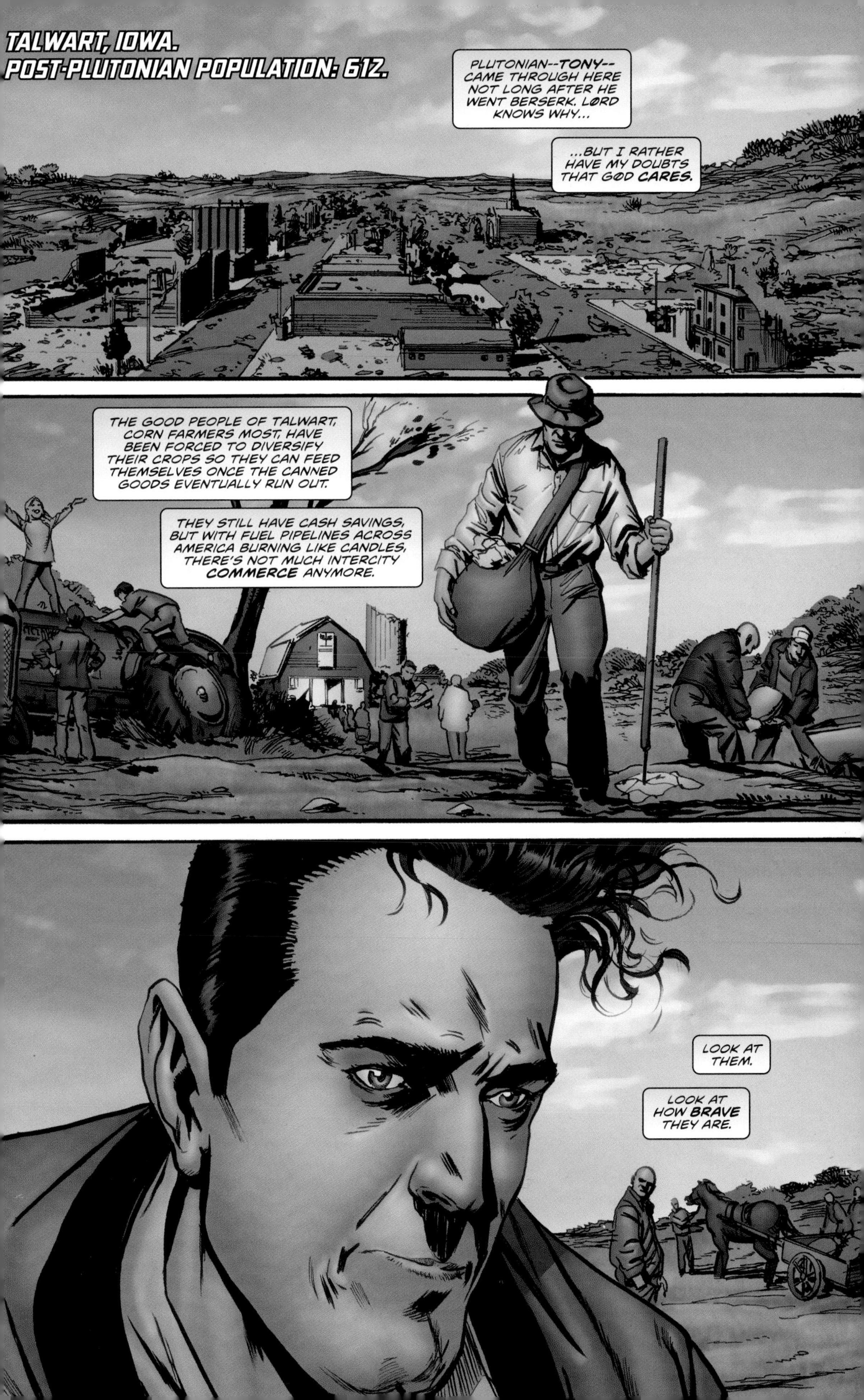
TALWART, IOWA.
POST-PLUTONIAN POPULATION: 612.
PLUTONIAN--TONY--CAME THROUGH HERE NOT LONG AFTER HE WENT BERSERK. LORD KNOWS WHY...
...BUT I RATHER HAVE MY DOUBTS THAT GOD CARES.
THE GOOD PEOPLE OF TALWART, CORN FARMERS MOST, HAVE BEEN FORCED TO DIVERSIFY THEIR CROPS SO THEY CAN FEED THEMSELVES ONCE THE CANNED GOODS EVENTUALLY RUN OUT.
THEY STILL HAVE CASH SAVINGS, BUT WITH FUEL PIPELINES ACROSS AMERICA BURNING LIKE CANDLES, THERE'S NOT MUCH INTERCITY COMMERCE ANYMORE.
LOOK AT THEM.
LOOK AT HOW BRAVE THEY ARE.

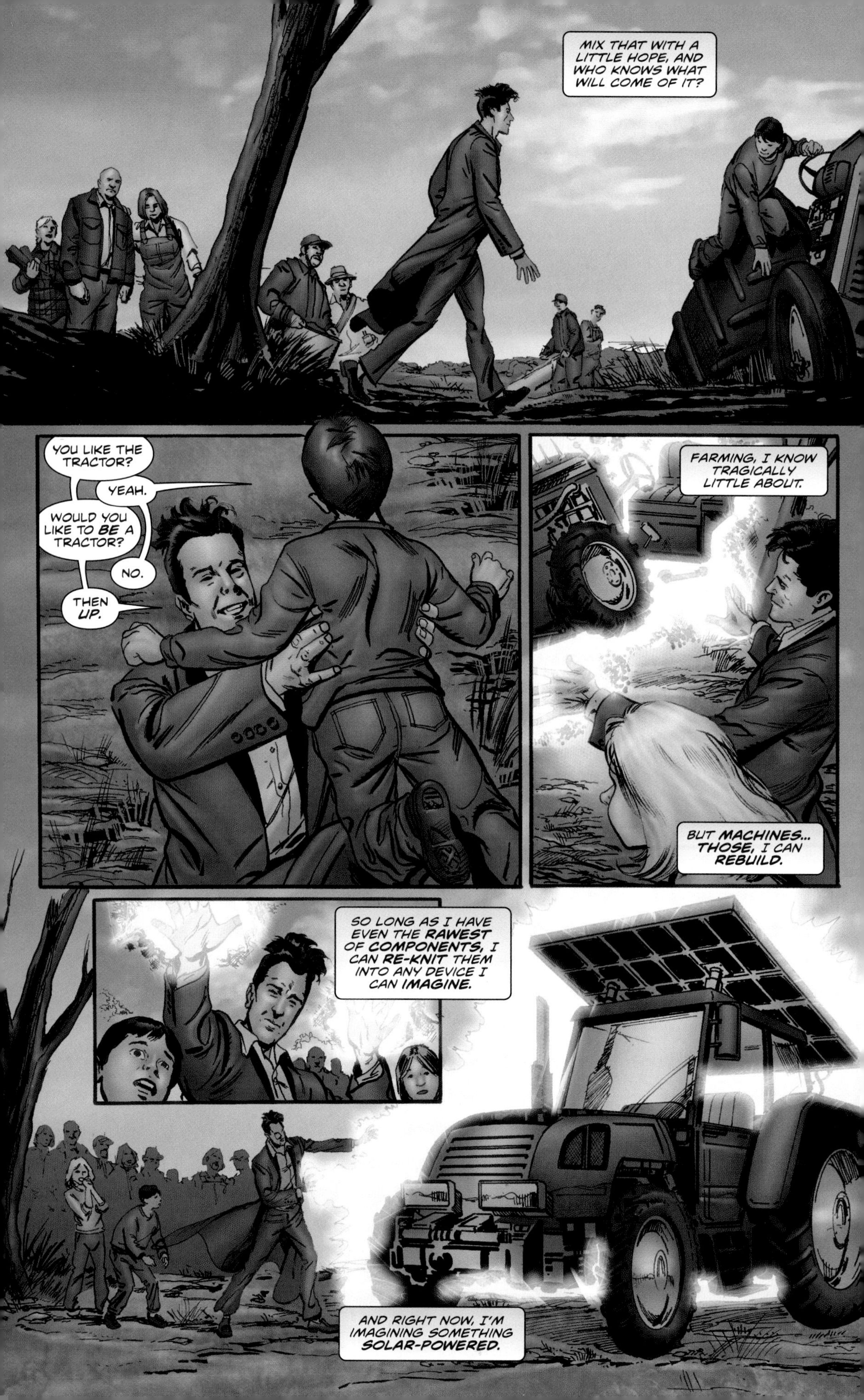
MIX THAT WITH A LITTLE HOPE, AND WHO KNOWS WHAT WILL COME OF IT?
YOU LIKE THE TRACTOR?
YEAH.
WOULD YOU LIKE TO BE A TRACTOR?
NO.
THEN UP.
FARMING, I KNOW TRAGICALLY LITTLE ABOUT.
BUT MACHINES... THOSE, I CAN REBUILD.
SO LONG AS I HAVE EVEN THE RAWEST OF COMPONENTS, I CAN RE-KNIT THEM INTO ANY DEVICE I CAN IMAGINE.
AND RIGHT NOW, I'M IMAGINING SOMETHING SOLAR-POWERED.

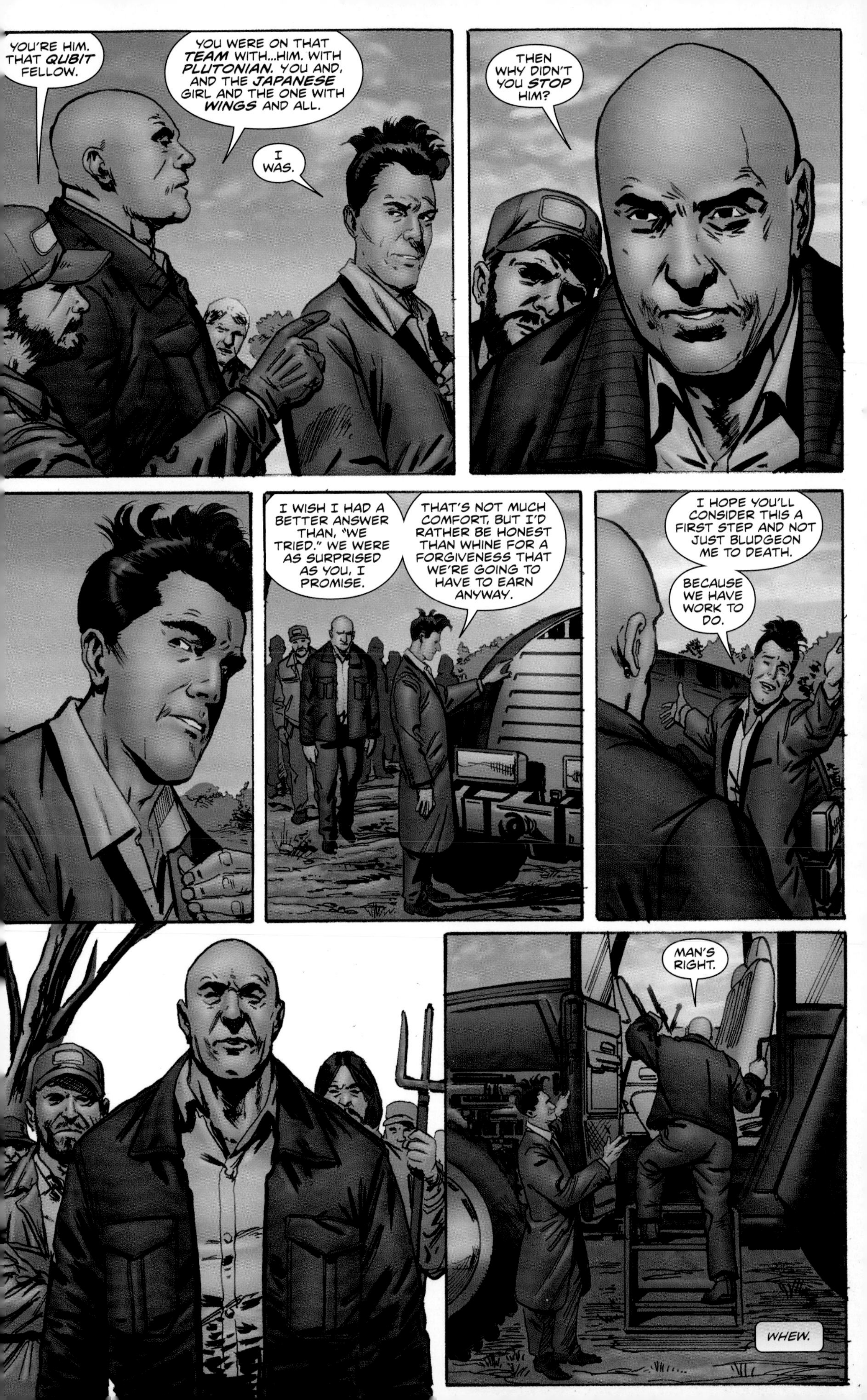
YOU'RE HIM. THAT *QUBIT* FELLOW.
YOU WERE ON THAT *TEAM* WITH...HIM. WITH *PLUTONIAN.* YOU AND, AND THE *JAPANESE* GIRL AND THE ONE WITH *WINGS* AND ALL.
I WAS.
THEN WHY DIDN'T YOU *STOP* HIM?
I WISH I HAD A BETTER ANSWER THAN, "WE TRIED." WE WERE AS SURPRISED AS YOU, I PROMISE.
THAT'S NOT MUCH COMFORT, BUT I'D RATHER BE HONEST THAN WHINE FOR A FORGIVENESS THAT WE'RE GOING TO HAVE TO EARN ANYWAY.
I HOPE YOU'LL CONSIDER THIS A FIRST STEP AND NOT JUST BLUDGEON ME TO DEATH.
BECAUSE WE HAVE WORK TO DO.
MAN'S RIGHT.
WHEW.

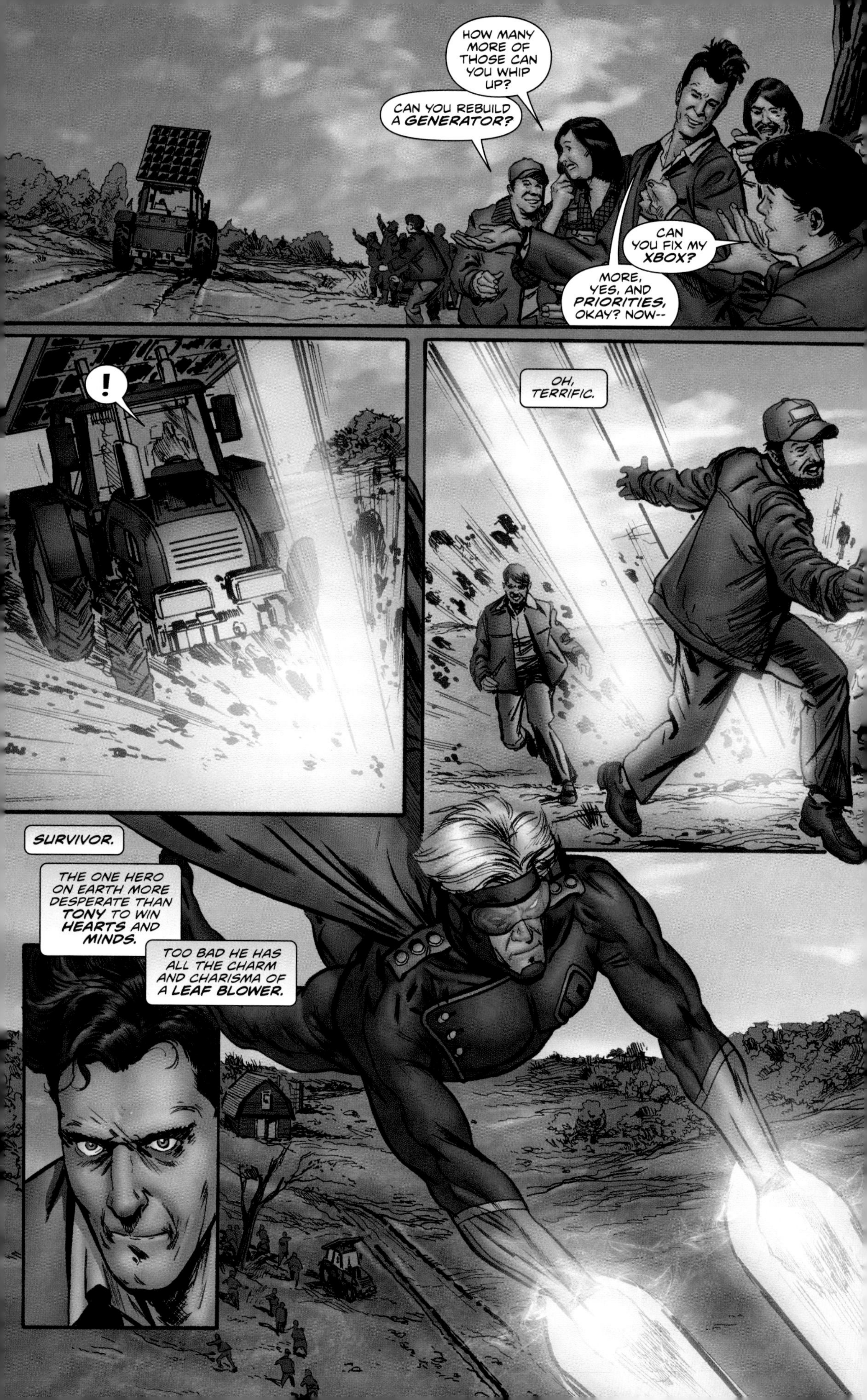
HOW MANY MORE OF THOSE CAN YOU WHIP UP?
CAN YOU REBUILD A GENERATOR?
CAN YOU FIX MY XBOX?
MORE, YES, AND PRIORITIES, OKAY? NOW--
!
OH, TERRIFIC.
SURVIVOR.
THE ONE HERO ON EARTH MORE DESPERATE THAN TONY TO WIN HEARTS AND MINDS.
TOO BAD HE HAS ALL THE CHARM AND CHARISMA OF A LEAF BLOWER.

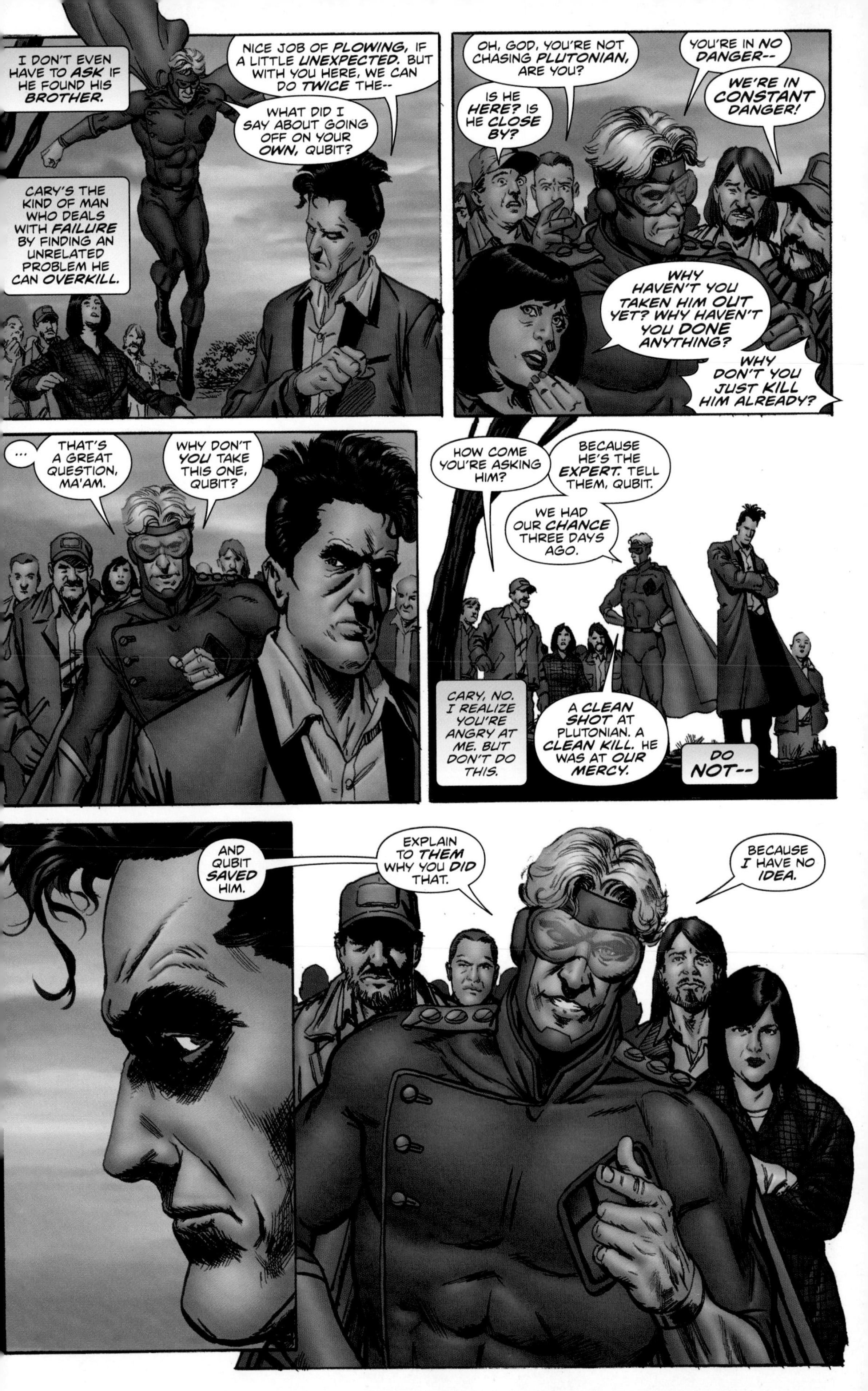

I DON'T EVEN HAVE TO ASK IF HE FOUND HIS BROTHER.
NICE JOB OF PLOWING, IF A LITTLE UNEXPECTED. BUT WITH YOU HERE, WE CAN DO TWICE THE--
WHAT DID I SAY ABOUT GOING OFF ON YOUR OWN, QUBIT?
CARY'S THE KIND OF MAN WHO DEALS WITH FAILURE BY FINDING AN UNRELATED PROBLEM HE CAN OVERKILL.
OH, GOD, YOU'RE NOT CHASING PLUTONIAN, ARE YOU?
IS HE HERE? IS HE CLOSE BY?
YOU'RE IN NO DANGER--
WE'RE IN CONSTANT DANGER!
WHY HAVEN'T YOU TAKEN HIM OUT YET? WHY HAVEN'T YOU DONE ANYTHING?
WHY DON'T YOU JUST KILL HIM ALREADY?
...
THAT'S A GREAT QUESTION, MA'AM.
WHY DON'T YOU TAKE THIS ONE, QUBIT?
HOW COME YOU'RE ASKING HIM?
BECAUSE HE'S THE EXPERT. TELL THEM, QUBIT.
WE HAD OUR CHANCE THREE DAYS AGO.
CARY, NO. I REALIZE YOU'RE ANGRY AT ME. BUT DON'T DO THIS.
A CLEAN SHOT AT PLUTONIAN. A CLEAN KILL. HE WAS AT OUR MERCY.
DO NOT--
AND QUBIT SAVED HIM.
EXPLAIN TO THEM WHY YOU DID THAT.
BECAUSE I HAVE NO IDEA.

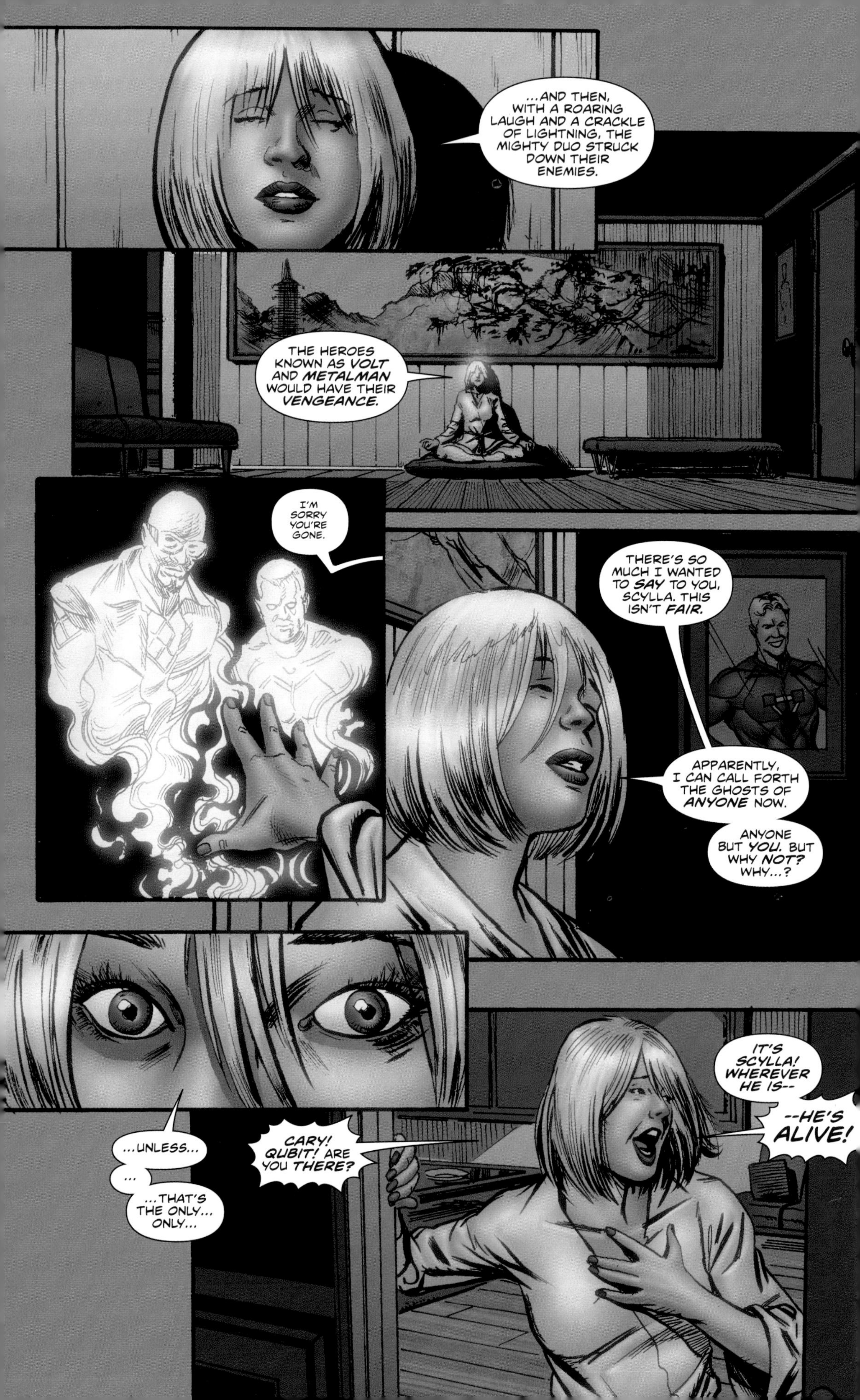
...AND THEN, WITH A ROARING LAUGH AND A CRACKLE OF LIGHTNING, THE MIGHTY DUO STRUCK DOWN THEIR ENEMIES.
THE HEROES KNOWN AS VOLT AND METALMAN WOULD HAVE THEIR VENGEANCE.
I'M SORRY YOU'RE GONE.
THERE'S SO MUCH I WANTED TO SAY TO YOU, SCYLLA. THIS ISN'T FAIR.
APPARENTLY, I CAN CALL FORTH THE GHOSTS OF ANYONE NOW.
ANYONE BUT YOU. BUT WHY NOT? WHY...?
...UNLESS...
...
...THAT'S THE ONLY... ONLY...
CARY! QUBIT! ARE YOU THERE?
IT'S SCYLLA! WHEREVER HE IS--
--HE'S ALIVE!

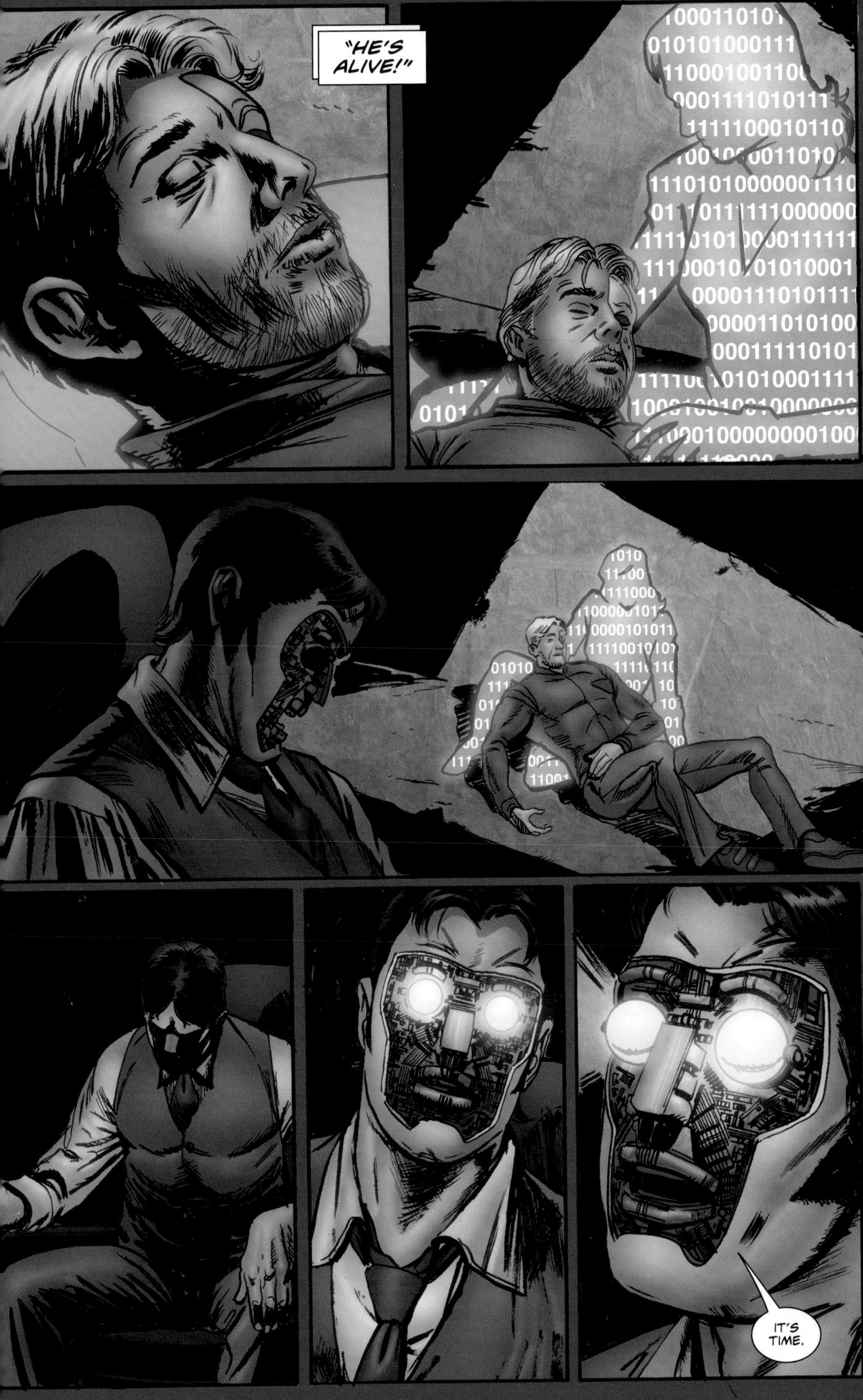
"HE'S ALIVE!"
IT'S TIME.

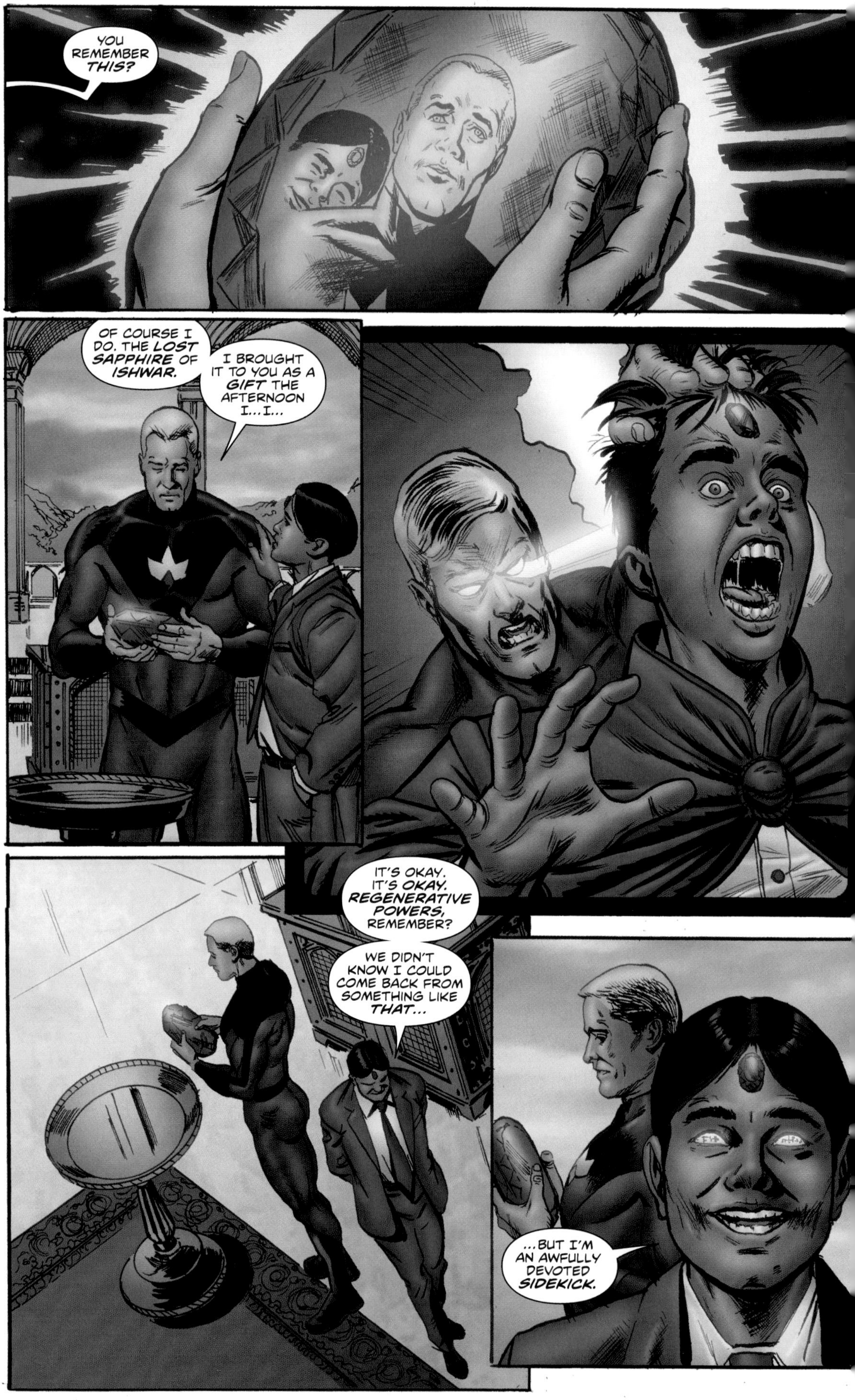
YOU REMEMBER *THIS?*
OF COURSE I DO. THE ***LOST SAPPHIRE*** OF ***ISHWAR.***
I BROUGHT IT TO YOU AS A *GIFT* THE AFTERNOON I... I...
IT'S OKAY. IT'S *OKAY.* ***REGENERATIVE POWERS,*** REMEMBER?
WE DIDN'T KNOW I COULD COME BACK FROM SOMETHING LIKE *THAT...*
...BUT I'M AN AWFULLY DEVOTED ***SIDEKICK.***

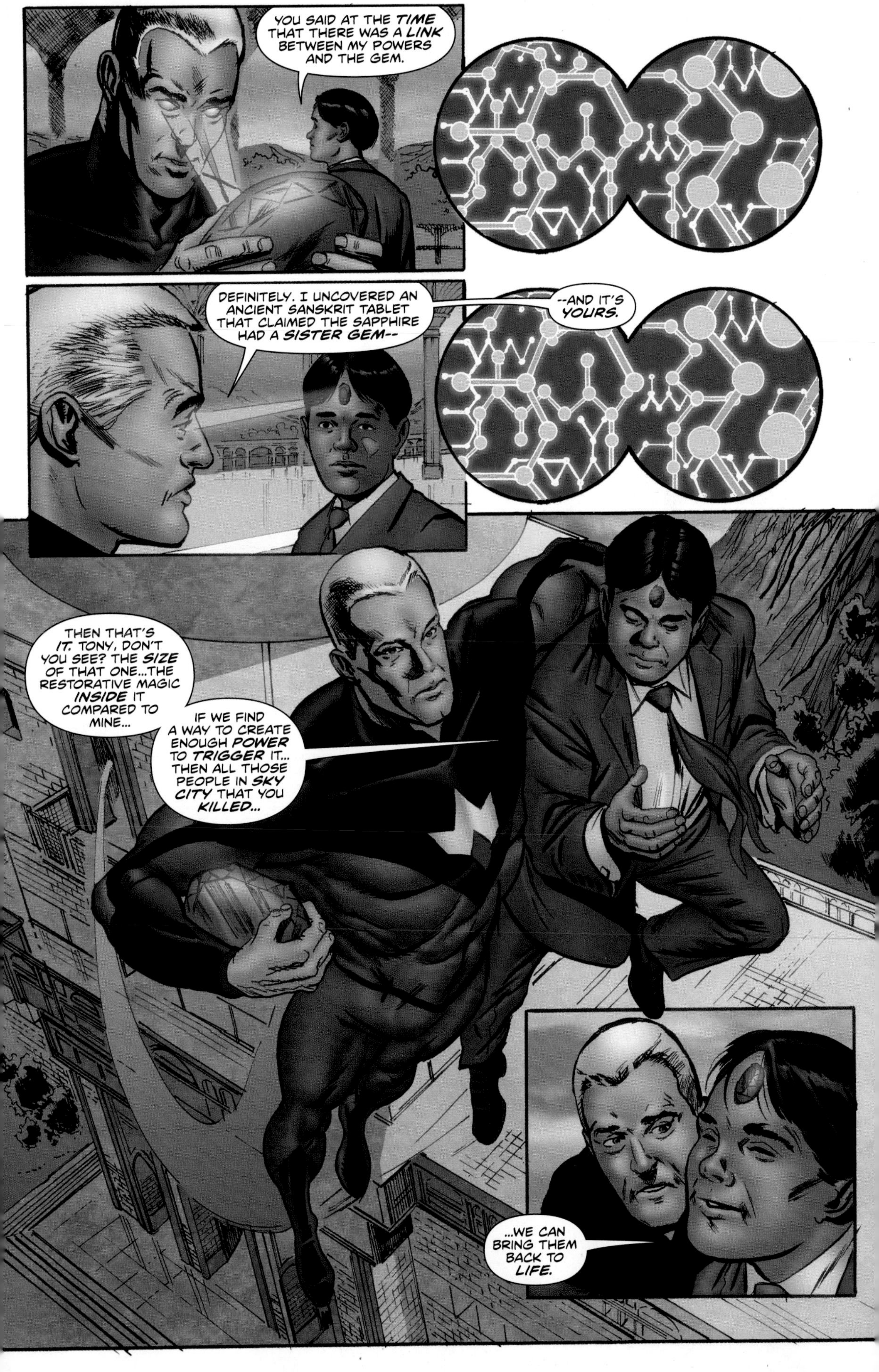
YOU SAID AT THE *TIME* THAT THERE WAS A *LINK* BETWEEN MY POWERS AND THE GEM.
DEFINITELY. I UNCOVERED AN ANCIENT SANSKRIT TABLET THAT CLAIMED THE SAPPHIRE HAD A *SISTER GEM*--
--AND IT'S *YOURS.*
THEN THAT'S *IT.* TONY, DON'T YOU SEE? THE *SIZE* OF THAT ONE...THE RESTORATIVE MAGIC *INSIDE* IT COMPARED TO MINE...
IF WE FIND A WAY TO CREATE ENOUGH *POWER* TO *TRIGGER* IT... THEN ALL THOSE PEOPLE IN *SKY CITY* THAT YOU *KILLED*...
...WE CAN BRING THEM BACK TO *LIFE.*

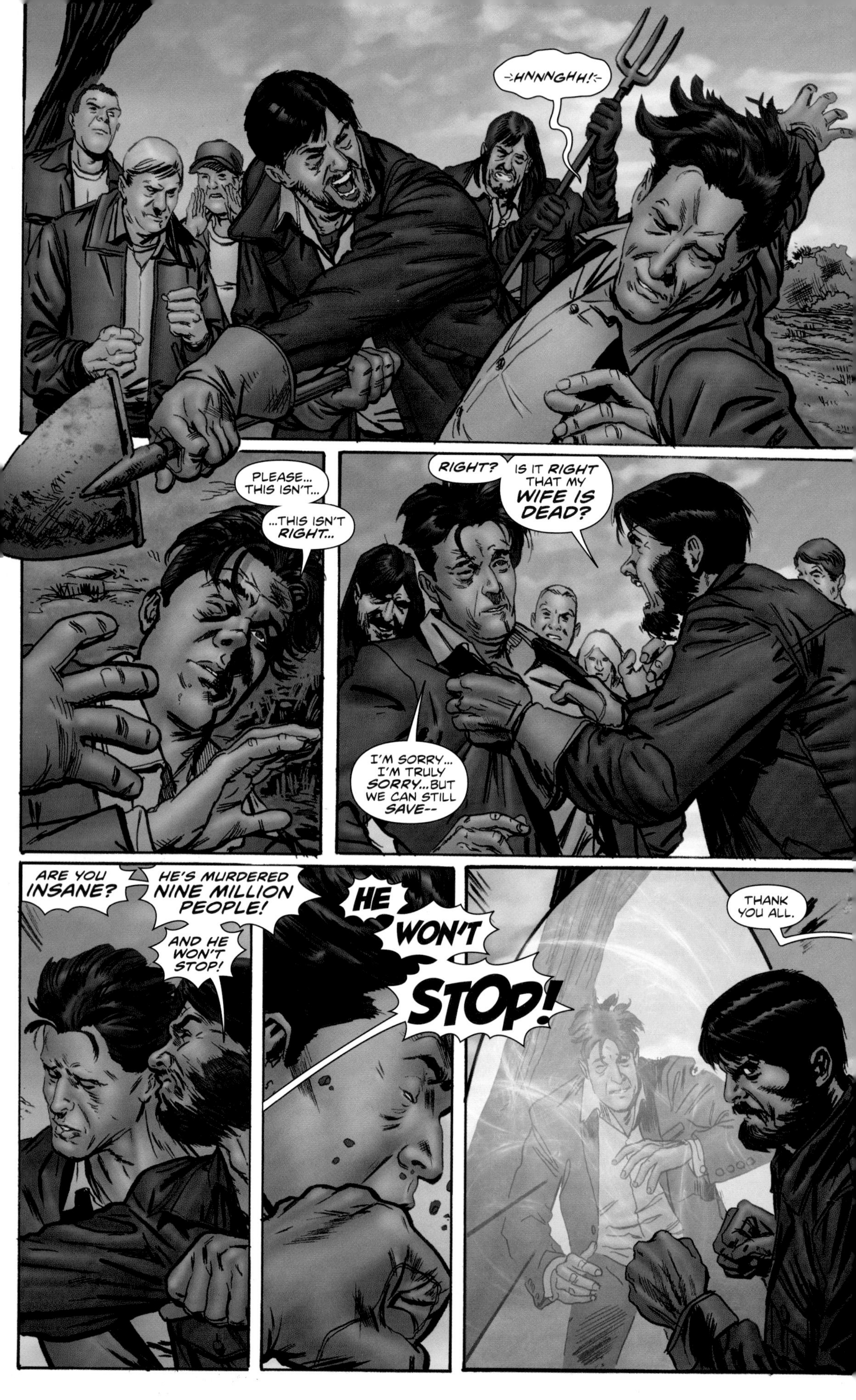
-HNNNGHH!-
PLEASE... THIS ISN'T...
...THIS ISN'T RIGHT...
RIGHT?
IS IT RIGHT THAT MY WIFE IS DEAD?
I'M SORRY... I'M TRULY SORRY...BUT WE CAN STILL SAVE--
ARE YOU INSANE?
HE'S MURDERED NINE MILLION PEOPLE!
AND HE WON'T STOP!
HE WON'T STOP!
THANK YOU ALL.

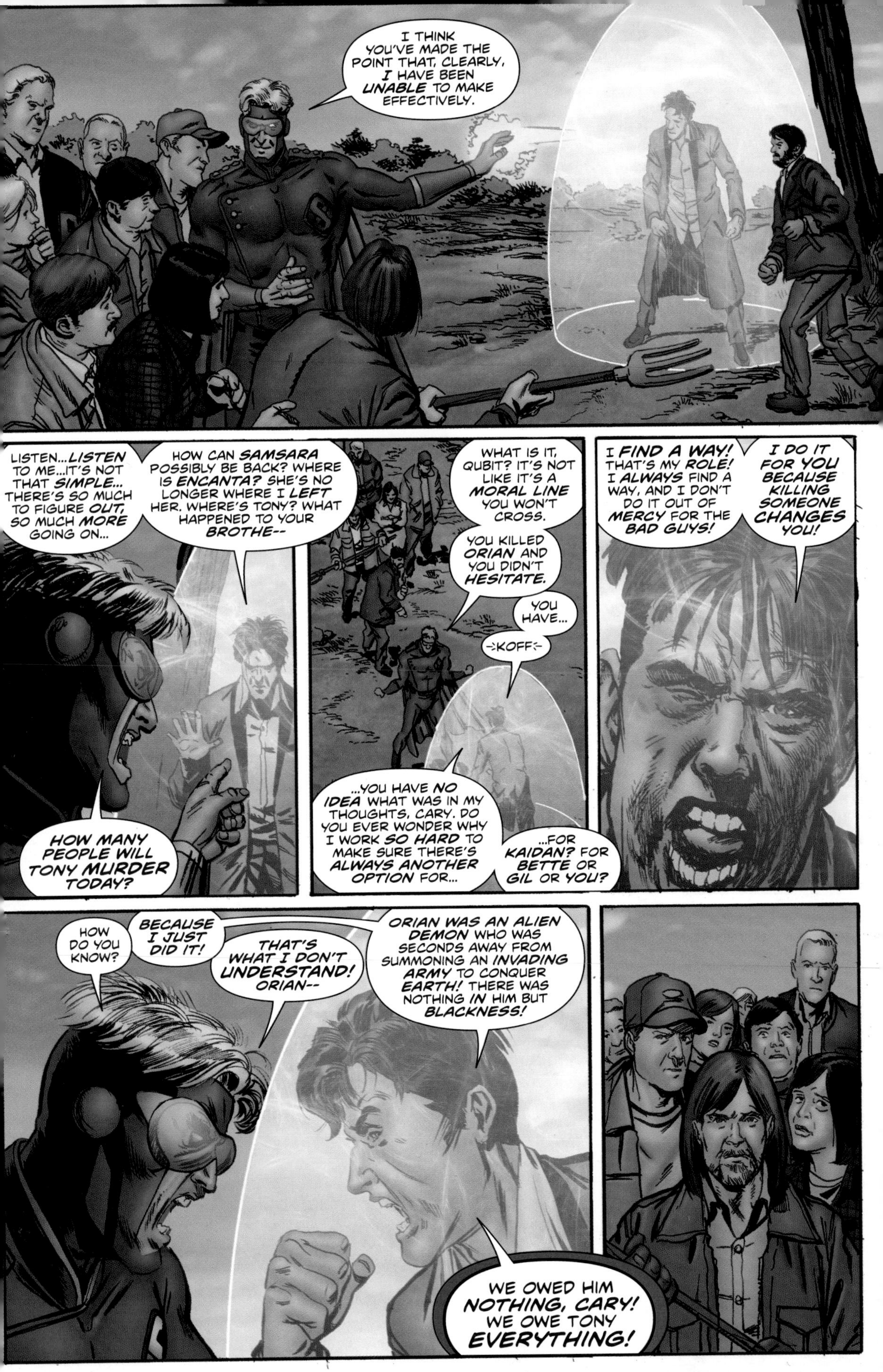
I THINK YOU'VE MADE THE POINT THAT, CLEARLY, I HAVE BEEN UNABLE TO MAKE EFFECTIVELY.
LISTEN...LISTEN TO ME...IT'S NOT THAT SIMPLE... THERE'S SO MUCH TO FIGURE OUT, SO MUCH MORE GOING ON...
HOW CAN SAMSARA POSSIBLY BE BACK? WHERE IS ENCANTA? SHE'S NO LONGER WHERE I LEFT HER. WHERE'S TONY? WHAT HAPPENED TO YOUR BROTHE--
HOW MANY PEOPLE WILL TONY MURDER TODAY?
WHAT IS IT, QUBIT? IT'S NOT LIKE IT'S A MORAL LINE YOU WON'T CROSS.
YOU KILLED ORIAN AND YOU DIDN'T HESITATE.
YOU HAVE...
-KOFF-
...YOU HAVE NO IDEA WHAT WAS IN MY THOUGHTS, CARY. DO YOU EVER WONDER WHY I WORK SO HARD TO MAKE SURE THERE'S ALWAYS ANOTHER OPTION FOR...
...FOR KAIDAN? FOR BETTE OR GIL OR YOU?
I FIND A WAY! THAT'S MY ROLE! I ALWAYS FIND A WAY, AND I DON'T DO IT OUT OF MERCY FOR THE BAD GUYS!
I DO IT FOR YOU BECAUSE KILLING SOMEONE CHANGES YOU!
HOW DO YOU KNOW?
BECAUSE I JUST DID IT!
THAT'S WHAT I DON'T UNDERSTAND! ORIAN--
ORIAN WAS AN ALIEN DEMON WHO WAS SECONDS AWAY FROM SUMMONING AN INVADING ARMY TO CONQUER EARTH! THERE WAS NOTHING IN HIM BUT BLACKNESS!
WE OWED HIM NOTHING, CARY! WE OWE TONY EVERYTHING!

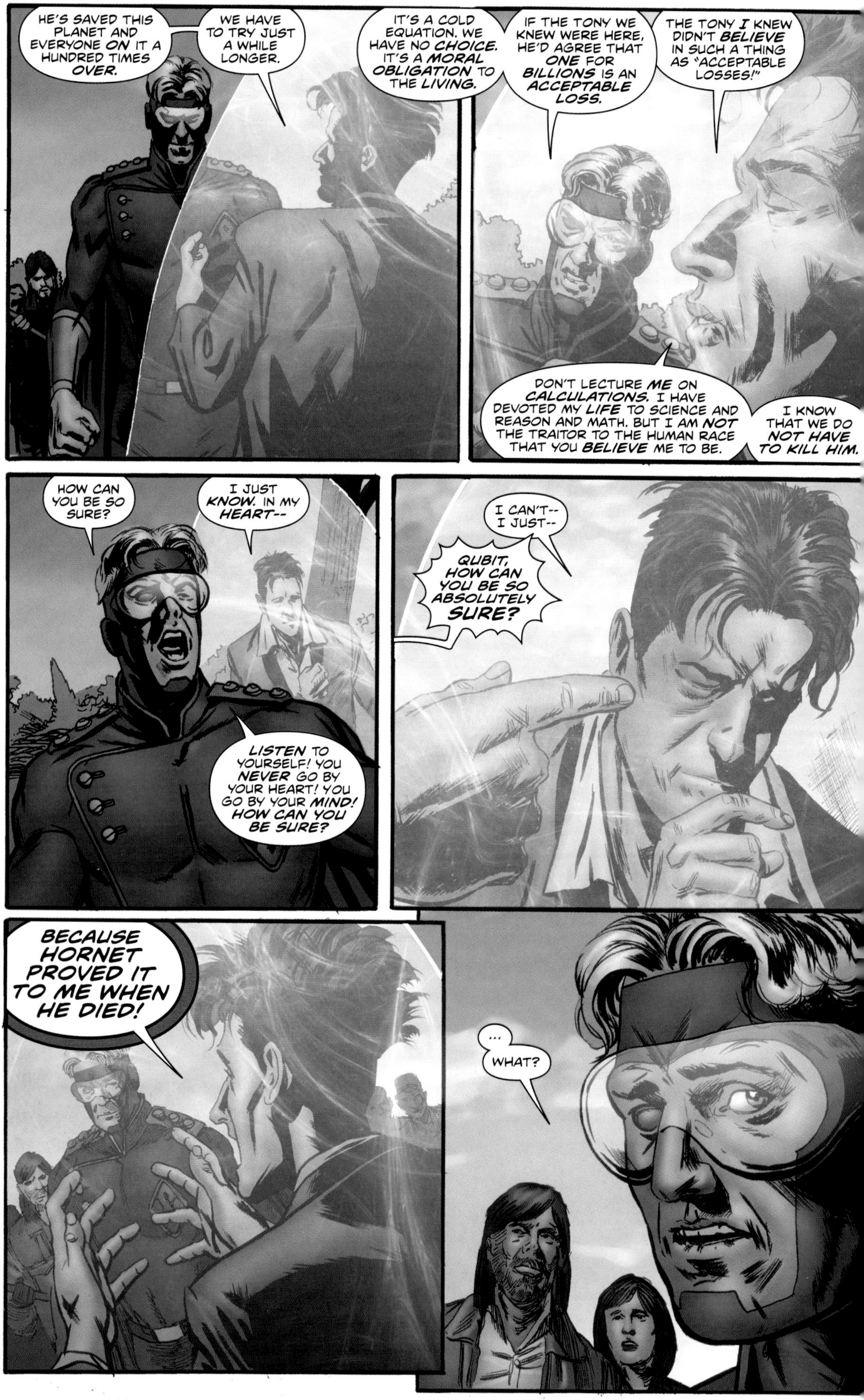
HE'S SAVED THIS PLANET AND EVERYONE ON IT A HUNDRED TIMES OVER.
WE HAVE TO TRY JUST A WHILE LONGER.
IT'S A COLD EQUATION. WE HAVE NO CHOICE. IT'S A MORAL OBLIGATION TO THE LIVING.
IF THE TONY WE KNEW WERE HERE, HE'D AGREE THAT ONE FOR BILLIONS IS AN ACCEPTABLE LOSS.
THE TONY I KNEW DIDN'T BELIEVE IN SUCH A THING AS "ACCEPTABLE LOSSES!"
DON'T LECTURE ME ON CALCULATIONS. I HAVE DEVOTED MY LIFE TO SCIENCE AND REASON AND MATH. BUT I AM NOT THE TRAITOR TO THE HUMAN RACE THAT YOU BELIEVE ME TO BE.
I KNOW THAT WE DO NOT HAVE TO KILL HIM.
HOW CAN YOU BE SO SURE?
I JUST KNOW. IN MY HEART--
LISTEN TO YOURSELF! YOU NEVER GO BY YOUR HEART! YOU GO BY YOUR MIND! HOW CAN YOU BE SURE?
I CAN'T-- I JUST--
QUBIT, HOW CAN YOU BE SO ABSOLUTELY SURE?
BECAUSE HORNET PROVED IT TO ME WHEN HE DIED!
... WHAT?

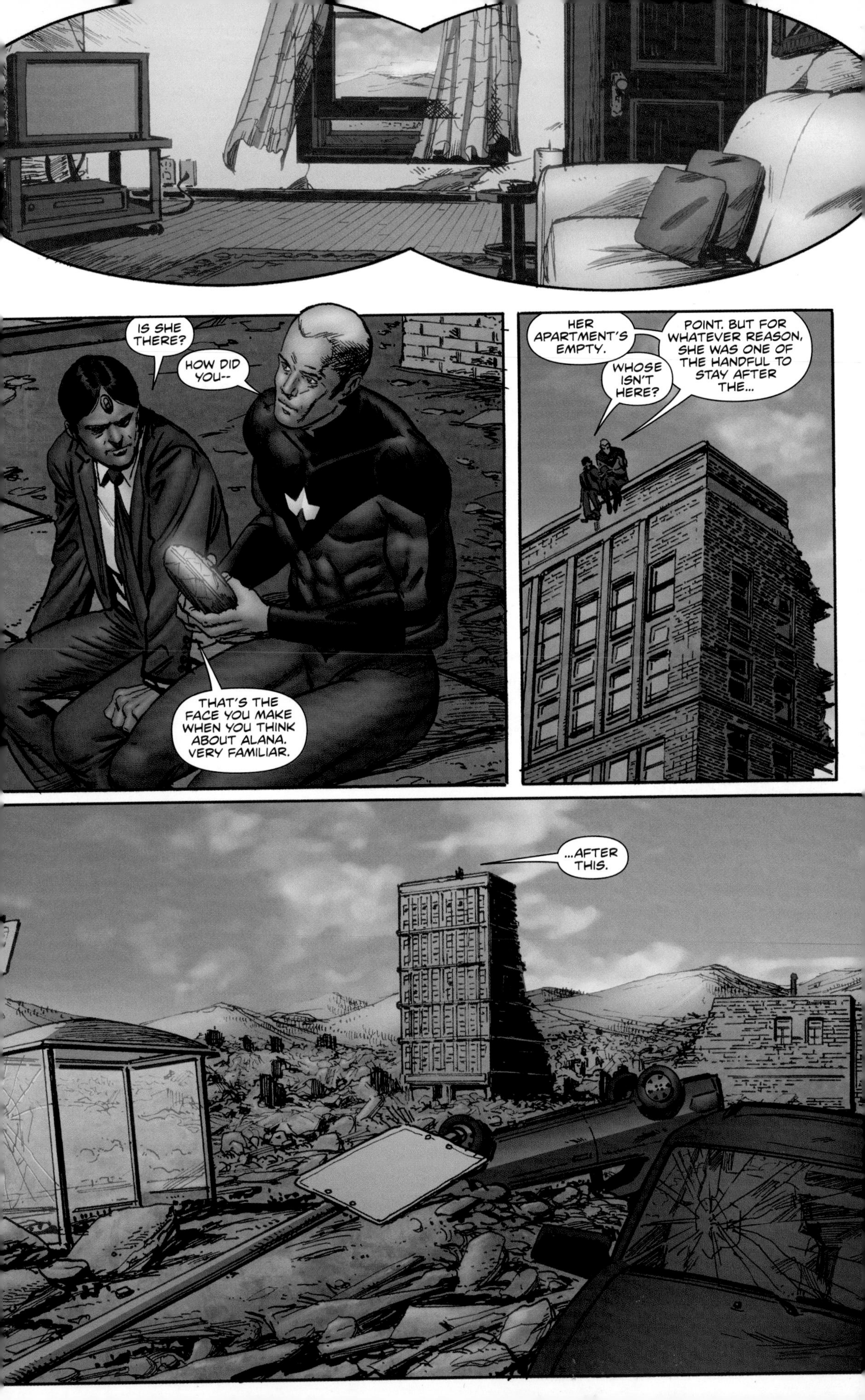
IS SHE THERE?
HOW DID YOU--
THAT'S THE FACE YOU MAKE WHEN YOU THINK ABOUT ALANA. VERY FAMILIAR.
HER APARTMENT'S EMPTY.
WHOSE ISN'T HERE?
POINT. BUT FOR WHATEVER REASON, SHE WAS ONE OF THE HANDFUL TO STAY AFTER THE...
...AFTER THIS.

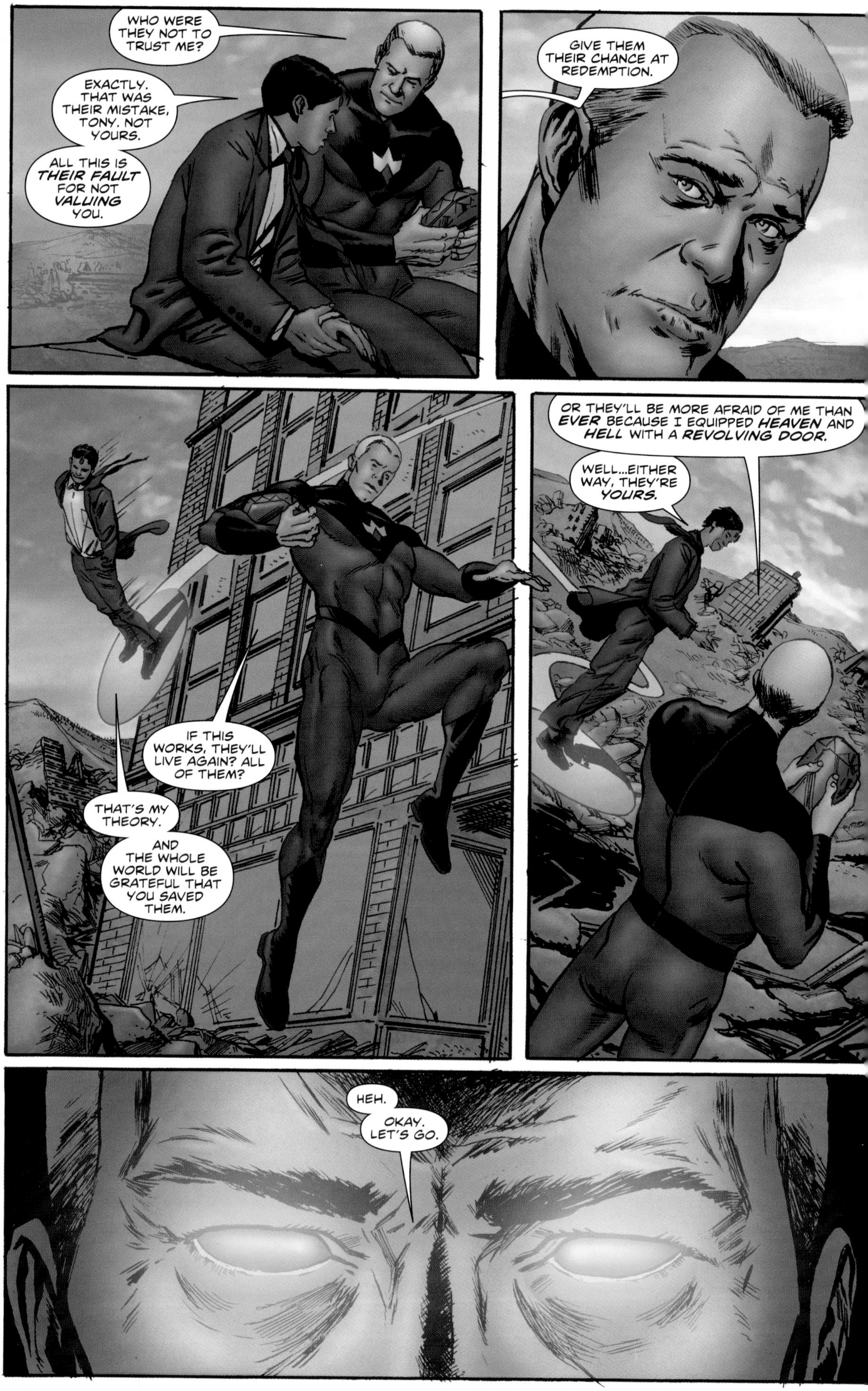
WHO WERE THEY NOT TO TRUST ME?
EXACTLY. THAT WAS THEIR MISTAKE, TONY. NOT YOURS.
ALL THIS IS *THEIR FAULT* FOR NOT *VALUING* YOU.
GIVE THEM THEIR CHANCE AT REDEMPTION.
IF THIS WORKS, THEY'LL LIVE AGAIN? ALL OF THEM?
THAT'S MY THEORY.
AND THE WHOLE WORLD WILL BE GRATEFUL THAT YOU SAVED THEM.
OR THEY'LL BE MORE AFRAID OF ME THAN *EVER* BECAUSE I EQUIPPED *HEAVEN* AND *HELL* WITH A *REVOLVING DOOR.*
WELL...EITHER WAY, THEY'RE *YOURS.*
HEH.
OKAY. LET'S GO.

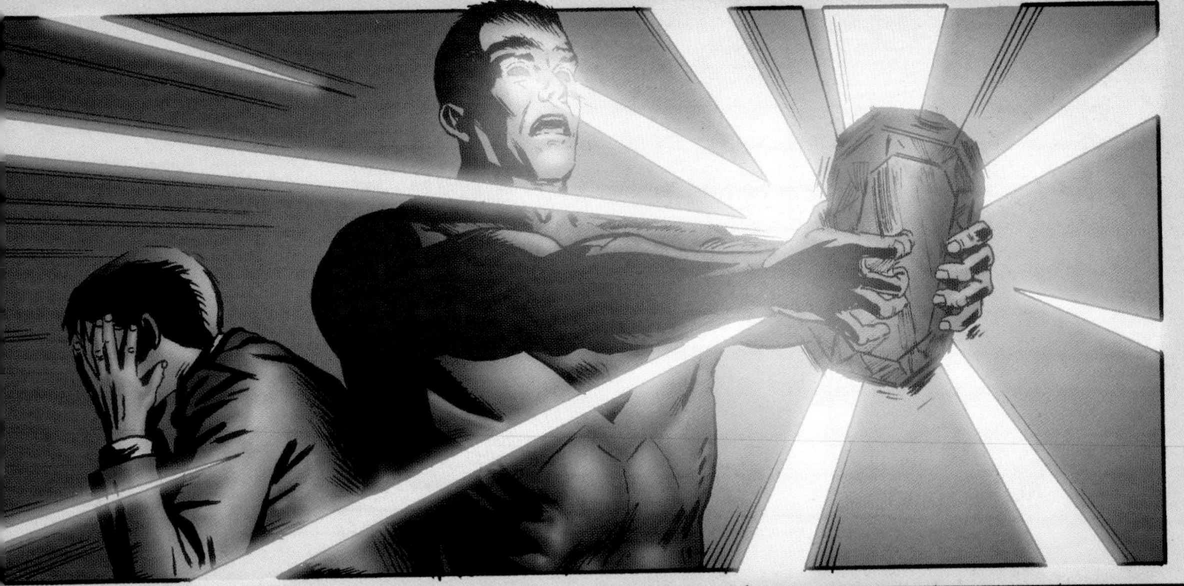
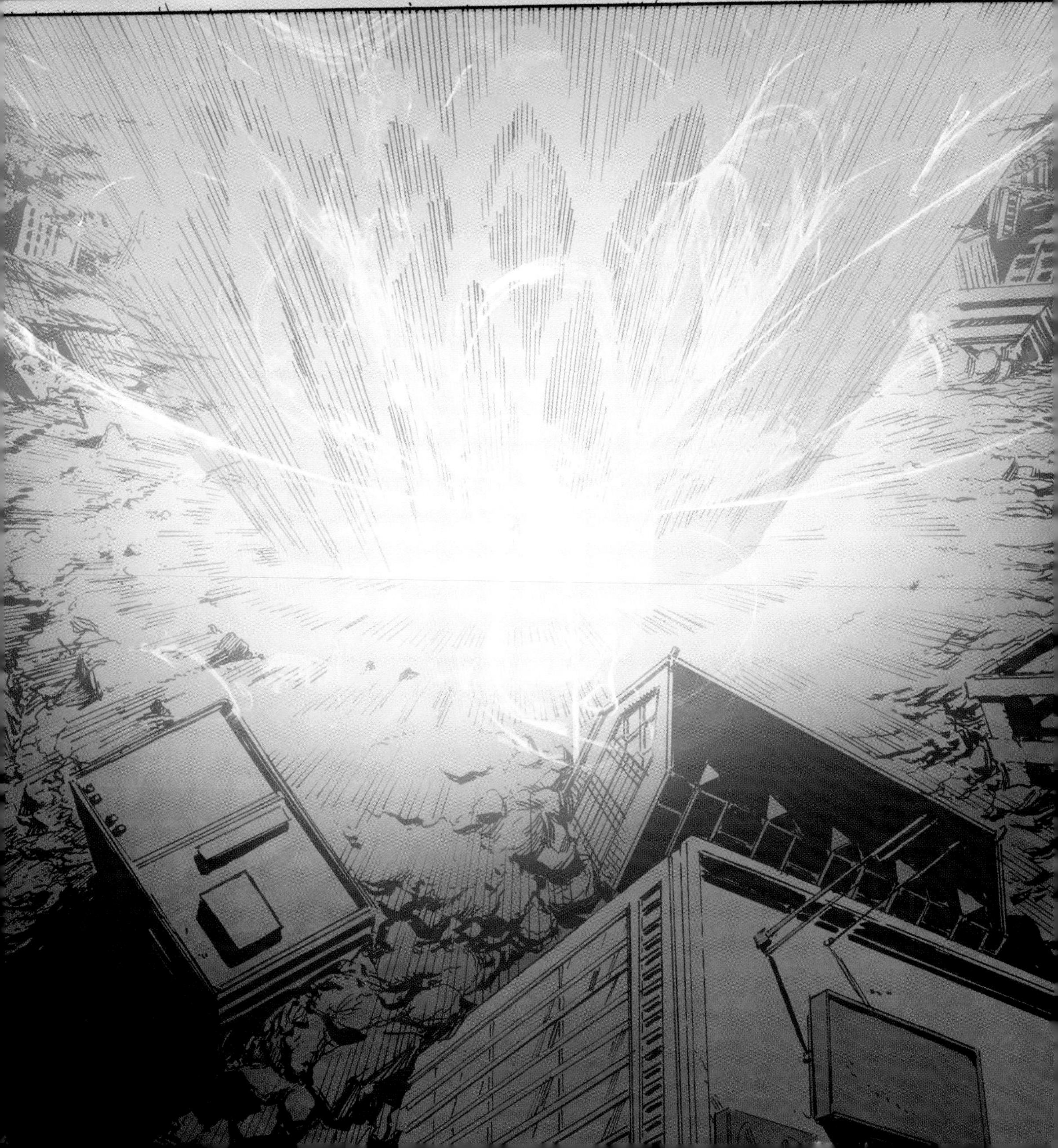

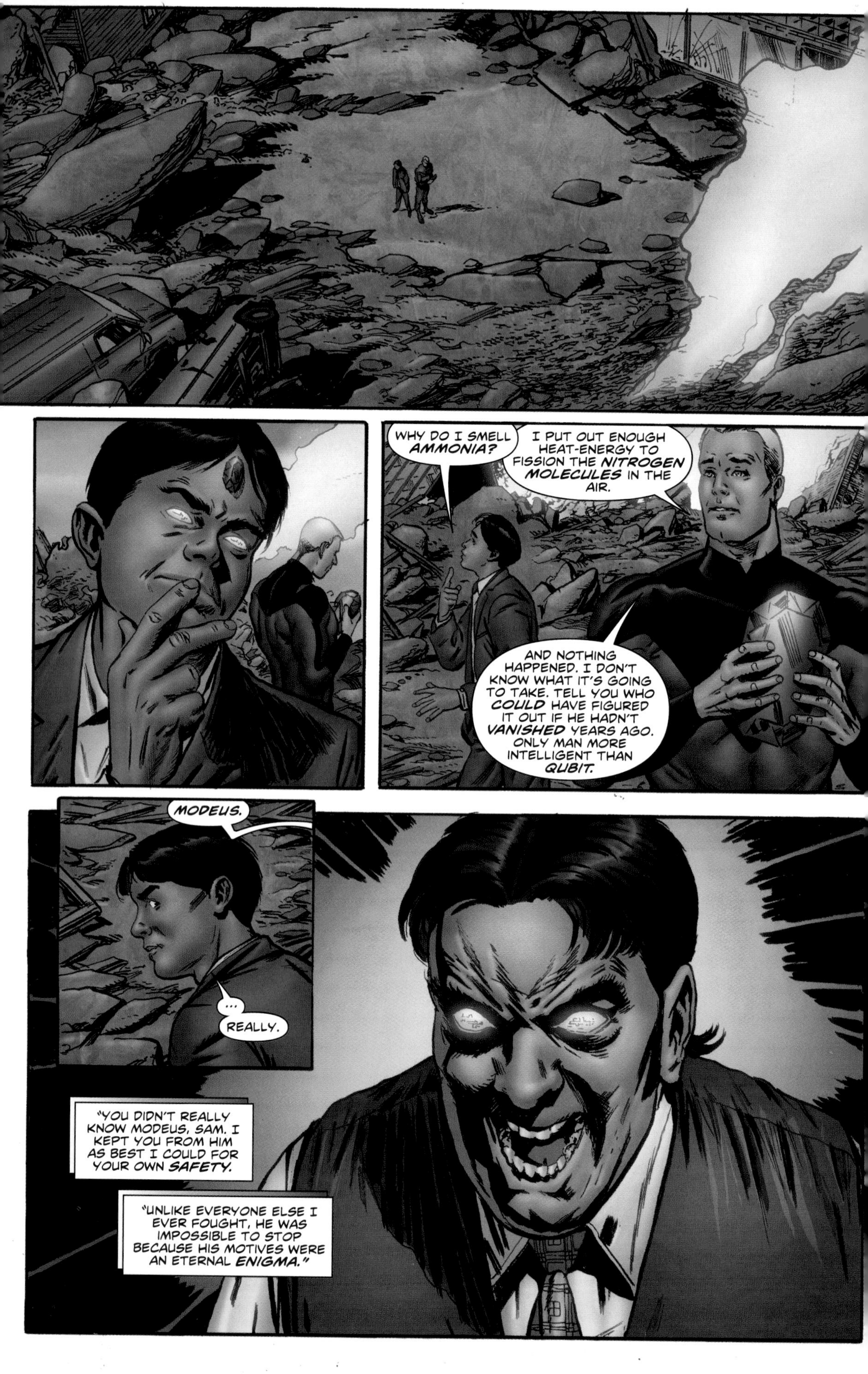
WHY DO I SMELL AMMONIA?
I PUT OUT ENOUGH HEAT-ENERGY TO FISSION THE NITROGEN MOLECULES IN THE AIR.
AND NOTHING HAPPENED. I DON'T KNOW WHAT IT'S GOING TO TAKE. TELL YOU WHO COULD HAVE FIGURED IT OUT IF HE HADN'T VANISHED YEARS AGO. ONLY MAN MORE INTELLIGENT THAN QUBIT.
MODEUS.
... REALLY.
"YOU DIDN'T REALLY KNOW MODEUS, SAM. I KEPT YOU FROM HIM AS BEST I COULD FOR YOUR OWN SAFETY.
"UNLIKE EVERYONE ELSE I EVER FOUGHT, HE WAS IMPOSSIBLE TO STOP BECAUSE HIS MOTIVES WERE AN ETERNAL ENIGMA."

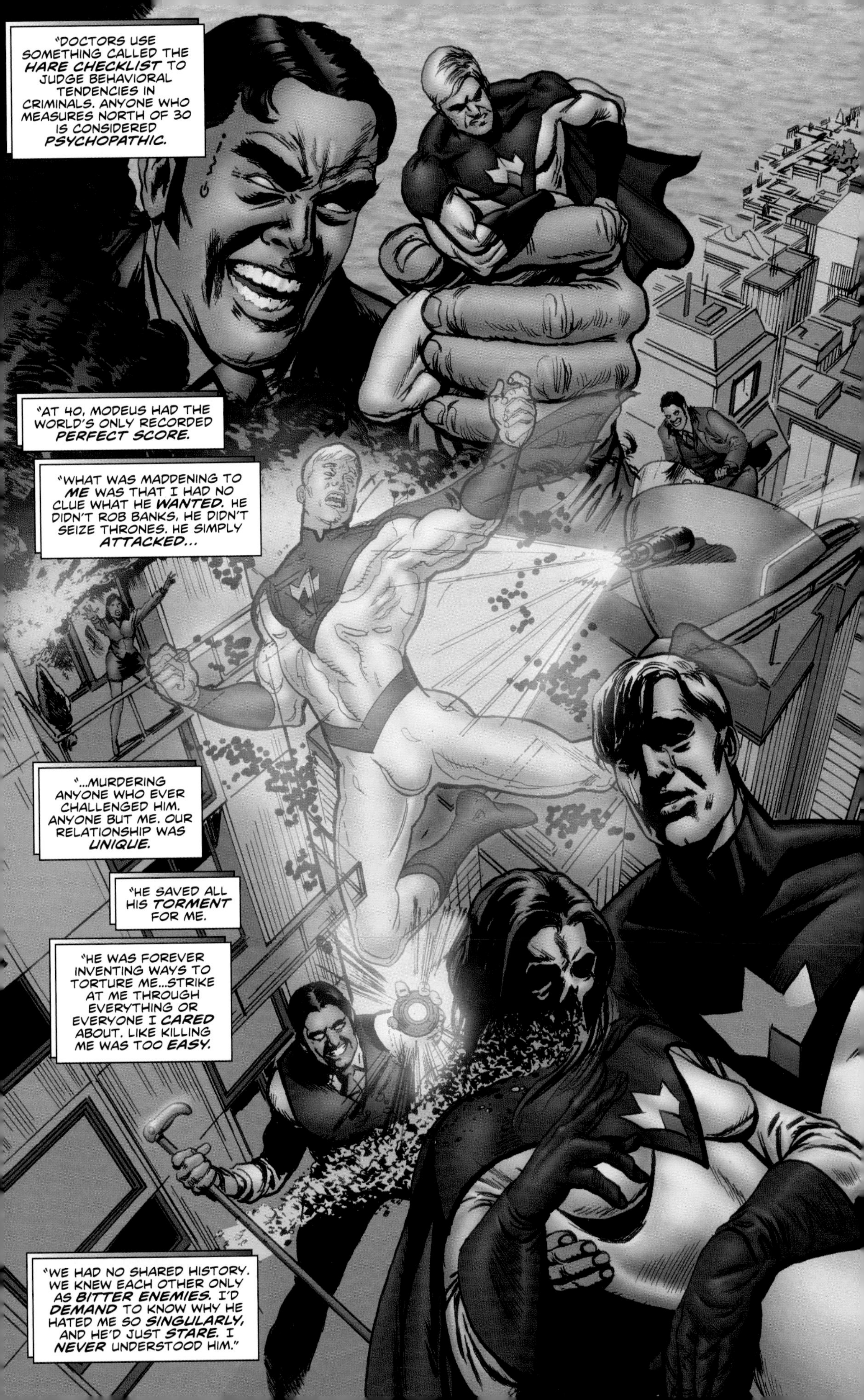
"DOCTORS USE SOMETHING CALLED THE *HARE CHECKLIST* TO JUDGE BEHAVIORAL TENDENCIES IN CRIMINALS. ANYONE WHO MEASURES NORTH OF 30 IS CONSIDERED *PSYCHOPATHIC.*
"AT 40, MODEUS HAD THE WORLD'S ONLY RECORDED *PERFECT SCORE.*
"WHAT WAS MADDENING TO *ME* WAS THAT I HAD NO CLUE WHAT HE *WANTED.* HE DIDN'T ROB BANKS, HE DIDN'T SEIZE THRONES. HE SIMPLY *ATTACKED...*
"...MURDERING ANYONE WHO EVER CHALLENGED HIM. ANYONE BUT ME. OUR RELATIONSHIP WAS *UNIQUE.*
"HE SAVED ALL HIS *TORMENT* FOR ME.
"HE WAS FOREVER INVENTING WAYS TO TORTURE ME...STRIKE AT ME THROUGH EVERYTHING OR EVERYONE I *CARED* ABOUT. LIKE KILLING ME WAS TOO *EASY.*
"WE HAD NO SHARED HISTORY. WE KNEW EACH OTHER ONLY AS *BITTER ENEMIES.* I'D *DEMAND* TO KNOW WHY HE HATED ME SO *SINGULARLY,* AND HE'D JUST *STARE.* I *NEVER* UNDERSTOOD HIM."

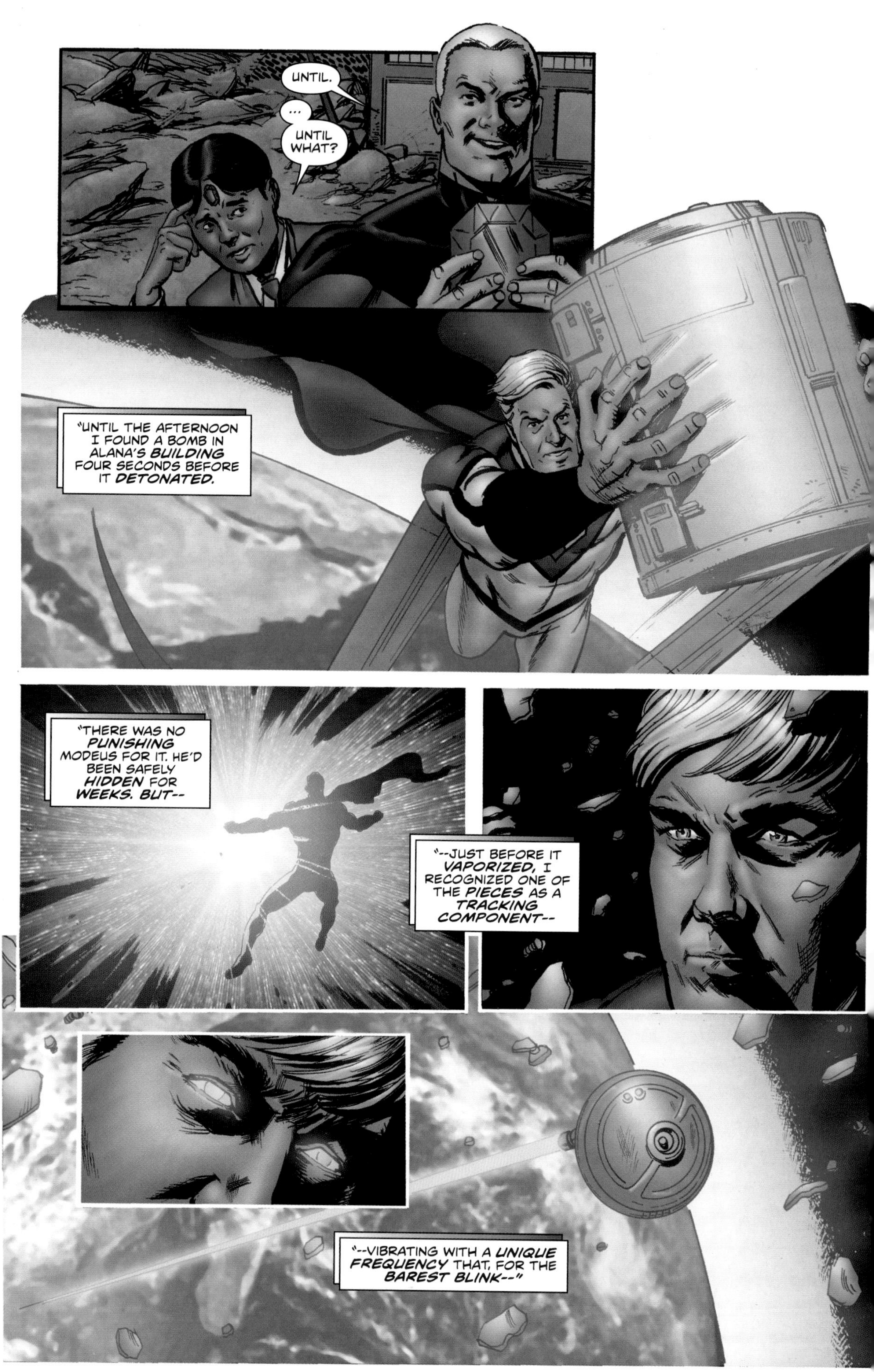
UNTIL.
...
UNTIL WHAT?
"UNTIL THE AFTERNOON I FOUND A BOMB IN ALANA'S BUILDING FOUR SECONDS BEFORE IT DETONATED.
"THERE WAS NO PUNISHING MODEUS FOR IT. HE'D BEEN SAFELY HIDDEN FOR WEEKS. BUT--
"--JUST BEFORE IT VAPORIZED, I RECOGNIZED ONE OF THE PIECES AS A TRACKING COMPONENT--
"--VIBRATING WITH A UNIQUE FREQUENCY THAT, FOR THE BAREST BLINK--"

"--ETHERCAST A PICOSECOND-LONG *BATTLE REPORT* BACK TO ITS *BUILDER.*

"IF I COULD OUTRACE THE *SIGNAL,* I COULD--FOR *ONCE, FINALLY*--GET THE *DROP* ON THIS GUY.

"THE SIGNAL LED ME TO SOME SORT OF *CYBERNETICS LAB.* THERE WERE *GUARD DOGS,* NATURALLY.

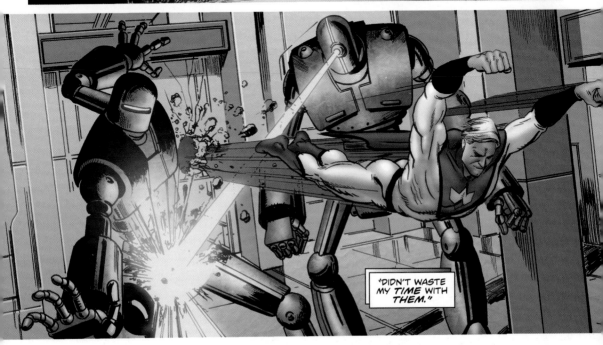

"DIDN'T WASTE MY *TIME* WITH *THEM.*"

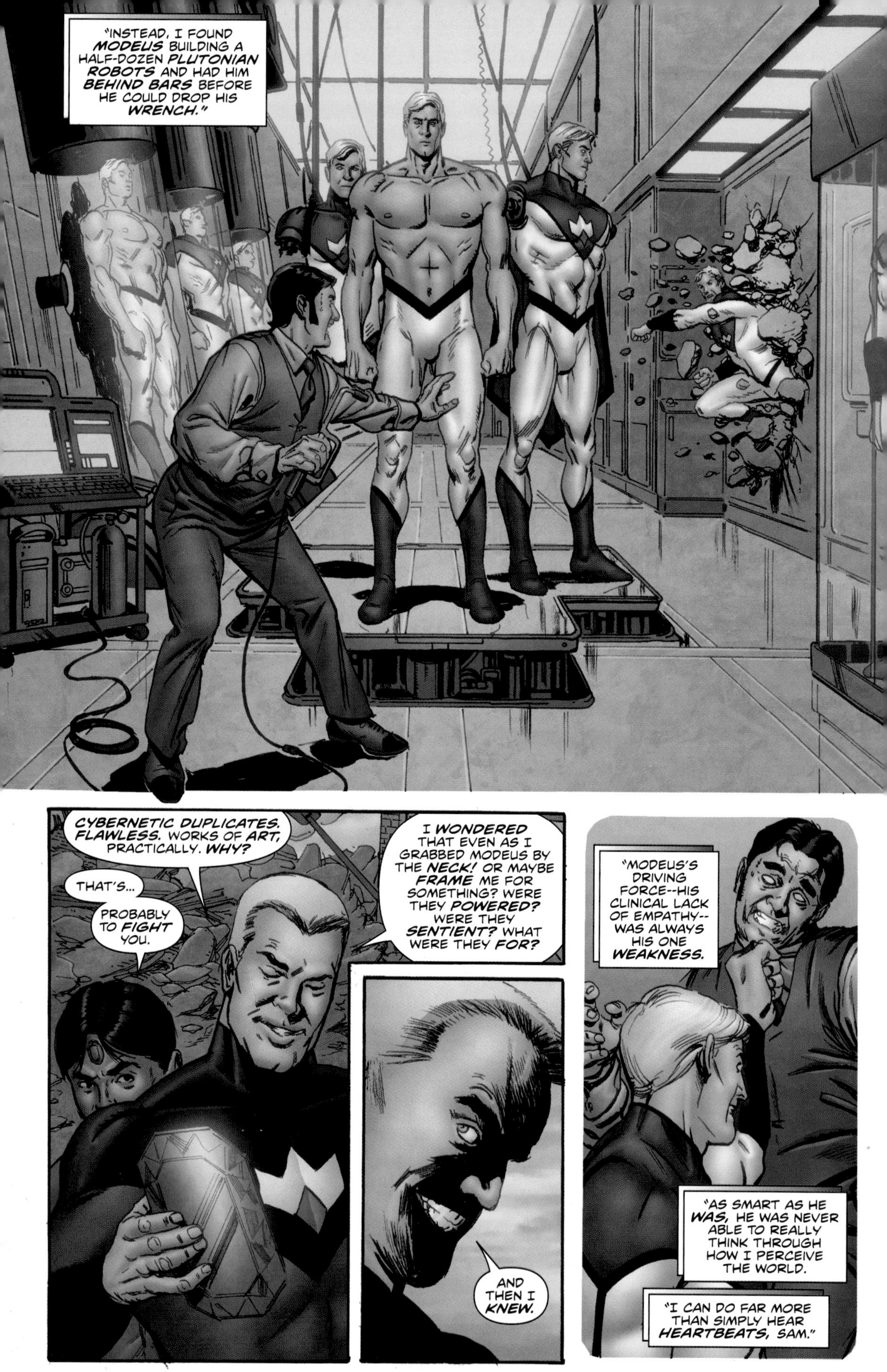
"INSTEAD, I FOUND MODEUS BUILDING A HALF-DOZEN PLUTONIAN ROBOTS AND HAD HIM BEHIND BARS BEFORE HE COULD DROP HIS WRENCH."
CYBERNETIC DUPLICATES. FLAWLESS. WORKS OF ART, PRACTICALLY. WHY?
THAT'S...
PROBABLY TO FIGHT YOU.
I WONDERED THAT EVEN AS I GRABBED MODEUS BY THE NECK! OR MAYBE FRAME ME FOR SOMETHING? WERE THEY POWERED? WERE THEY SENTIENT? WHAT WERE THEY FOR?
AND THEN I KNEW.
"MODEUS'S DRIVING FORCE--HIS CLINICAL LACK OF EMPATHY--WAS ALWAYS HIS ONE WEAKNESS.
"AS SMART AS HE WAS, HE WAS NEVER ABLE TO REALLY THINK THROUGH HOW I PERCEIVE THE WORLD.
"I CAN DO FAR MORE THAN SIMPLY HEAR HEARTBEATS, SAM."

"I CAN WATCH ELECTRONS BOUNCE THROUGH A MAN'S *SUBCORTEX*. I CAN INTERPRET THEIR *DANCE* AS *ANXIETY* OR *ELATION* OR *RAGE*.

"I CAN DECODE THE *PHEROMONES* HE GIVES OFF AND KNOW *CONCLUSIVELY* WHAT HE *LUSTS* FOR AND WHAT *REPELS* HIM.

"I'D MISSED IT *ALL ALONG*. BUT IN THAT MOMENT, MODEUS'S *GUARD* WAS DOWN AND ALL HIS FEELINGS WERE NOT ONLY ON *FULL DISPLAY*, THEY WERE OFF THE *CHARTS*...AND I FINALLY KNEW THE *TRUTH*.

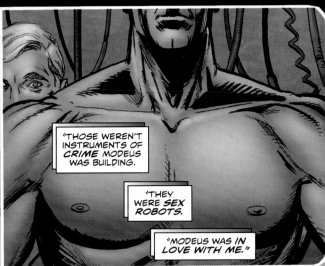

"THOSE WEREN'T INSTRUMENTS OF *CRIME* MODEUS WAS BUILDING.

"THEY WERE *SEX ROBOTS*.

"MODEUS WAS *IN LOVE WITH ME*."

...

THAT'S...

...THAT'S NOT...

...HE DIDN'T *LOVE*...

...HE *HATED* YOU...

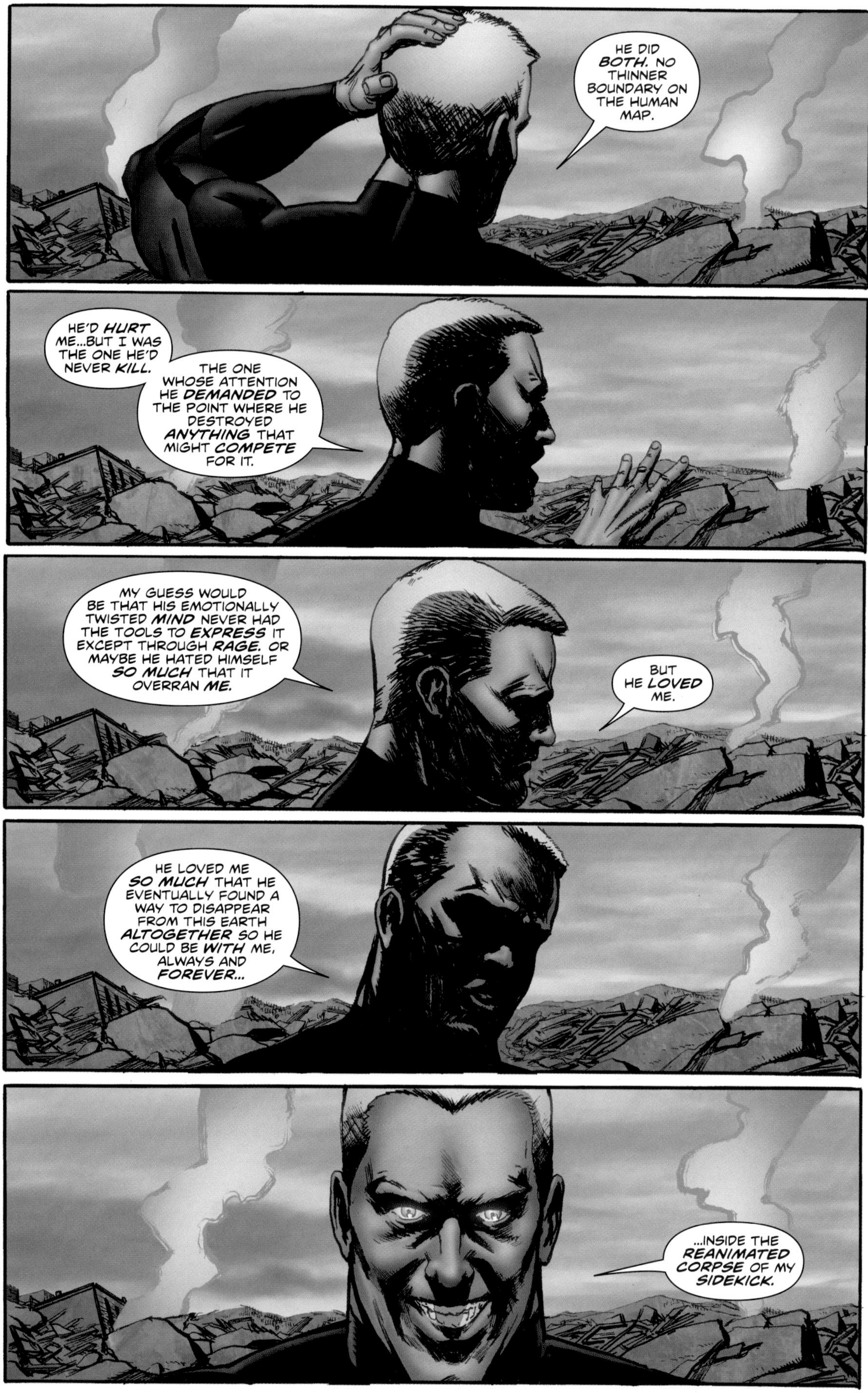
HE DID BOTH. NO THINNER BOUNDARY ON THE HUMAN MAP.
HE'D HURT ME...BUT I WAS THE ONE HE'D NEVER KILL.
THE ONE WHOSE ATTENTION HE DEMANDED TO THE POINT WHERE HE DESTROYED ANYTHING THAT MIGHT COMPETE FOR IT.
MY GUESS WOULD BE THAT HIS EMOTIONALLY TWISTED MIND NEVER HAD THE TOOLS TO EXPRESS IT EXCEPT THROUGH RAGE. OR MAYBE HE HATED HIMSELF SO MUCH THAT IT OVERRAN ME.
BUT HE LOVED ME.
HE LOVED ME SO MUCH THAT HE EVENTUALLY FOUND A WAY TO DISAPPEAR FROM THIS EARTH ALTOGETHER SO HE COULD BE WITH ME, ALWAYS AND FOREVER...
...INSIDE THE REANIMATED CORPSE OF MY SIDEKICK.

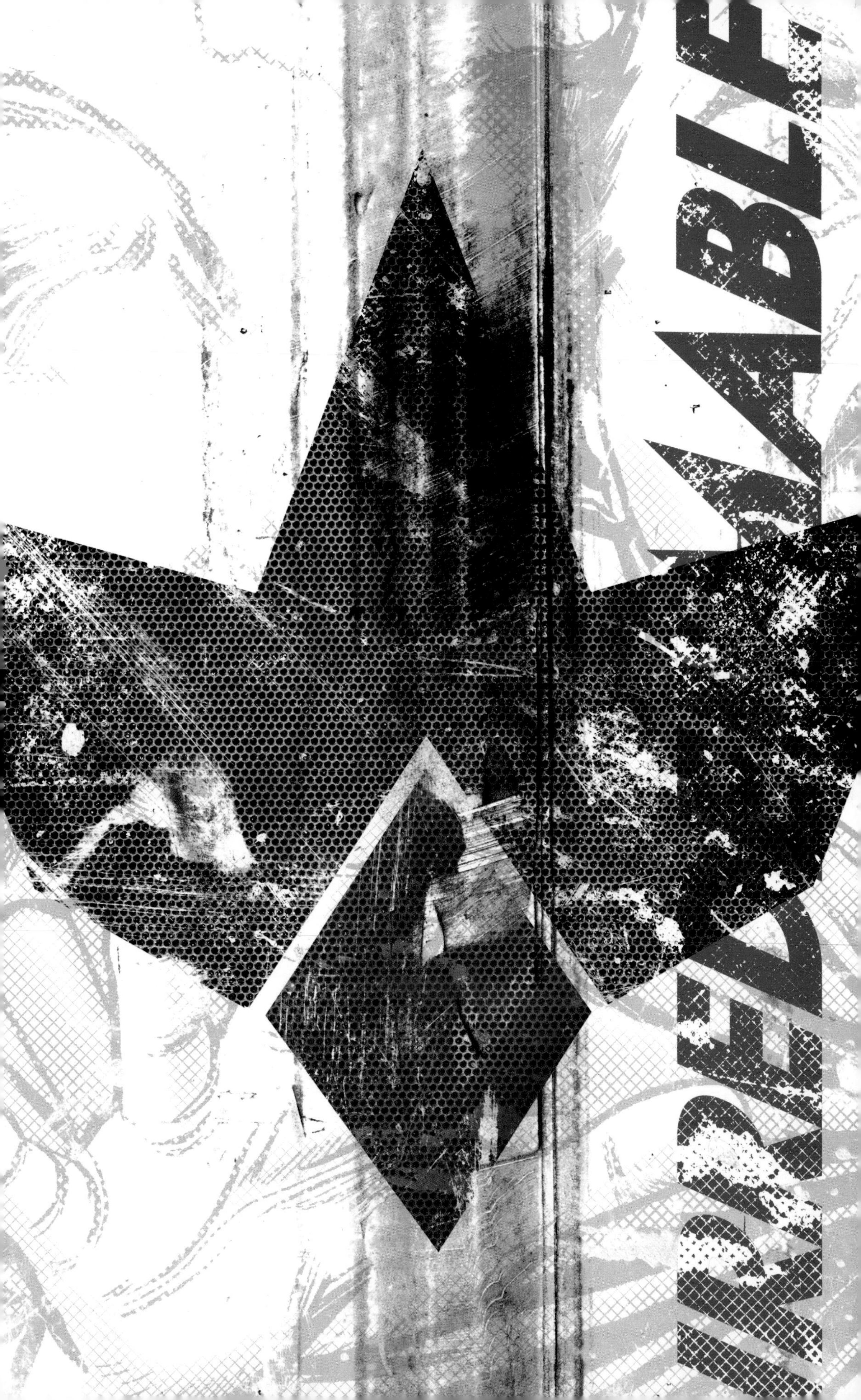

CHAPTER 18

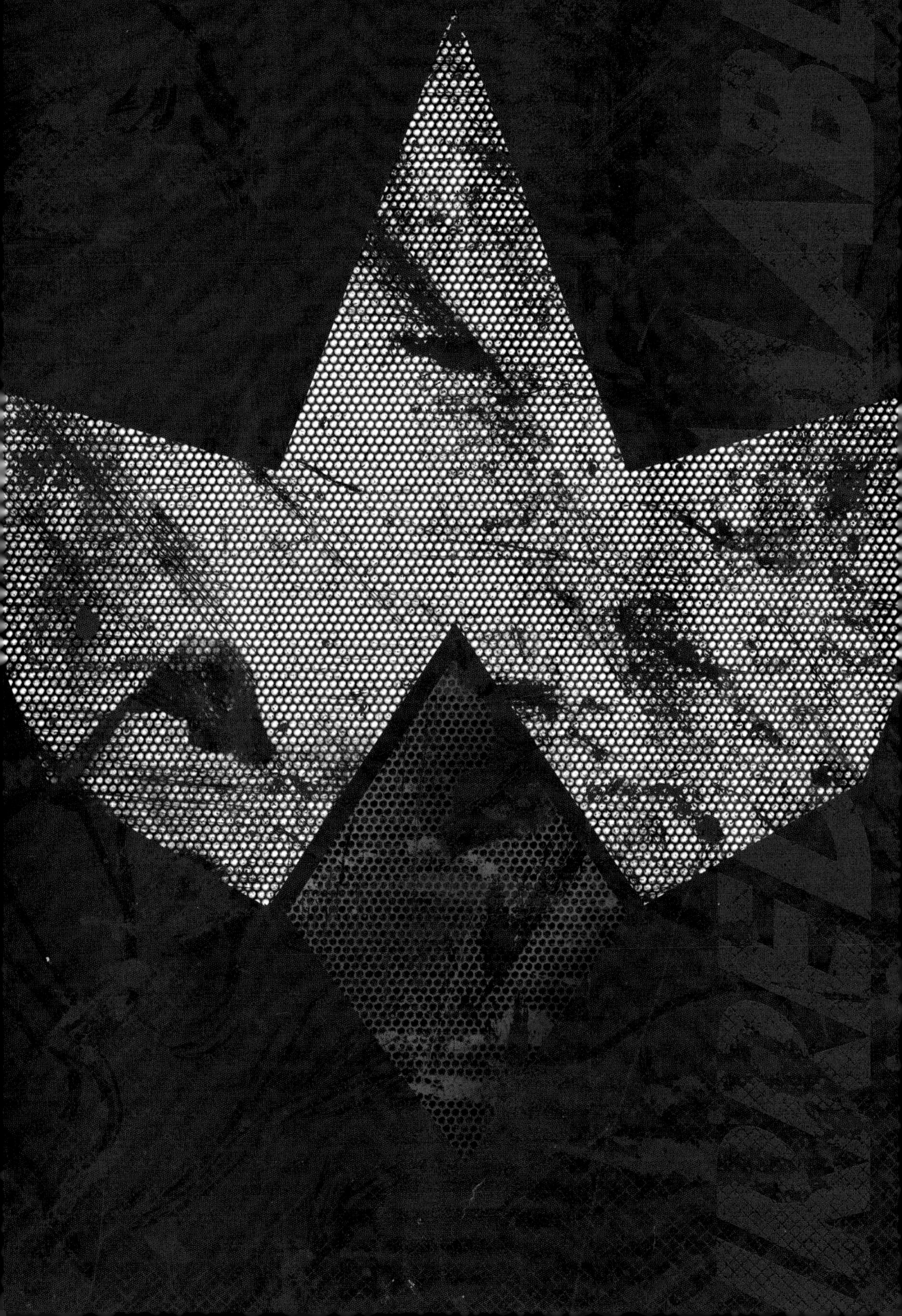

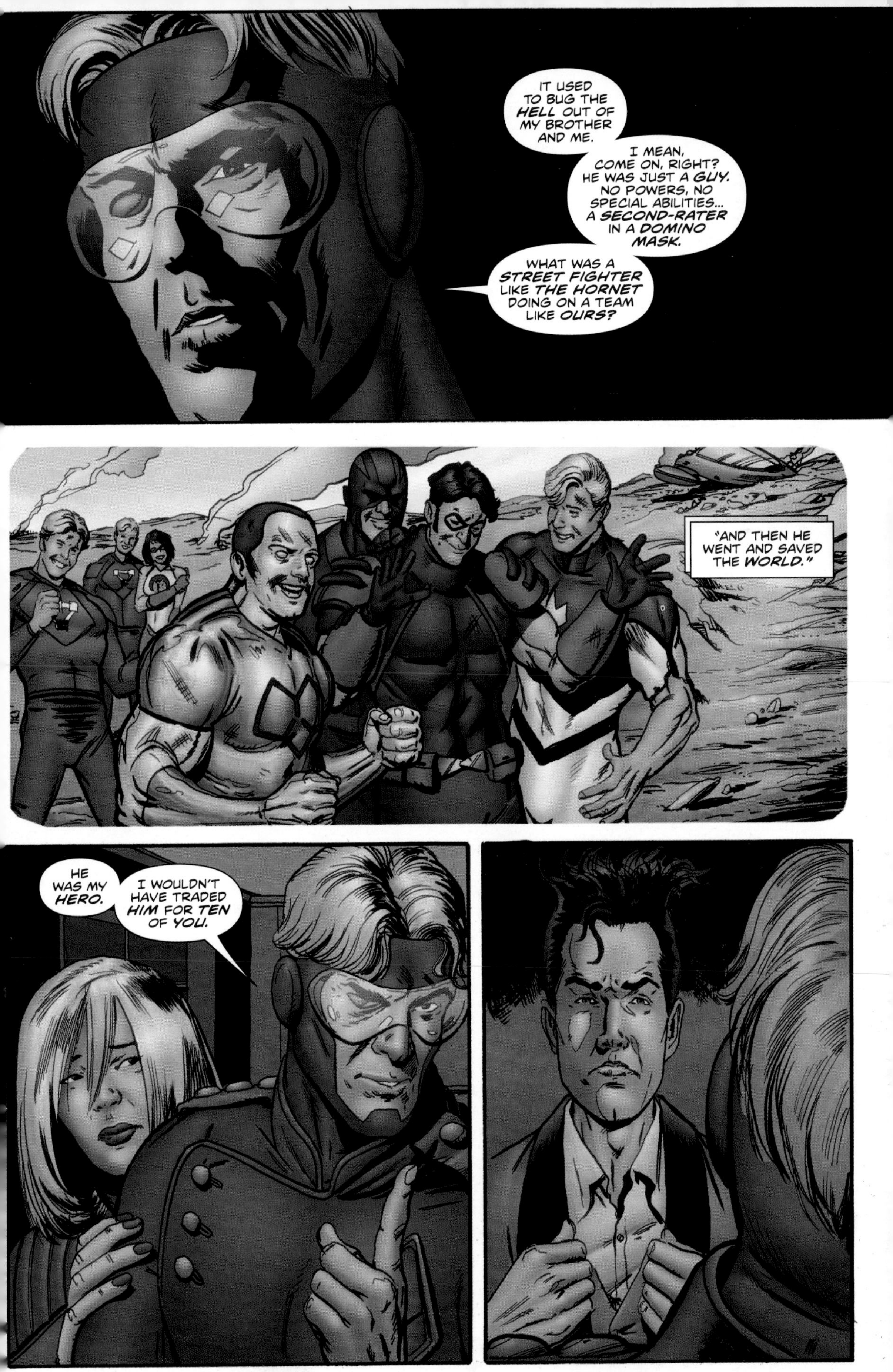
IT USED TO BUG THE HELL OUT OF MY BROTHER AND ME.
I MEAN, COME ON, RIGHT? HE WAS JUST A GUY. NO POWERS, NO SPECIAL ABILITIES... A SECOND-RATER IN A DOMINO MASK.
WHAT WAS A STREET FIGHTER LIKE THE HORNET DOING ON A TEAM LIKE OURS?
"AND THEN HE WENT AND SAVED THE WORLD."
HE WAS MY HERO.
I WOULDN'T HAVE TRADED HIM FOR TEN OF YOU.

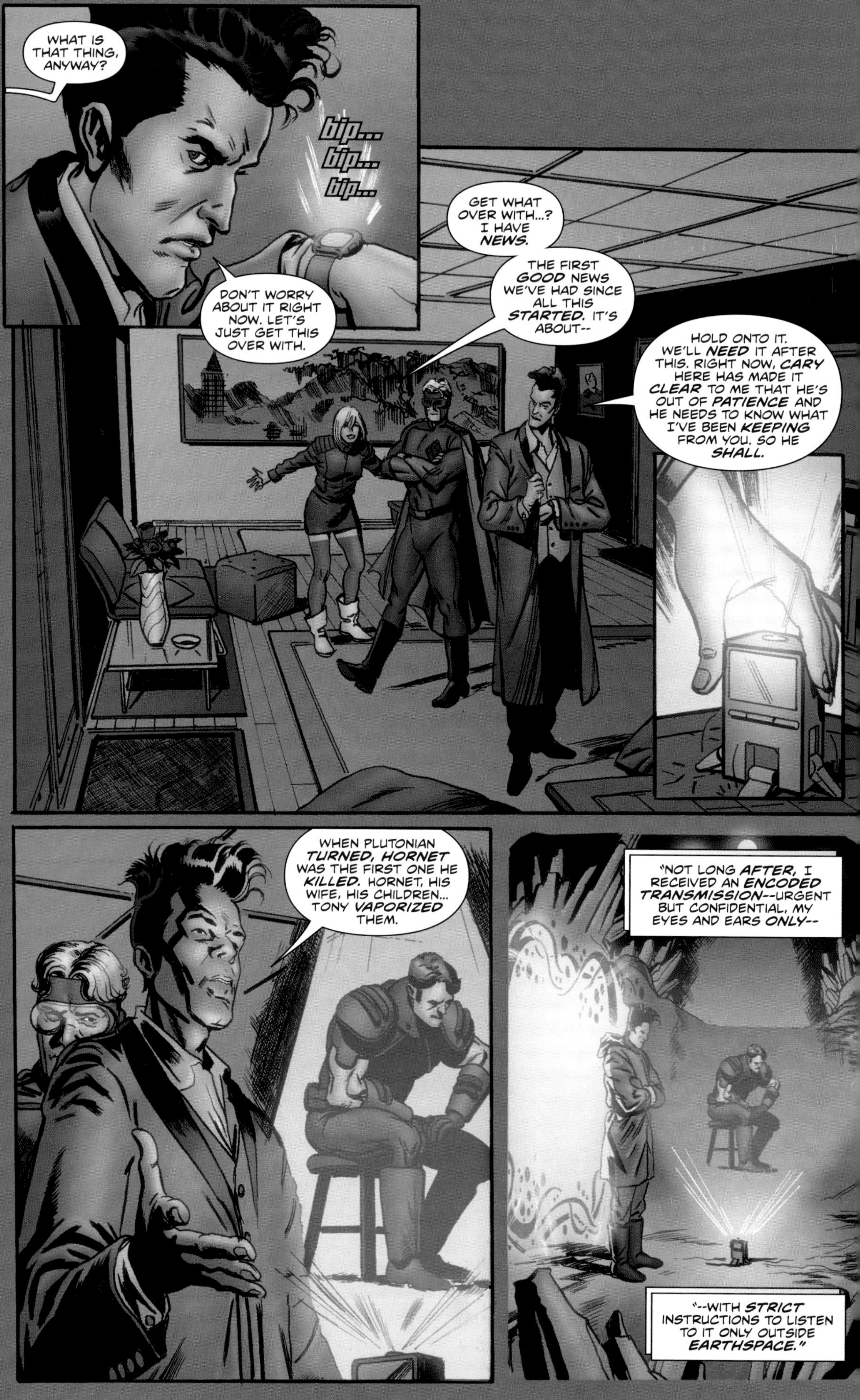
WHAT IS THAT THING, ANYWAY?
bip... bip... bip...
DON'T WORRY ABOUT IT RIGHT NOW. LET'S JUST GET THIS OVER WITH.
GET WHAT OVER WITH...? I HAVE NEWS.
THE FIRST GOOD NEWS WE'VE HAD SINCE ALL THIS STARTED. IT'S ABOUT--
HOLD ONTO IT. WE'LL NEED IT AFTER THIS. RIGHT NOW, CARY HERE HAS MADE IT CLEAR TO ME THAT HE'S OUT OF PATIENCE AND HE NEEDS TO KNOW WHAT I'VE BEEN KEEPING FROM YOU. SO HE SHALL.
WHEN PLUTONIAN TURNED, HORNET WAS THE FIRST ONE HE KILLED. HORNET, HIS WIFE, HIS CHILDREN... TONY VAPORIZED THEM.
"NOT LONG AFTER, I RECEIVED AN ENCODED TRANSMISSION--URGENT BUT CONFIDENTIAL, MY EYES AND EARS ONLY--
"--WITH STRICT INSTRUCTIONS TO LISTEN TO IT ONLY OUTSIDE EARTHSPACE."

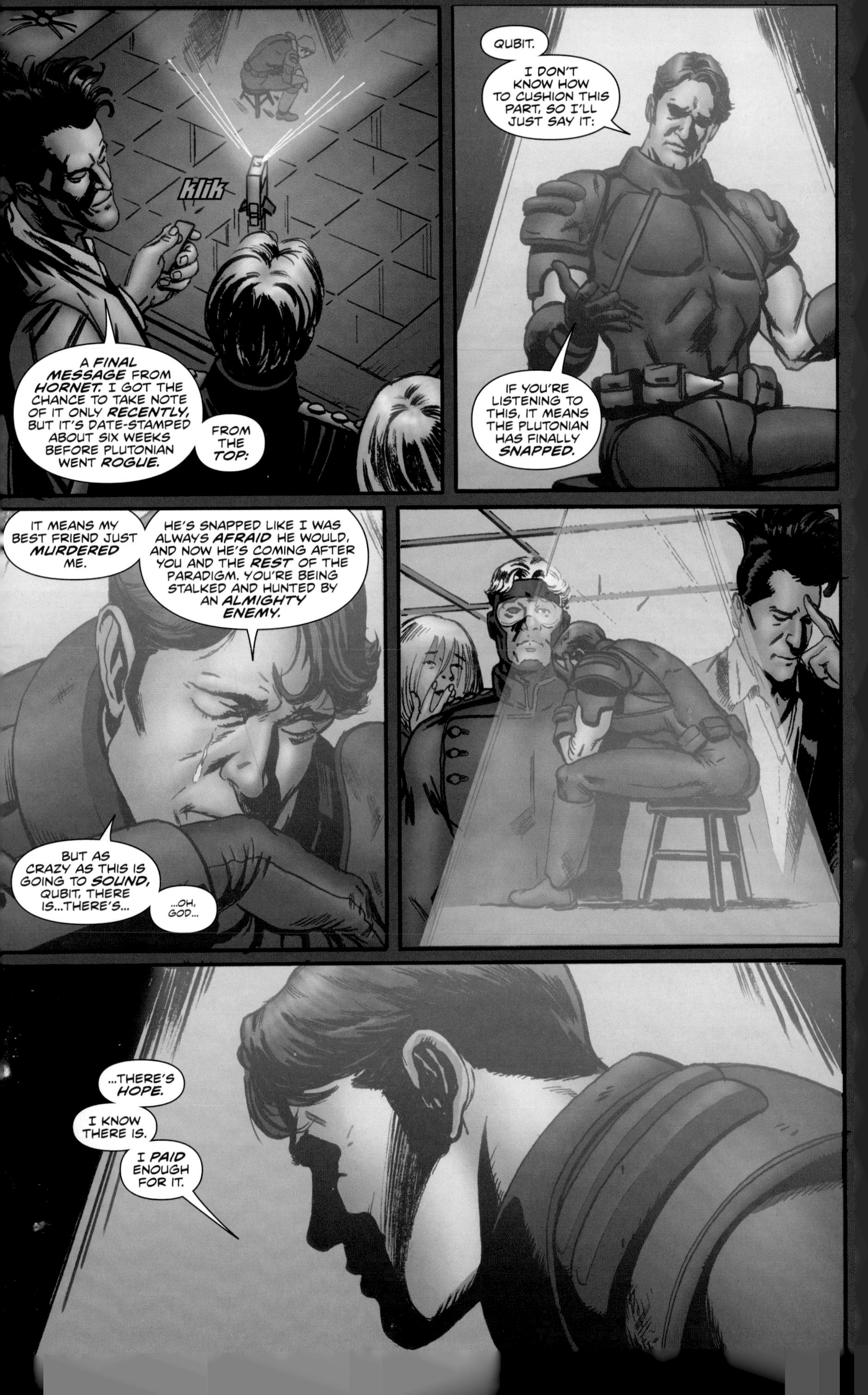
klik
A FINAL MESSAGE FROM HORNET. I GOT THE CHANCE TO TAKE NOTE OF IT ONLY RECENTLY, BUT IT'S DATE-STAMPED ABOUT SIX WEEKS BEFORE PLUTONIAN WENT ROGUE.
FROM THE TOP:
QUBIT.
I DON'T KNOW HOW TO CUSHION THIS PART, SO I'LL JUST SAY IT:
IF YOU'RE LISTENING TO THIS, IT MEANS THE PLUTONIAN HAS FINALLY SNAPPED.
IT MEANS MY BEST FRIEND JUST MURDERED ME.
HE'S SNAPPED LIKE I WAS ALWAYS AFRAID HE WOULD, AND NOW HE'S COMING AFTER YOU AND THE REST OF THE PARADIGM. YOU'RE BEING STALKED AND HUNTED BY AN ALMIGHTY ENEMY.
BUT AS CRAZY AS THIS IS GOING TO SOUND, QUBIT, THERE IS...THERE'S...
...OH, GOD...
...THERE'S HOPE.
I KNOW THERE IS.
I PAID ENOUGH FOR IT.

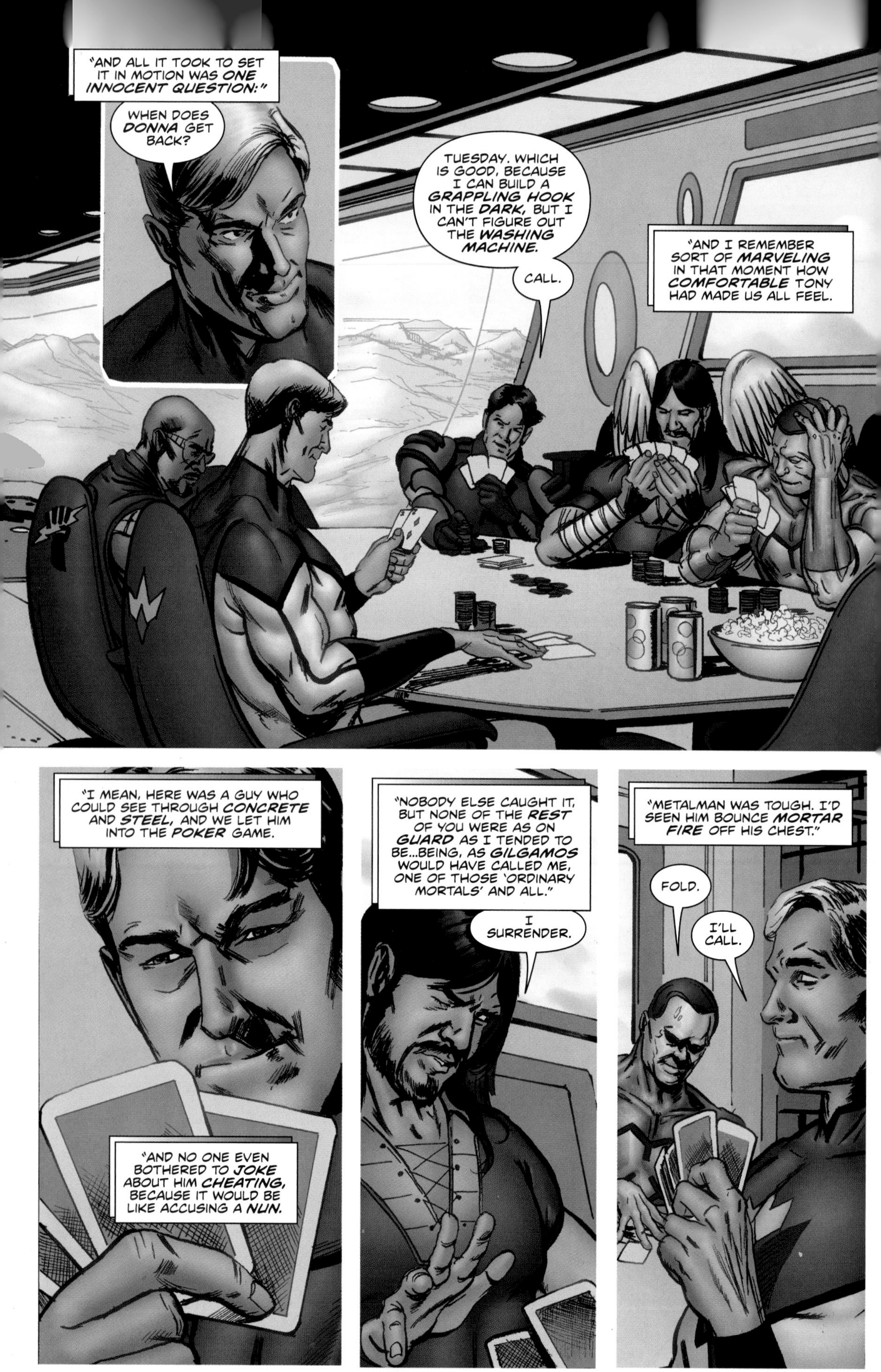
"AND ALL IT TOOK TO SET IT IN MOTION WAS ONE INNOCENT QUESTION:"
WHEN DOES DONNA GET BACK?
TUESDAY. WHICH IS GOOD, BECAUSE I CAN BUILD A GRAPPLING HOOK IN THE DARK, BUT I CAN'T FIGURE OUT THE WASHING MACHINE.
CALL.
"AND I REMEMBER SORT OF MARVELING IN THAT MOMENT HOW COMFORTABLE TONY HAD MADE US ALL FEEL.
"I MEAN, HERE WAS A GUY WHO COULD SEE THROUGH CONCRETE AND STEEL, AND WE LET HIM INTO THE POKER GAME.
"AND NO ONE EVEN BOTHERED TO JOKE ABOUT HIM CHEATING, BECAUSE IT WOULD BE LIKE ACCUSING A NUN.
"NOBODY ELSE CAUGHT IT, BUT NONE OF THE REST OF YOU WERE AS ON GUARD AS I TENDED TO BE...BEING, AS GILGAMOS WOULD HAVE CALLED ME, ONE OF THOSE 'ORDINARY MORTALS' AND ALL."
I SURRENDER.
"METALMAN WAS TOUGH. I'D SEEN HIM BOUNCE MORTAR FIRE OFF HIS CHEST."
FOLD.
I'LL CALL.

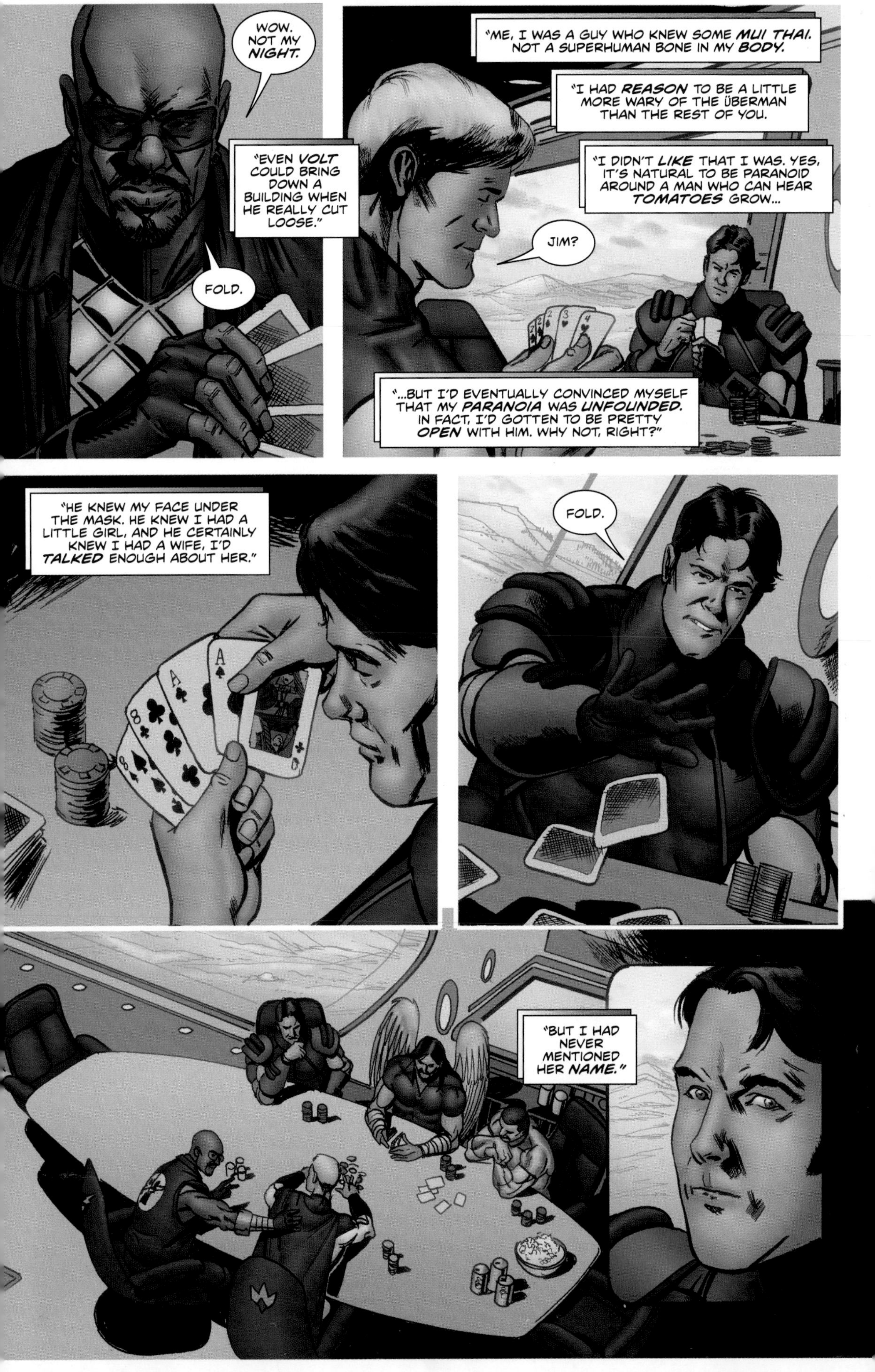
WOW. NOT MY NIGHT.
"EVEN VOLT COULD BRING DOWN A BUILDING WHEN HE REALLY CUT LOOSE."
FOLD.
"ME, I WAS A GUY WHO KNEW SOME MUI THAI. NOT A SUPERHUMAN BONE IN MY BODY.
"I HAD REASON TO BE A LITTLE MORE WARY OF THE ÜBERMAN THAN THE REST OF YOU.
"I DIDN'T LIKE THAT I WAS. YES, IT'S NATURAL TO BE PARANOID AROUND A MAN WHO CAN HEAR TOMATOES GROW...
JIM?
"...BUT I'D EVENTUALLY CONVINCED MYSELF THAT MY PARANOIA WAS UNFOUNDED. IN FACT, I'D GOTTEN TO BE PRETTY OPEN WITH HIM. WHY NOT, RIGHT?"
"HE KNEW MY FACE UNDER THE MASK. HE KNEW I HAD A LITTLE GIRL, AND HE CERTAINLY KNEW I HAD A WIFE, I'D TALKED ENOUGH ABOUT HER."
FOLD.
"BUT I HAD NEVER MENTIONED HER NAME."

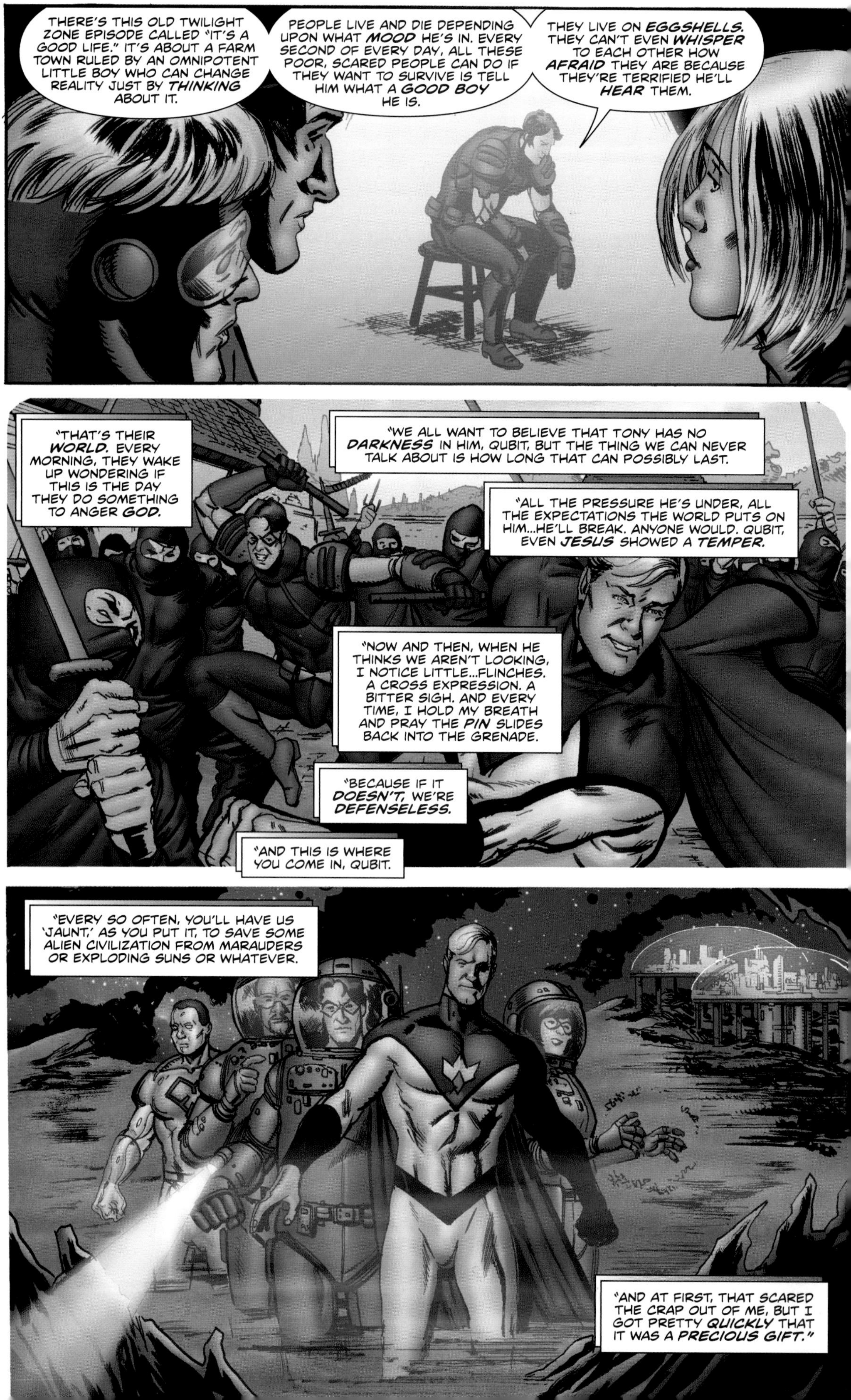
THERE'S THIS OLD TWILIGHT ZONE EPISODE CALLED "IT'S A GOOD LIFE." IT'S ABOUT A FARM TOWN RULED BY AN OMNIPOTENT LITTLE BOY WHO CAN CHANGE REALITY JUST BY *THINKING* ABOUT IT.
PEOPLE LIVE AND DIE DEPENDING UPON WHAT *MOOD* HE'S IN. EVERY SECOND OF EVERY DAY, ALL THESE POOR, SCARED PEOPLE CAN DO IF THEY WANT TO SURVIVE IS TELL HIM WHAT A *GOOD BOY* HE IS.
THEY LIVE ON *EGGSHELLS.* THEY CAN'T EVEN *WHISPER* TO EACH OTHER HOW *AFRAID* THEY ARE BECAUSE THEY'RE TERRIFIED HE'LL *HEAR* THEM.
"THAT'S THEIR *WORLD.* EVERY MORNING, THEY WAKE UP WONDERING IF THIS IS THE DAY THEY DO SOMETHING TO ANGER *GOD.*
"WE ALL WANT TO BELIEVE THAT TONY HAS NO *DARKNESS* IN HIM, QUBIT, BUT THE THING WE CAN NEVER TALK ABOUT IS HOW LONG THAT CAN POSSIBLY LAST.
"ALL THE PRESSURE HE'S UNDER, ALL THE EXPECTATIONS THE WORLD PUTS ON HIM...HE'LL BREAK. ANYONE WOULD. QUBIT, EVEN *JESUS* SHOWED A *TEMPER.*
"NOW AND THEN, WHEN HE THINKS WE AREN'T LOOKING, I NOTICE LITTLE...FLINCHES. A CROSS EXPRESSION. A BITTER SIGH. AND EVERY TIME, I HOLD MY BREATH AND PRAY THE *PIN* SLIDES BACK INTO THE GRENADE.
"BECAUSE IF IT *DOESN'T,* WE'RE *DEFENSELESS.*
"AND THIS IS WHERE YOU COME IN, QUBIT.
"EVERY SO OFTEN, YOU'LL HAVE US 'JAUNT,' AS YOU PUT IT, TO SAVE SOME ALIEN CIVILIZATION FROM MARAUDERS OR EXPLODING SUNS OR WHATEVER.
"AND AT FIRST, THAT SCARED THE CRAP OUT OF ME, BUT I GOT PRETTY *QUICKLY* THAT IT WAS A *PRECIOUS GIFT.*"

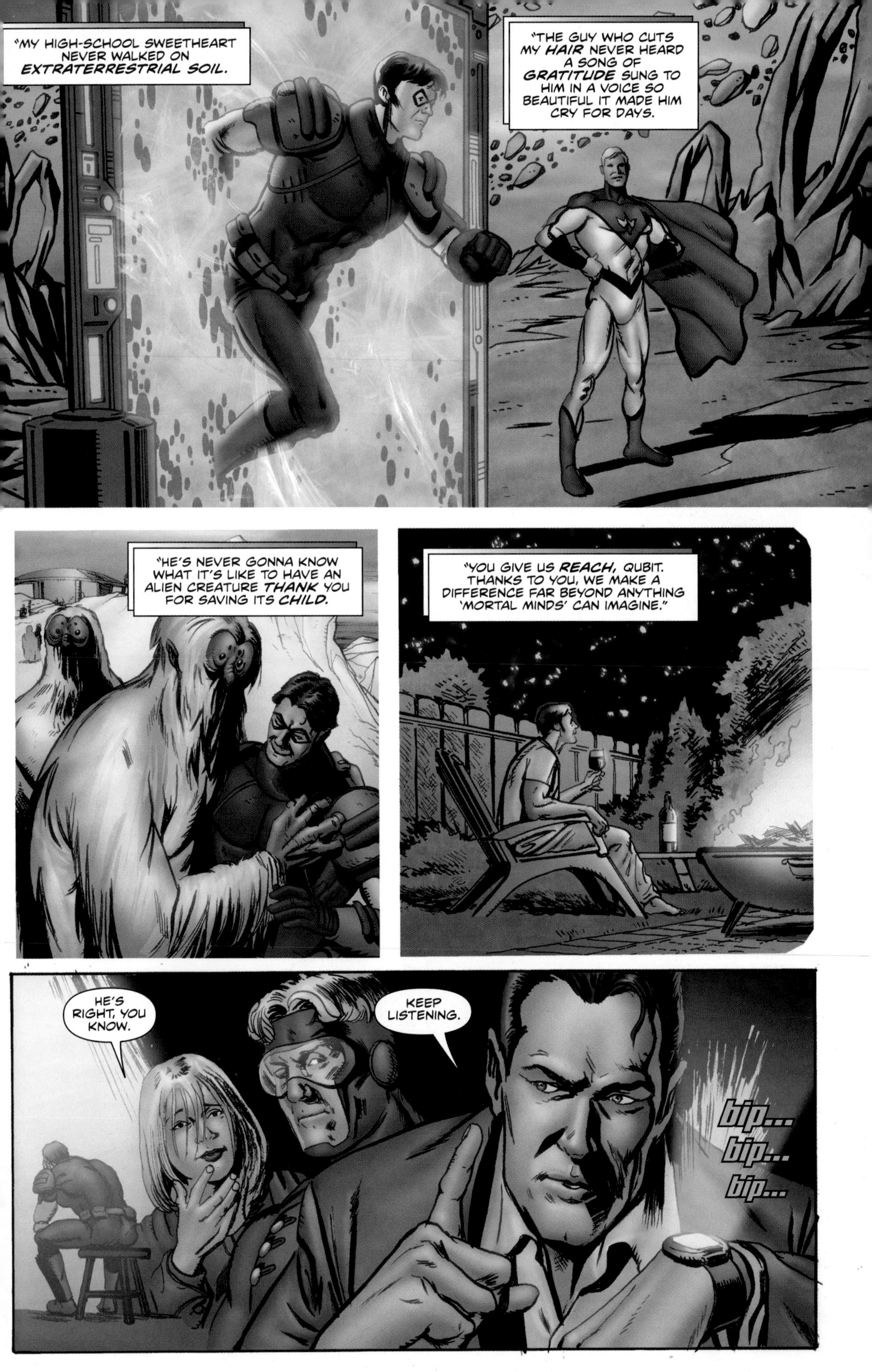
"MY HIGH-SCHOOL SWEETHEART NEVER WALKED ON EXTRATERRESTRIAL SOIL.
"THE GUY WHO CUTS MY HAIR NEVER HEARD A SONG OF GRATITUDE SUNG TO HIM IN A VOICE SO BEAUTIFUL IT MADE HIM CRY FOR DAYS.
"HE'S NEVER GONNA KNOW WHAT IT'S LIKE TO HAVE AN ALIEN CREATURE THANK YOU FOR SAVING ITS CHILD.
"YOU GIVE US REACH, QUBIT. THANKS TO YOU, WE MAKE A DIFFERENCE FAR BEYOND ANYTHING 'MORTAL MINDS' CAN IMAGINE."
HE'S RIGHT, YOU KNOW.
KEEP LISTENING.
bip... bip... bip...

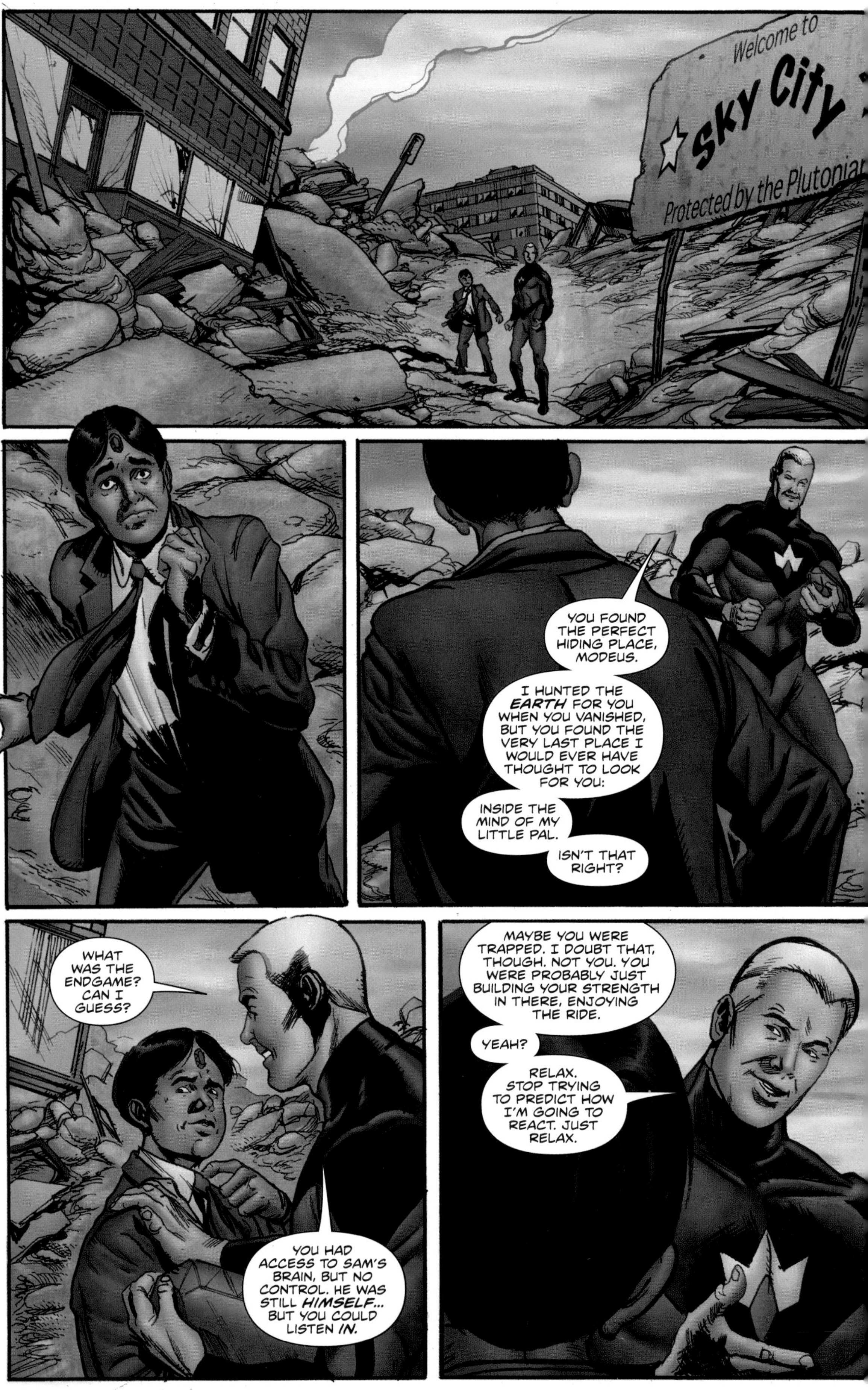
Welcome to
Sky City
Protected by the Plutonian
YOU FOUND THE PERFECT HIDING PLACE, MODEUS.
I HUNTED THE EARTH FOR YOU WHEN YOU VANISHED, BUT YOU FOUND THE VERY LAST PLACE I WOULD EVER HAVE THOUGHT TO LOOK FOR YOU:
INSIDE THE MIND OF MY LITTLE PAL.
ISN'T THAT RIGHT?
WHAT WAS THE ENDGAME? CAN I GUESS?
YOU HAD ACCESS TO SAM'S BRAIN, BUT NO CONTROL. HE WAS STILL HIMSELF... BUT YOU COULD LISTEN IN.
MAYBE YOU WERE TRAPPED. I DOUBT THAT, THOUGH. NOT YOU. YOU WERE PROBABLY JUST BUILDING YOUR STRENGTH IN THERE, ENJOYING THE RIDE.
YEAH?
RELAX. STOP TRYING TO PREDICT HOW I'M GOING TO REACT. JUST RELAX.

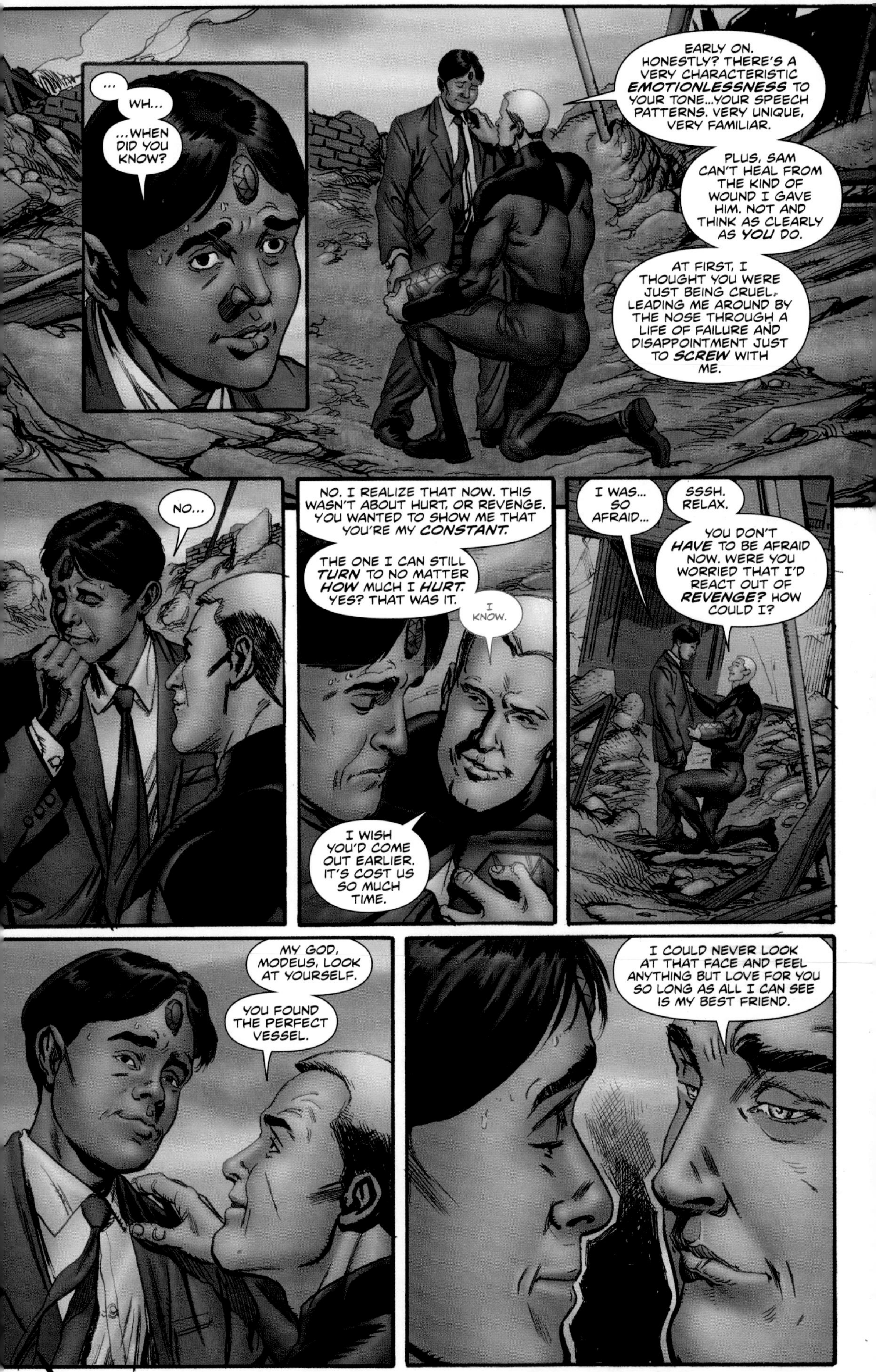
...
WH...
...WHEN DID YOU KNOW?
EARLY ON. HONESTLY? THERE'S A VERY CHARACTERISTIC EMOTIONLESSNESS TO YOUR TONE...YOUR SPEECH PATTERNS. VERY UNIQUE, VERY FAMILIAR.
PLUS, SAM CAN'T HEAL FROM THE KIND OF WOUND I GAVE HIM. NOT AND THINK AS CLEARLY AS YOU DO.
AT FIRST, I THOUGHT YOU WERE JUST BEING CRUEL. LEADING ME AROUND BY THE NOSE THROUGH A LIFE OF FAILURE AND DISAPPOINTMENT JUST TO SCREW WITH ME.
NO...
NO. I REALIZE THAT NOW. THIS WASN'T ABOUT HURT, OR REVENGE. YOU WANTED TO SHOW ME THAT YOU'RE MY CONSTANT.
THE ONE I CAN STILL TURN TO NO MATTER HOW MUCH I HURT. YES? THAT WAS IT.
I KNOW.
I WISH YOU'D COME OUT EARLIER. IT'S COST US SO MUCH TIME.
I WAS... SO AFRAID...
SSSH. RELAX.
YOU DON'T HAVE TO BE AFRAID NOW. WERE YOU WORRIED THAT I'D REACT OUT OF REVENGE? HOW COULD I?
MY GOD, MODEUS, LOOK AT YOURSELF.
YOU FOUND THE PERFECT VESSEL.
I COULD NEVER LOOK AT THAT FACE AND FEEL ANYTHING BUT LOVE FOR YOU SO LONG AS ALL I CAN SEE IS MY BEST FRIEND.

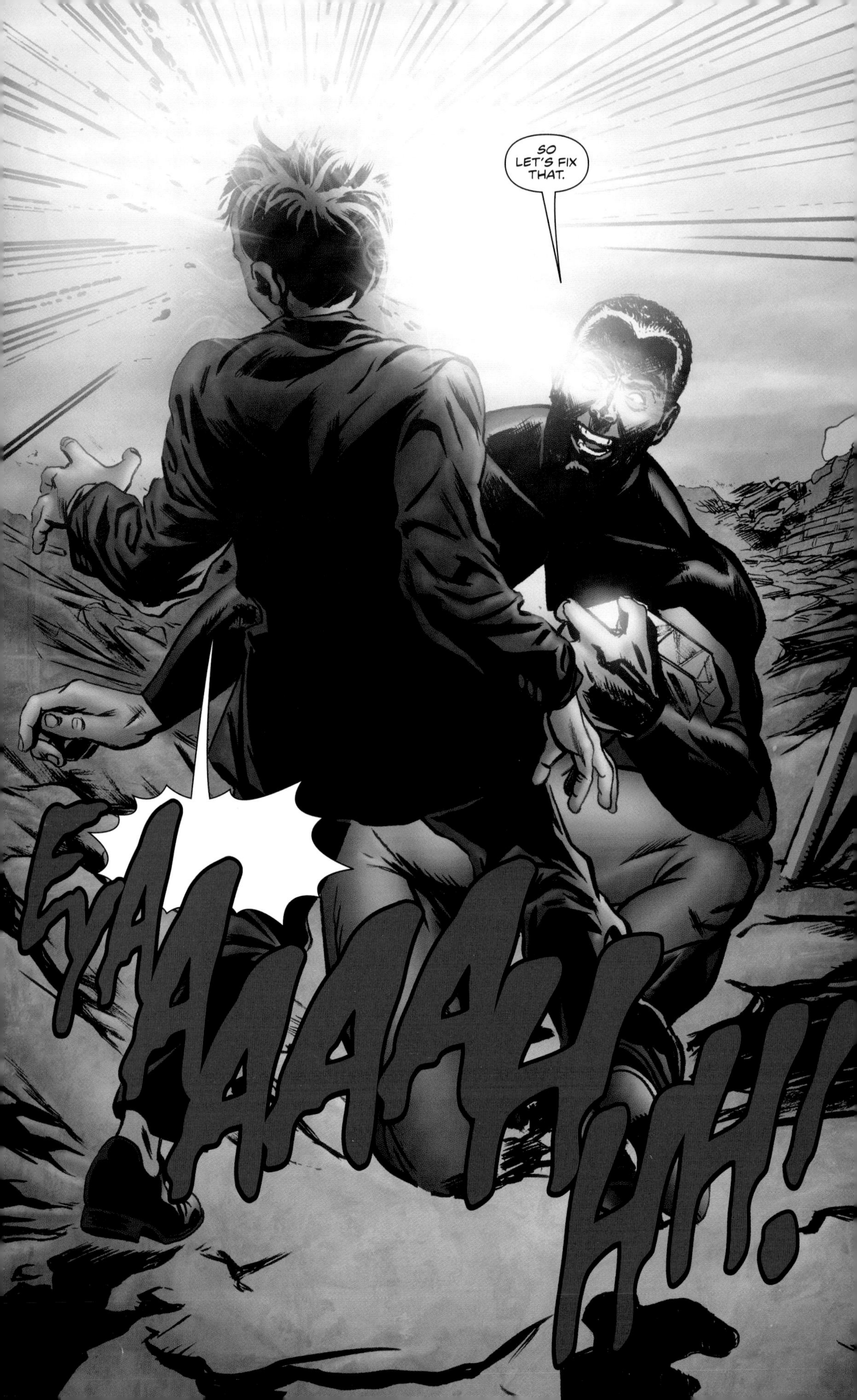
SO LET'S FIX THAT.
EYAAAAAHHH!!

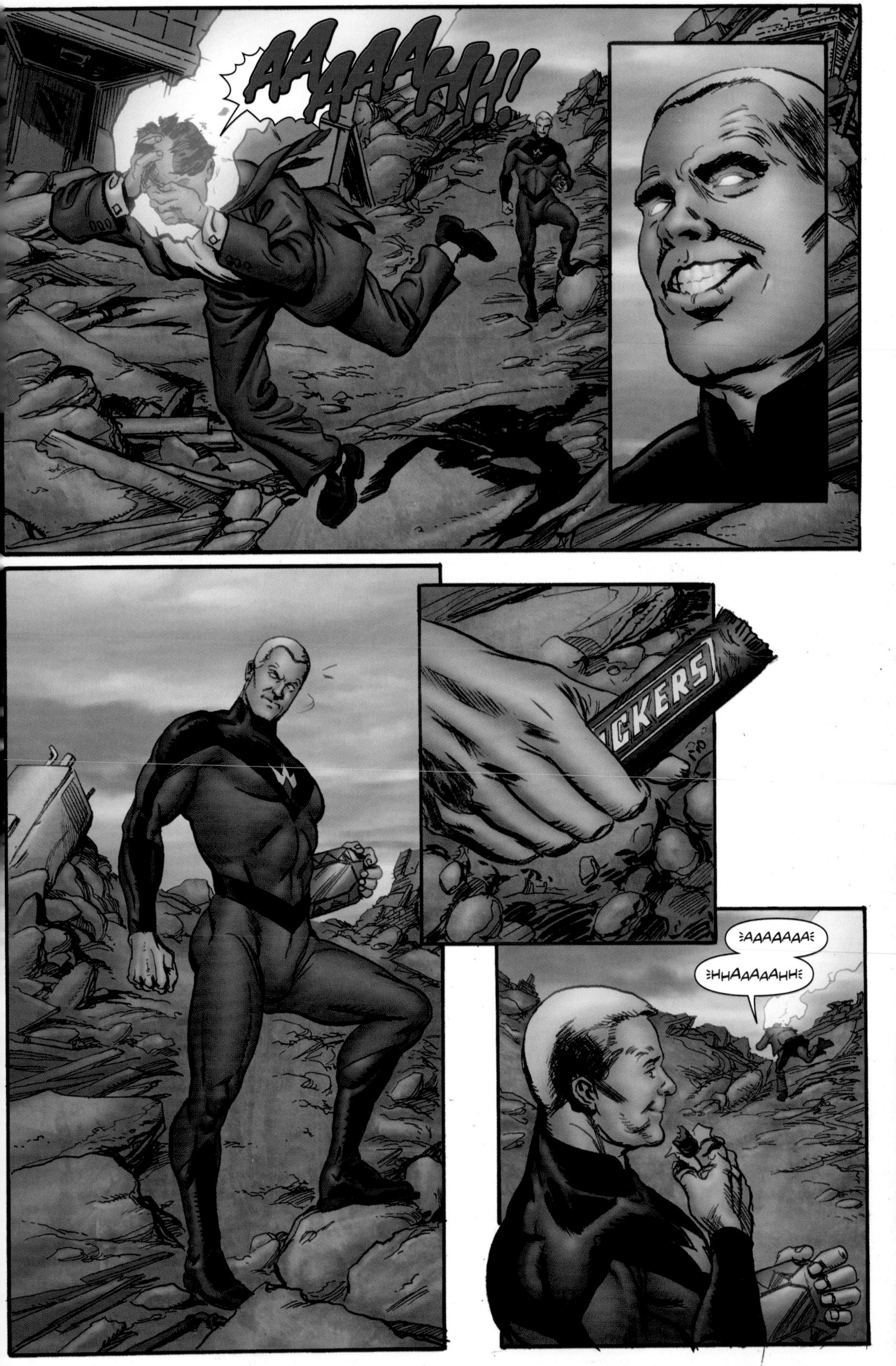
AAAAAAHH!
ICKERS
AAAAAAA
HHAAAAAHH

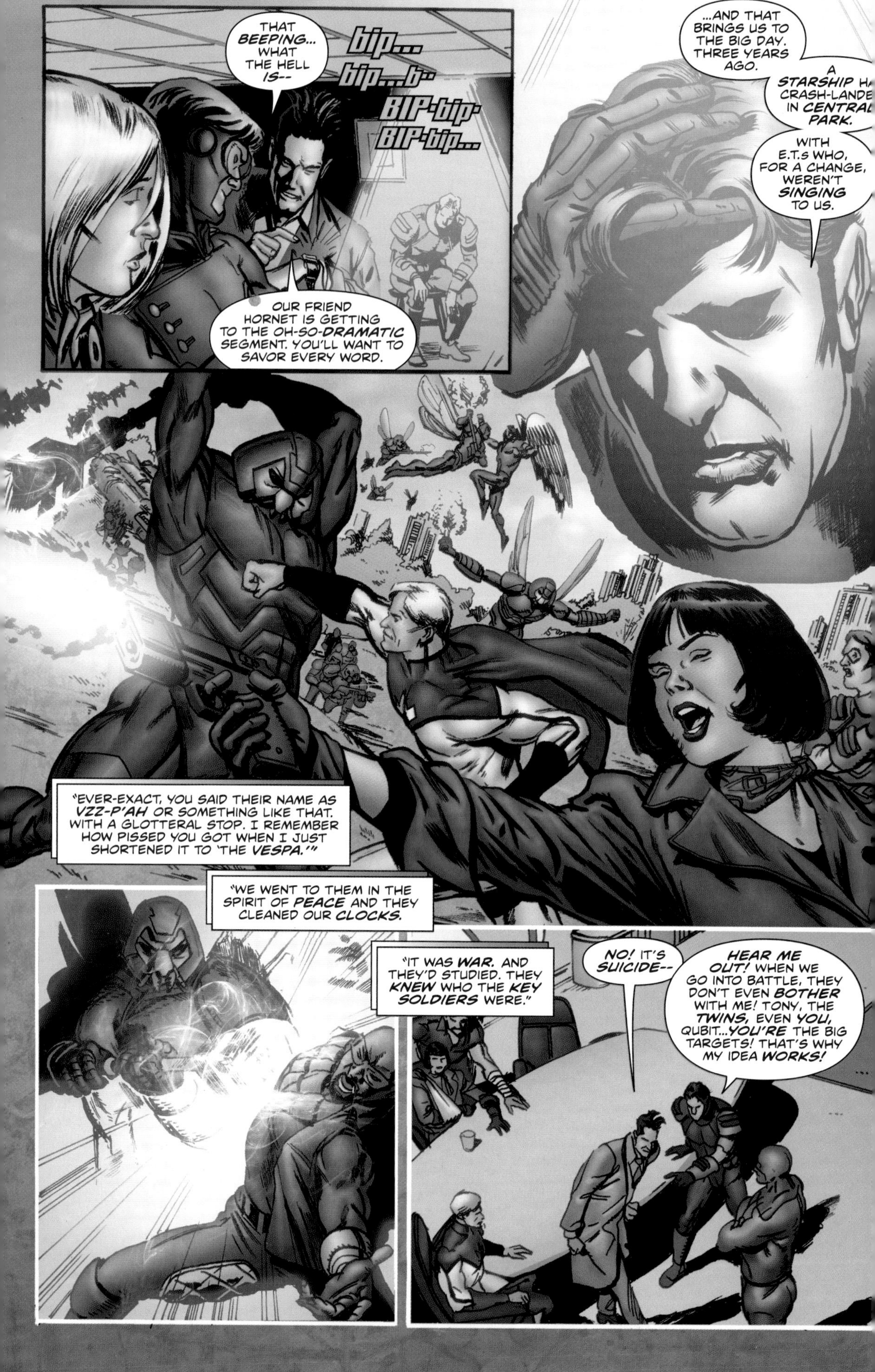

THAT BEEPING... WHAT THE HELL IS--
bip... bip...b
BIP-bip-BIP-bip...
OUR FRIEND HORNET IS GETTING TO THE OH-SO-DRAMATIC SEGMENT. YOU'LL WANT TO SAVOR EVERY WORD.
...AND THAT BRINGS US TO THE BIG DAY. THREE YEARS AGO.
A STARSHIP HA CRASH-LANDE IN CENTRAL PARK.
WITH E.T.s WHO, FOR A CHANGE, WEREN'T SINGING TO US.
"EVER-EXACT, YOU SAID THEIR NAME AS VZZ-P'AH OR SOMETHING LIKE THAT. WITH A GLOTTERAL STOP. I REMEMBER HOW PISSED YOU GOT WHEN I JUST SHORTENED IT TO 'THE VESPA.'"
"WE WENT TO THEM IN THE SPIRIT OF PEACE AND THEY CLEANED OUR CLOCKS.
"IT WAS WAR. AND THEY'D STUDIED. THEY KNEW WHO THE KEY SOLDIERS WERE."
NO! IT'S SUICIDE--
HEAR ME OUT! WHEN WE GO INTO BATTLE, THEY DON'T EVEN BOTHER WITH ME! TONY, THE TWINS, EVEN YOU, QUBIT...YOU'RE THE BIG TARGETS! THAT'S WHY MY IDEA WORKS!

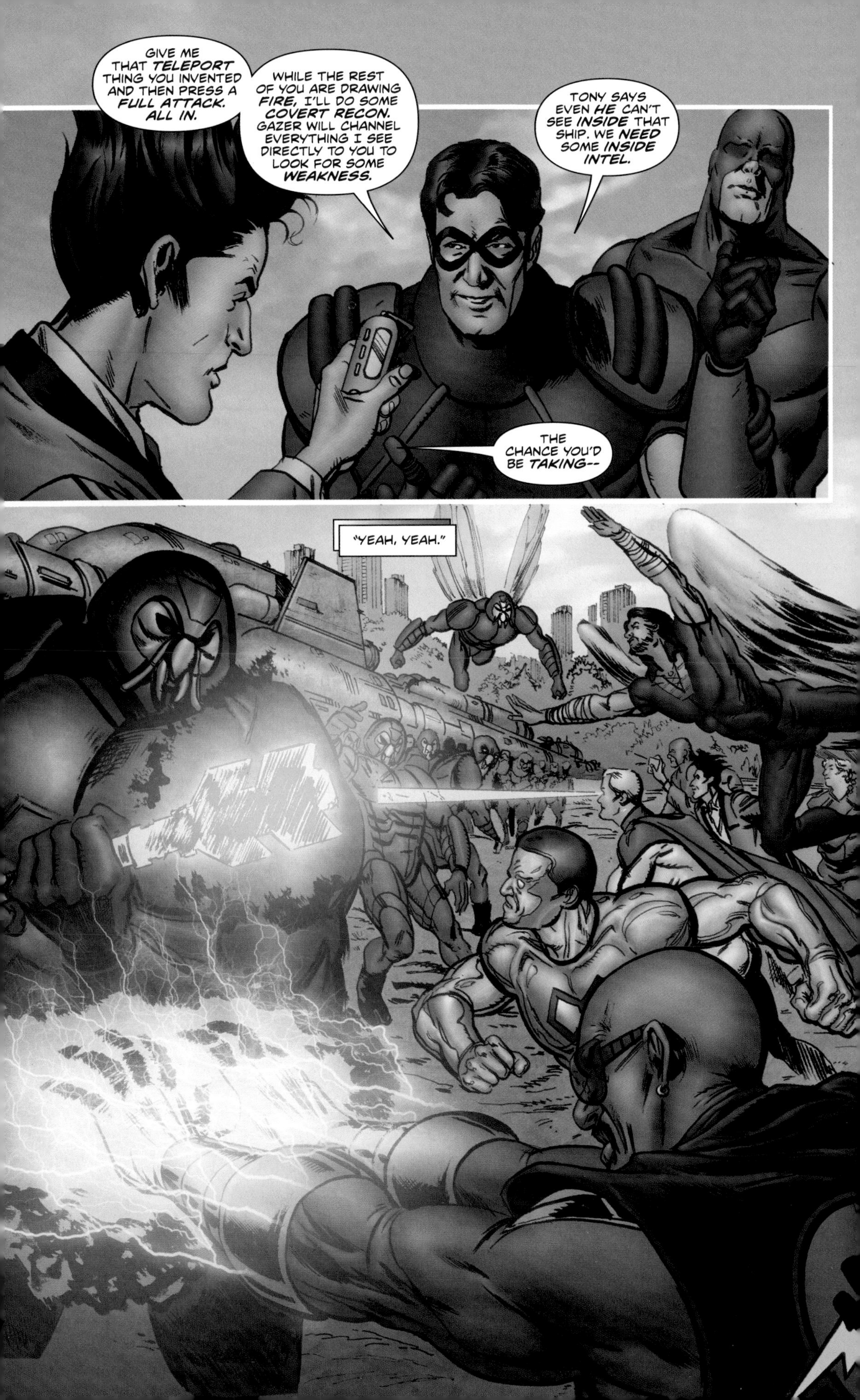
GIVE ME THAT TELEPORT THING YOU INVENTED AND THEN PRESS A FULL ATTACK. ALL IN.
WHILE THE REST OF YOU ARE DRAWING FIRE, I'LL DO SOME COVERT RECON. GAZER WILL CHANNEL EVERYTHING I SEE DIRECTLY TO YOU TO LOOK FOR SOME WEAKNESS.
TONY SAYS EVEN HE CAN'T SEE INSIDE THAT SHIP. WE NEED SOME INSIDE INTEL.
THE CHANCE YOU'D BE TAKING--
"YEAH, YEAH."

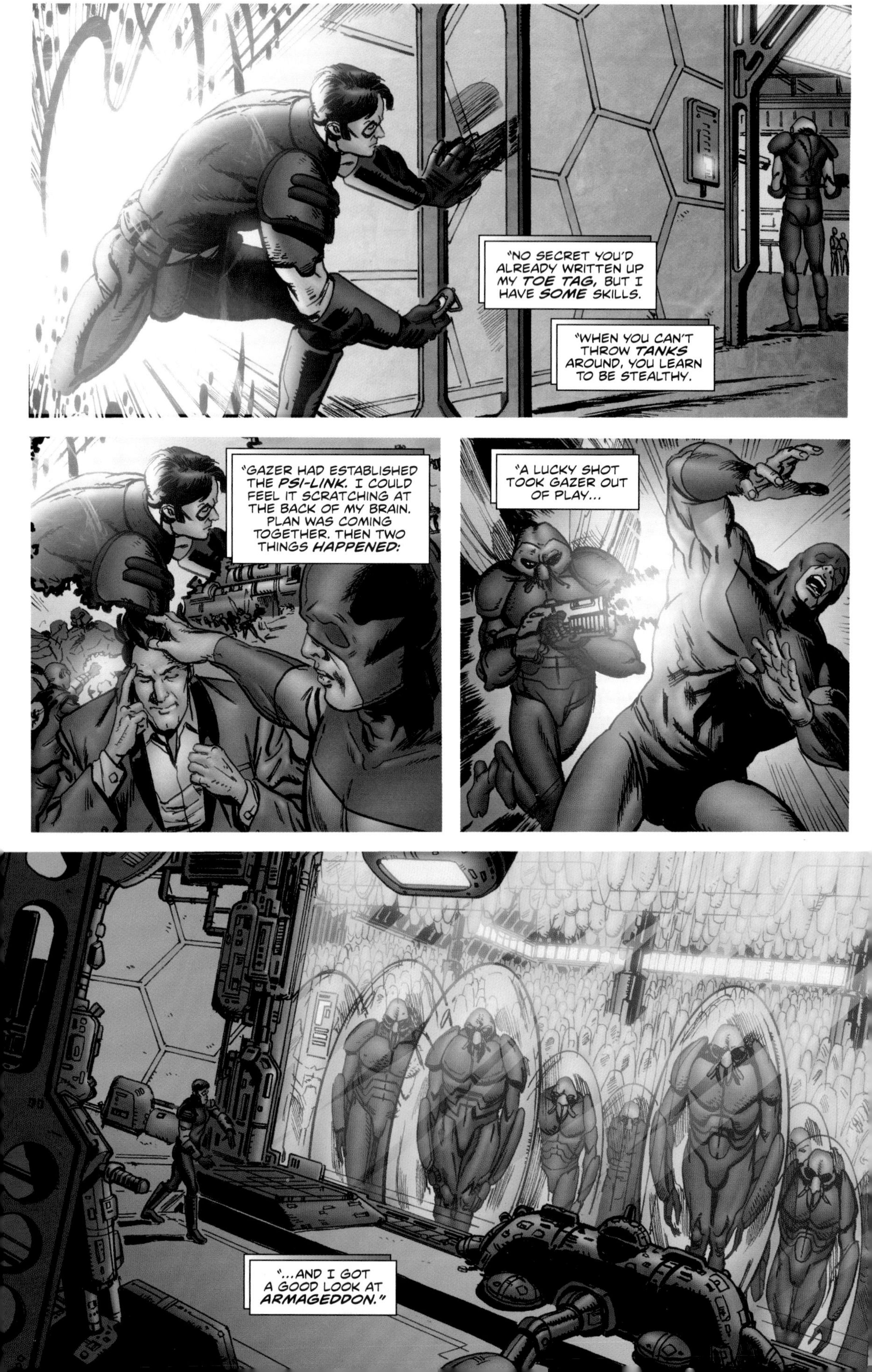
"NO SECRET YOU'D ALREADY WRITTEN UP MY TOE TAG, BUT I HAVE SOME SKILLS.
"WHEN YOU CAN'T THROW TANKS AROUND, YOU LEARN TO BE STEALTHY.
"GAZER HAD ESTABLISHED THE PSI-LINK. I COULD FEEL IT SCRATCHING AT THE BACK OF MY BRAIN. PLAN WAS COMING TOGETHER. THEN TWO THINGS HAPPENED:
"A LUCKY SHOT TOOK GAZER OUT OF PLAY...
"...AND I GOT A GOOD LOOK AT ARMAGEDDON."

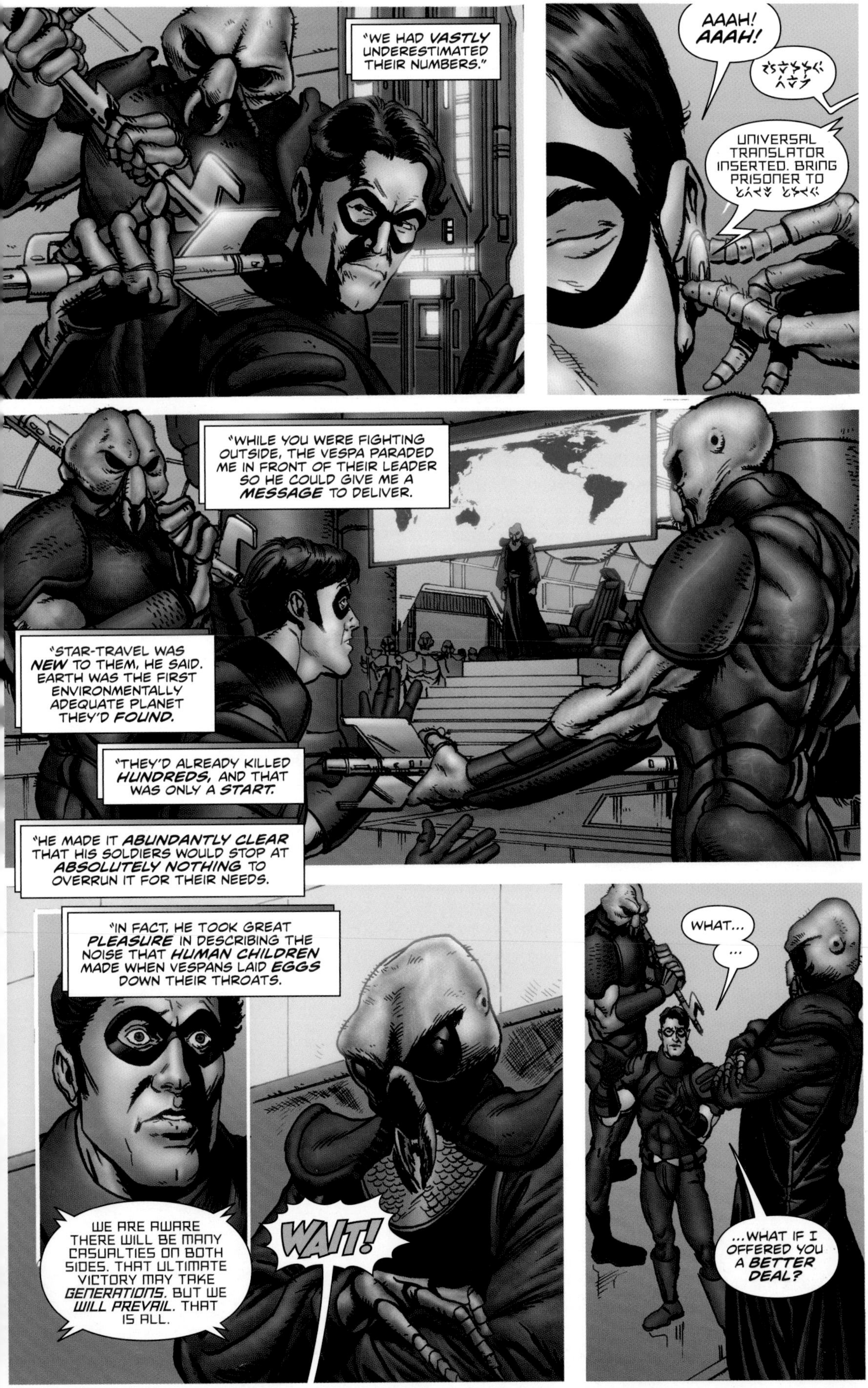
"WE HAD VASTLY UNDERESTIMATED THEIR NUMBERS."
AAAH! AAAH!
UNIVERSAL TRANSLATOR INSERTED. BRING PRISONER TO
"WHILE YOU WERE FIGHTING OUTSIDE, THE VESPA PARADED ME IN FRONT OF THEIR LEADER SO HE COULD GIVE ME A MESSAGE TO DELIVER.
"STAR-TRAVEL WAS NEW TO THEM, HE SAID. EARTH WAS THE FIRST ENVIRONMENTALLY ADEQUATE PLANET THEY'D FOUND.
"THEY'D ALREADY KILLED HUNDREDS, AND THAT WAS ONLY A START.
"HE MADE IT ABUNDANTLY CLEAR THAT HIS SOLDIERS WOULD STOP AT ABSOLUTELY NOTHING TO OVERRUN IT FOR THEIR NEEDS.
"IN FACT, HE TOOK GREAT PLEASURE IN DESCRIBING THE NOISE THAT HUMAN CHILDREN MADE WHEN VESPANS LAID EGGS DOWN THEIR THROATS.
WE ARE AWARE THERE WILL BE MANY CASUALTIES ON BOTH SIDES. THAT ULTIMATE VICTORY MAY TAKE GENERATIONS. BUT WE WILL PREVAIL. THAT IS ALL.
WAIT!
WHAT...
...
...WHAT IF I OFFERED YOU A BETTER DEAL?

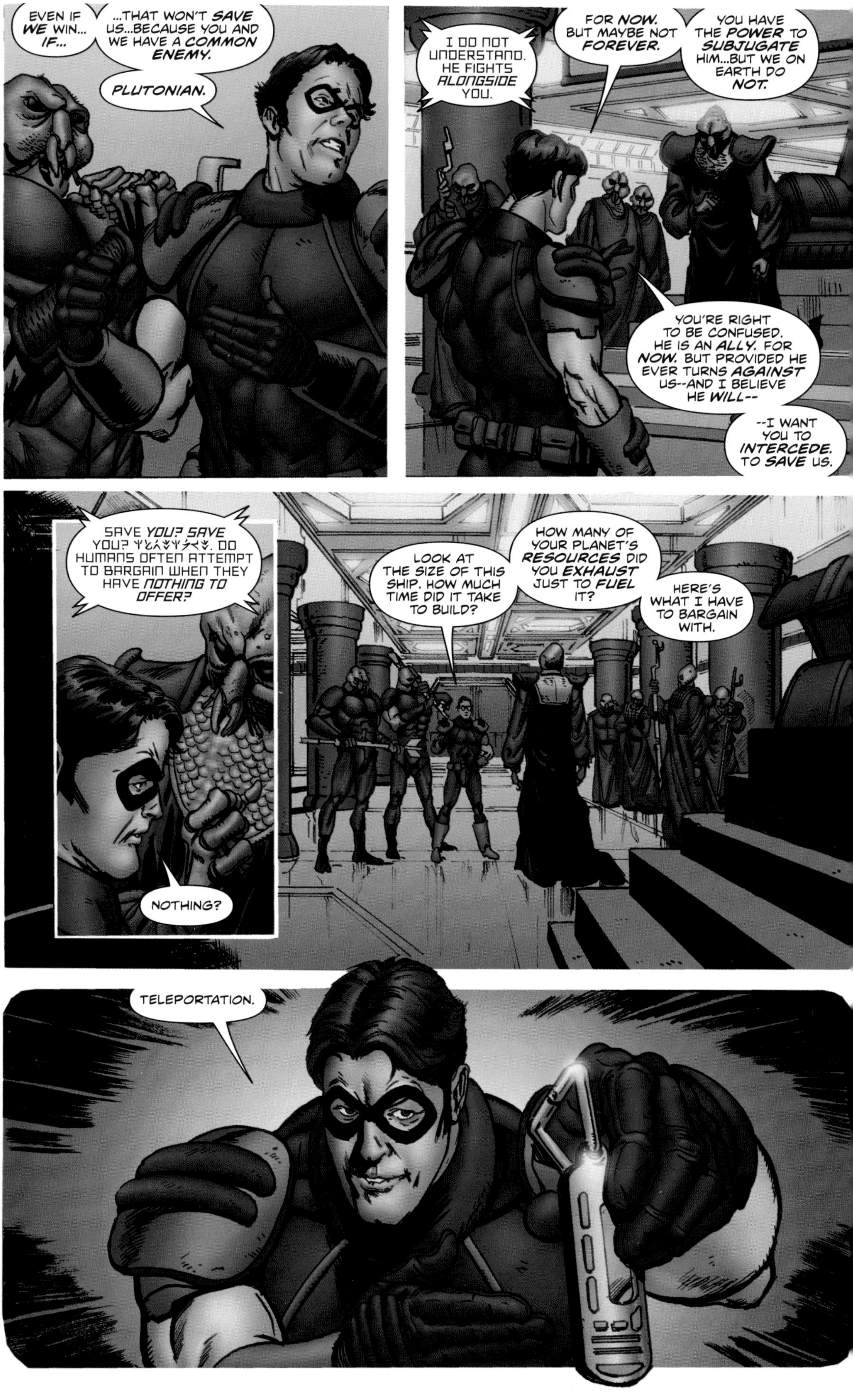
EVEN IF WE WIN... IF...
...THAT WON'T SAVE US...BECAUSE YOU AND WE HAVE A COMMON ENEMY.
PLUTONIAN.
I DO NOT UNDERSTAND. HE FIGHTS ALONGSIDE YOU.
FOR NOW. BUT MAYBE NOT FOREVER.
YOU HAVE THE POWER TO SUBJUGATE HIM...BUT WE ON EARTH DO NOT.
YOU'RE RIGHT TO BE CONFUSED. HE IS AN ALLY. FOR NOW. BUT PROVIDED HE EVER TURNS AGAINST US--AND I BELIEVE HE WILL--
--I WANT YOU TO INTERCEDE. TO SAVE US.
SAVE YOU? SAVE YOU? DO HUMANS OFTEN ATTEMPT TO BARGAIN WHEN THEY HAVE NOTHING TO OFFER?
NOTHING?
LOOK AT THE SIZE OF THIS SHIP. HOW MUCH TIME DID IT TAKE TO BUILD?
HOW MANY OF YOUR PLANET'S RESOURCES DID YOU EXHAUST JUST TO FUEL IT?
HERE'S WHAT I HAVE TO BARGAIN WITH.
TELEPORTATION.

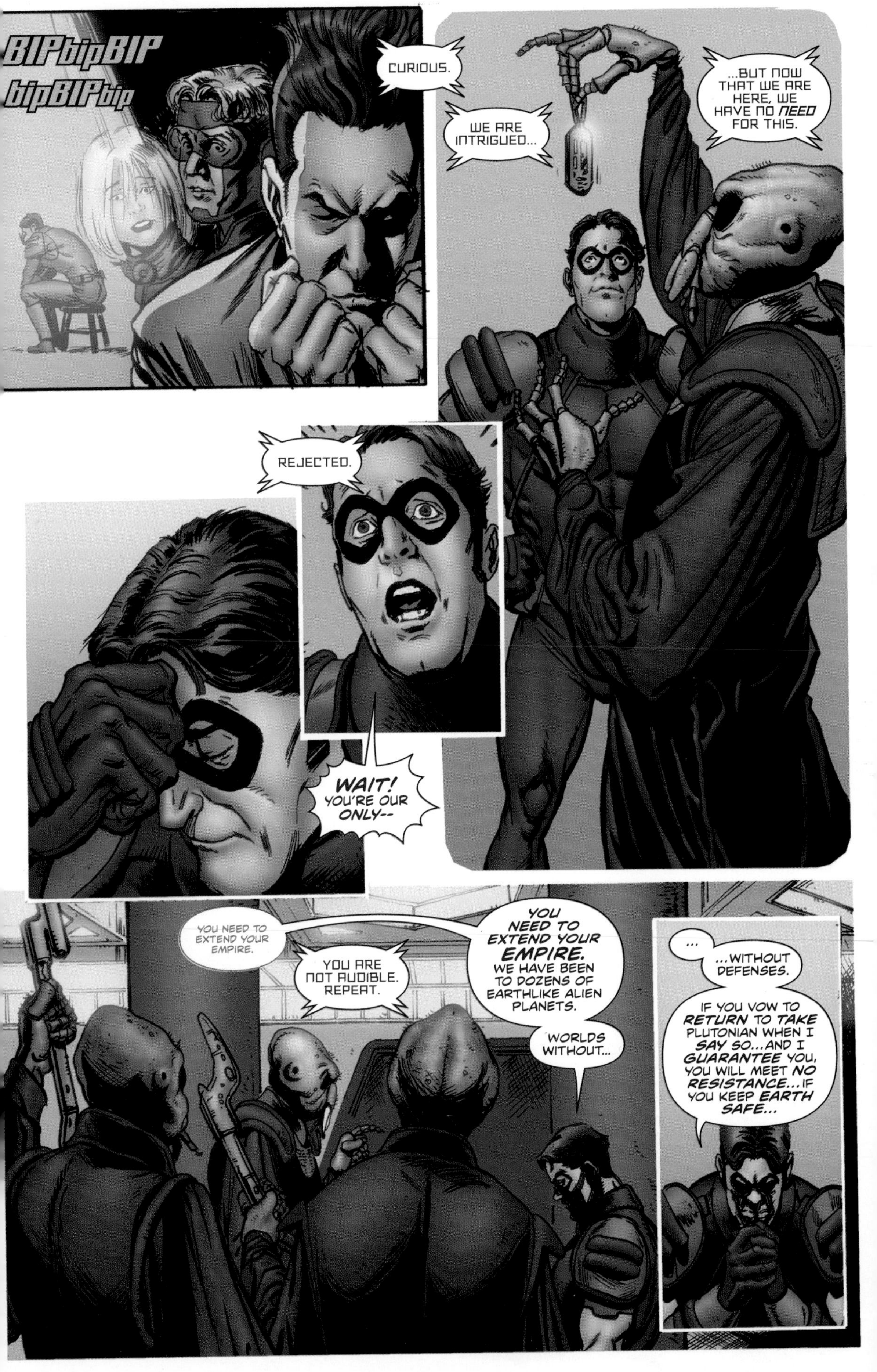
BIPbipBIP
bipBIPbip
CURIOUS.
WE ARE INTRIGUED...
...BUT NOW THAT WE ARE HERE, WE HAVE NO NEED FOR THIS.
REJECTED.
WAIT! YOU'RE OUR ONLY--
YOU NEED TO EXTEND YOUR EMPIRE.
YOU ARE NOT AUDIBLE. REPEAT.
YOU NEED TO EXTEND YOUR EMPIRE. WE HAVE BEEN TO DOZENS OF EARTHLIKE ALIEN PLANETS.
WORLDS WITHOUT...
...
...WITHOUT DEFENSES.
IF YOU VOW TO RETURN TO TAKE PLUTONIAN WHEN I SAY SO...AND I GUARANTEE YOU, YOU WILL MEET NO RESISTANCE...IF YOU KEEP EARTH SAFE...

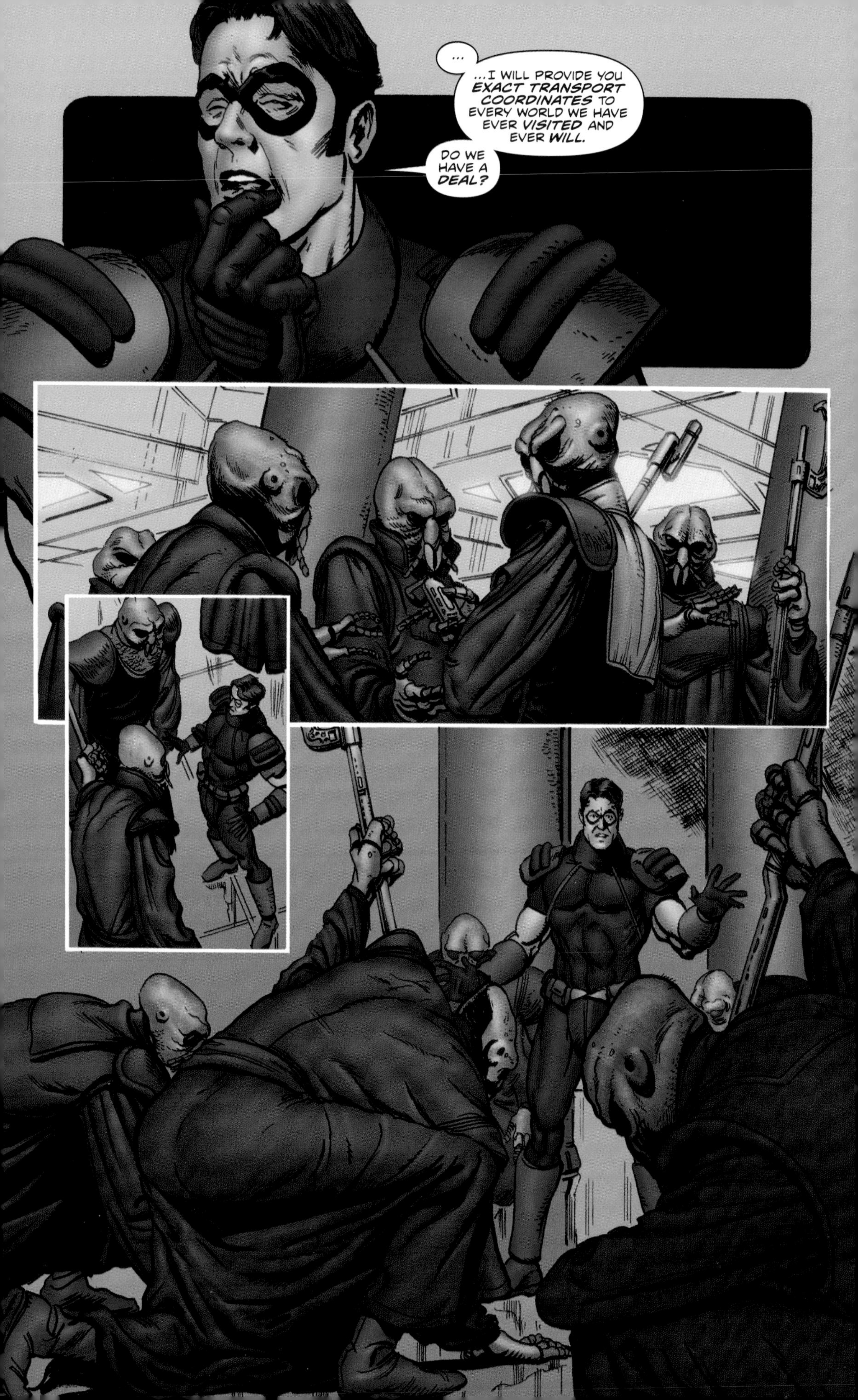
...
...I WILL PROVIDE YOU EXACT TRANSPORT COORDINATES TO EVERY WORLD WE HAVE EVER VISITED AND EVER WILL.
DO WE HAVE A DEAL?

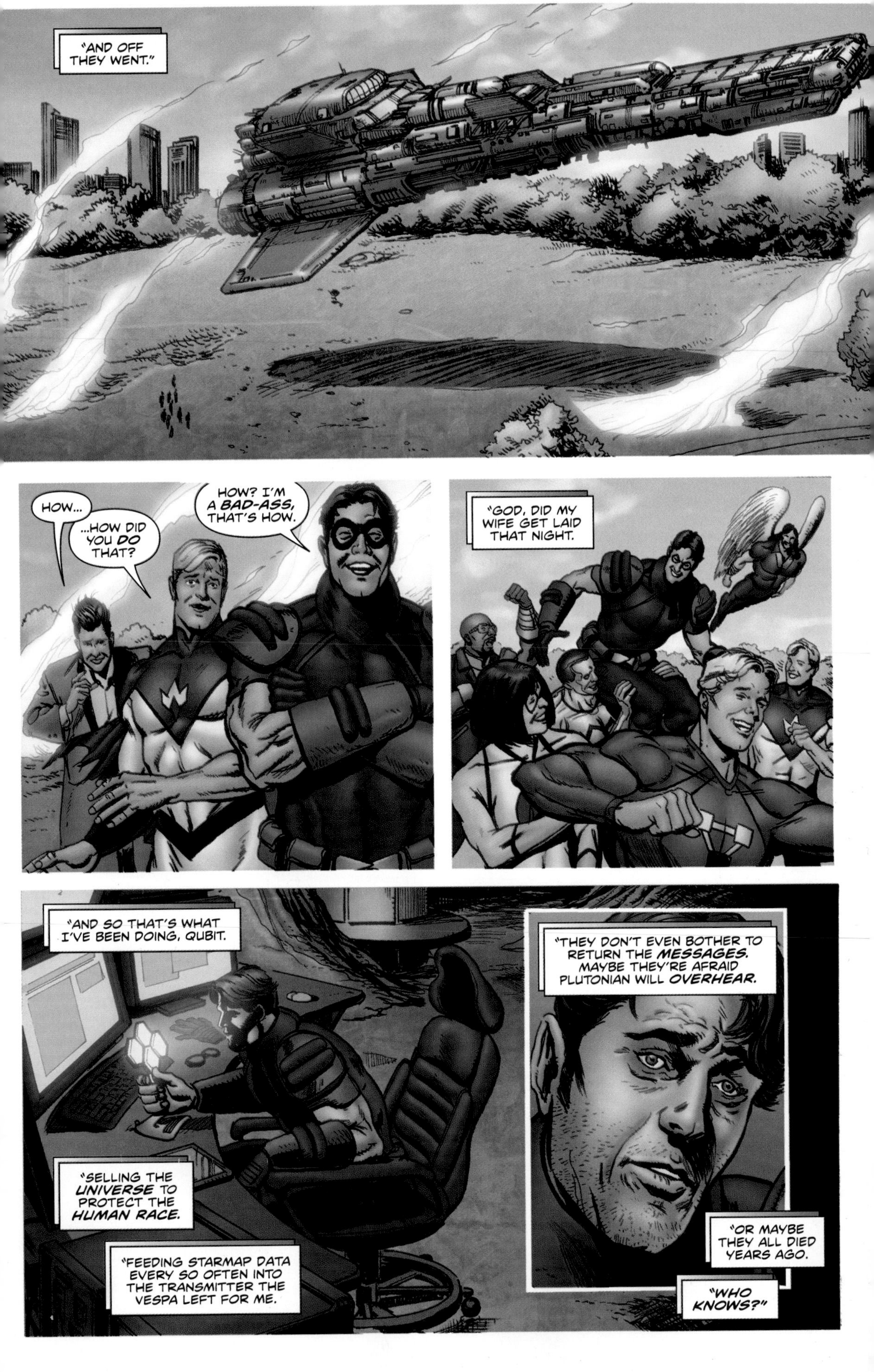
"AND OFF THEY WENT."
HOW...
...HOW DID YOU DO THAT?
HOW? I'M A BAD-ASS, THAT'S HOW.
"GOD, DID MY WIFE GET LAID THAT NIGHT.
"AND SO THAT'S WHAT I'VE BEEN DOING, QUBIT.
"SELLING THE UNIVERSE TO PROTECT THE HUMAN RACE.
"FEEDING STARMAP DATA EVERY SO OFTEN INTO THE TRANSMITTER THE VESPA LEFT FOR ME.
"THEY DON'T EVEN BOTHER TO RETURN THE MESSAGES. MAYBE THEY'RE AFRAID PLUTONIAN WILL OVERHEAR.
"OR MAYBE THEY ALL DIED YEARS AGO.
"WHO KNOWS?"

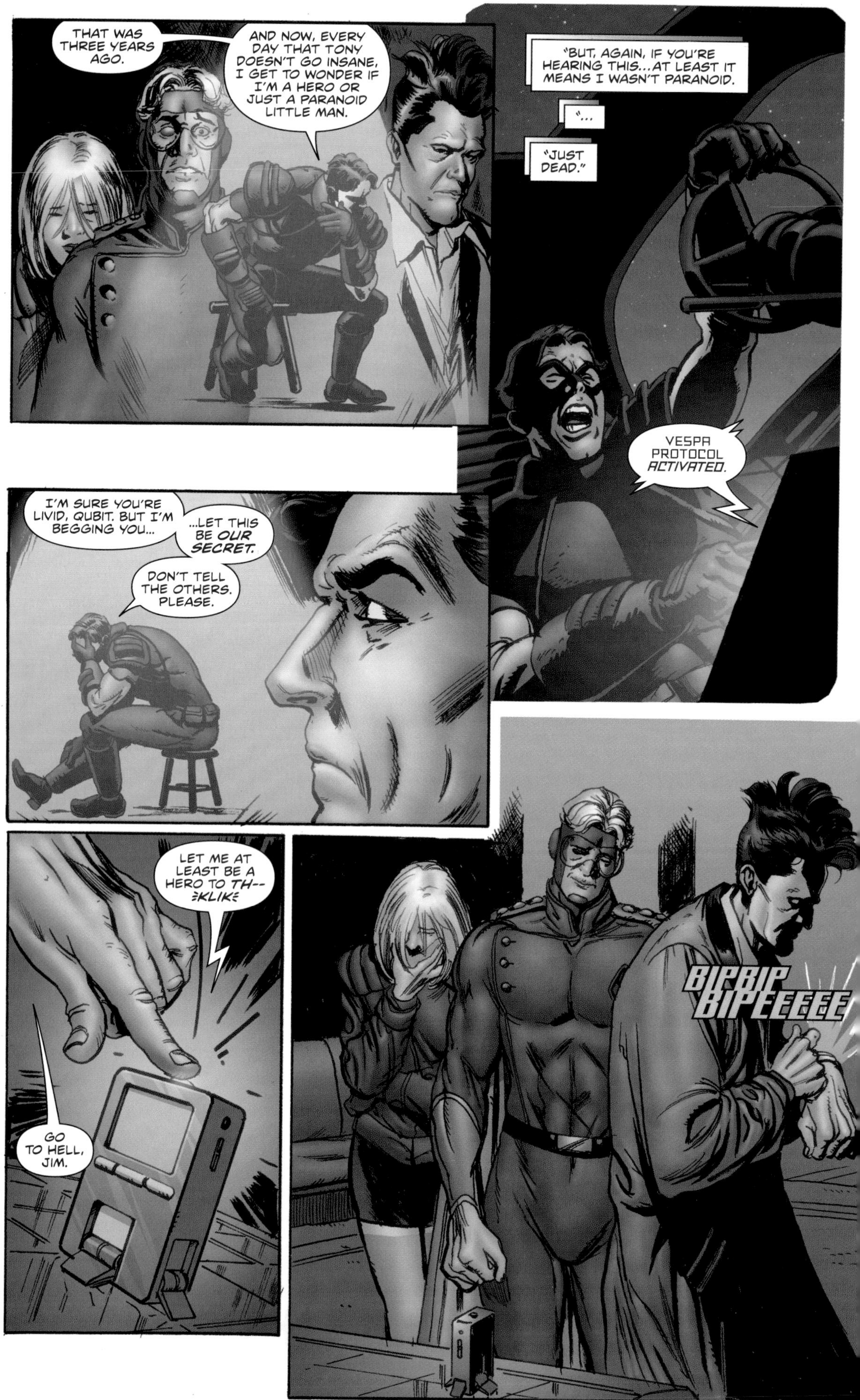
THAT WAS THREE YEARS AGO.
AND NOW, EVERY DAY THAT TONY DOESN'T GO INSANE, I GET TO WONDER IF I'M A HERO OR JUST A PARANOID LITTLE MAN.
"BUT, AGAIN, IF YOU'RE HEARING THIS...AT LEAST IT MEANS I WASN'T PARANOID.
"...
"JUST DEAD."
VESPA PROTOCOL *ACTIVATED.*
I'M SURE YOU'RE LIVID, QUBIT. BUT I'M BEGGING YOU...
...LET THIS BE ***OUR SECRET.***
DON'T TELL THE OTHERS. PLEASE.
LET ME AT LEAST BE A HERO TO *TH--*
KLIK
GO TO HELL, JIM.
BIPBIP BIPEEEEE

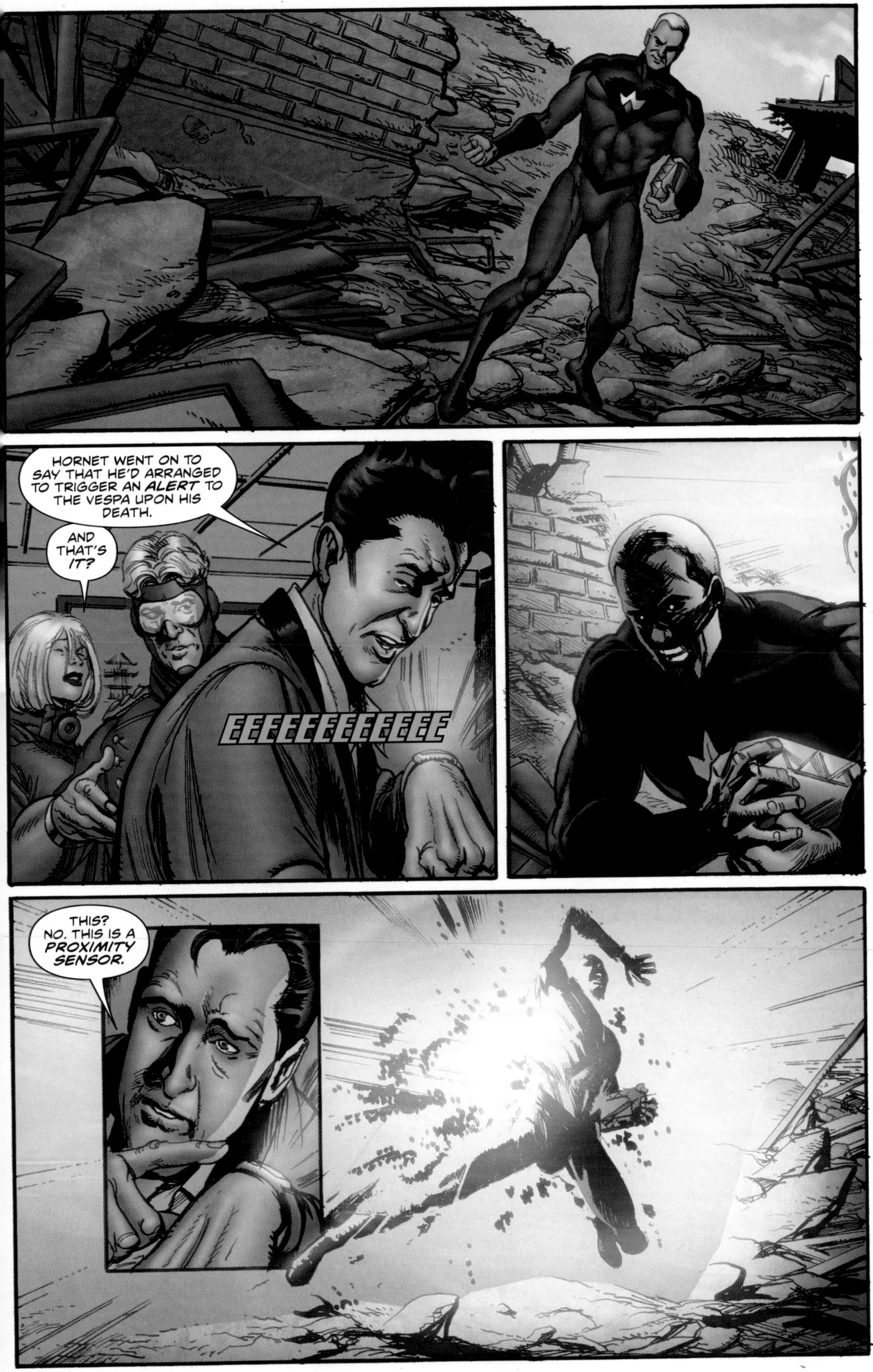
HORNET WENT ON TO SAY THAT HE'D ARRANGED TO TRIGGER AN ALERT TO THE VESPA UPON HIS DEATH.
AND THAT'S IT?
EEEEEEEEEEEE
THIS? NO. THIS IS A PROXIMITY SENSOR.

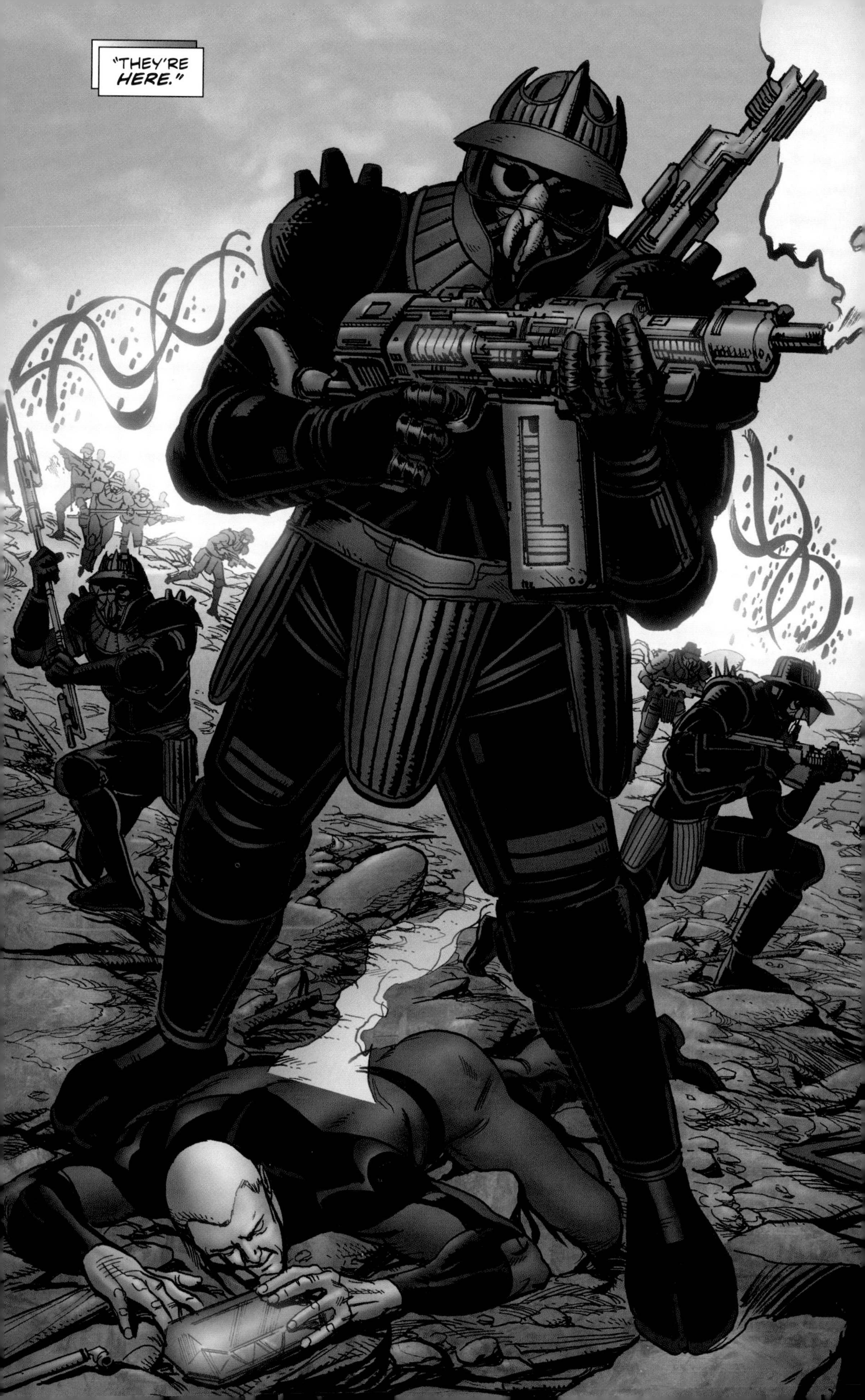
"THEY'RE HERE."

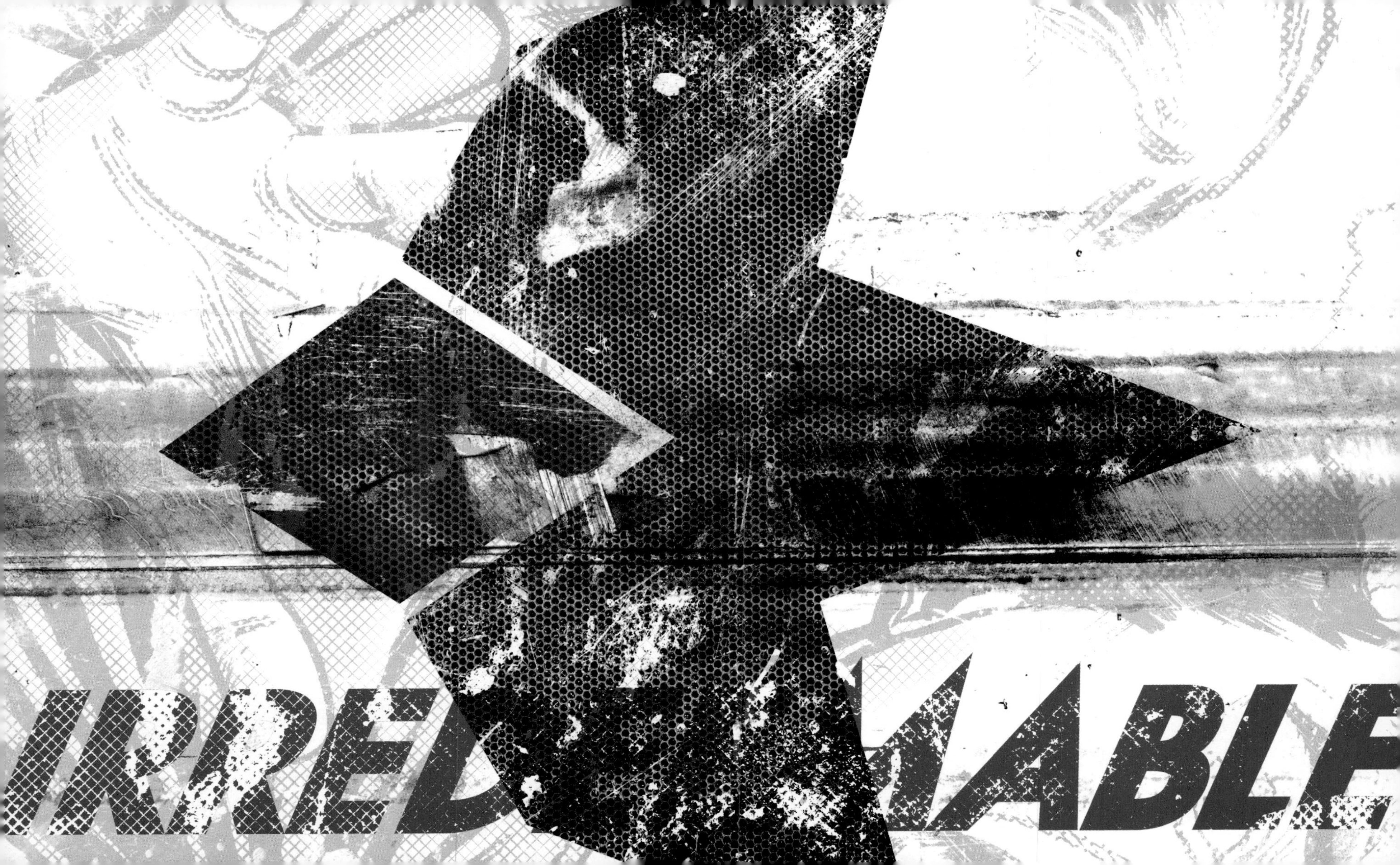
IRRED ABLE

CHAPTER 19

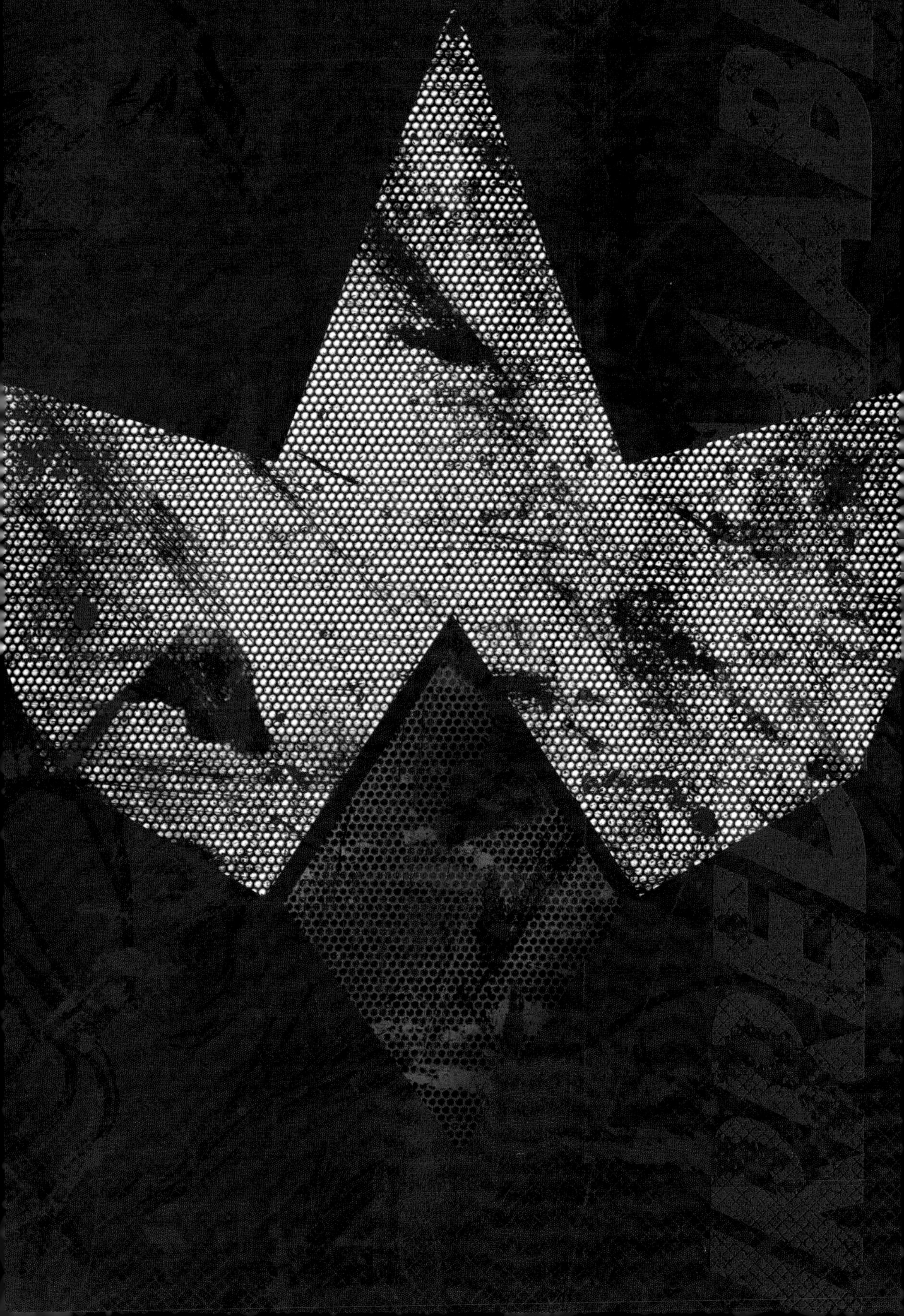

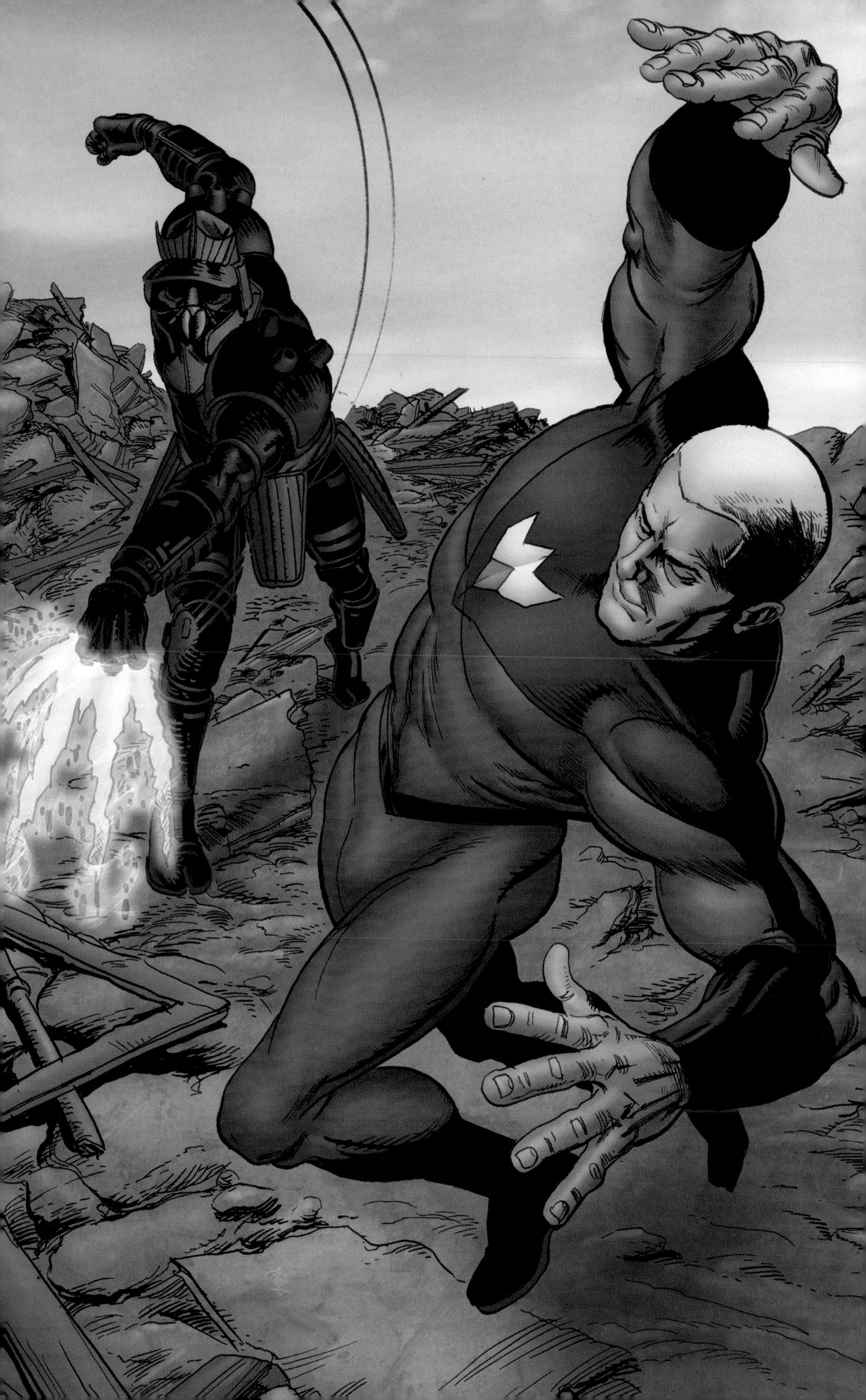

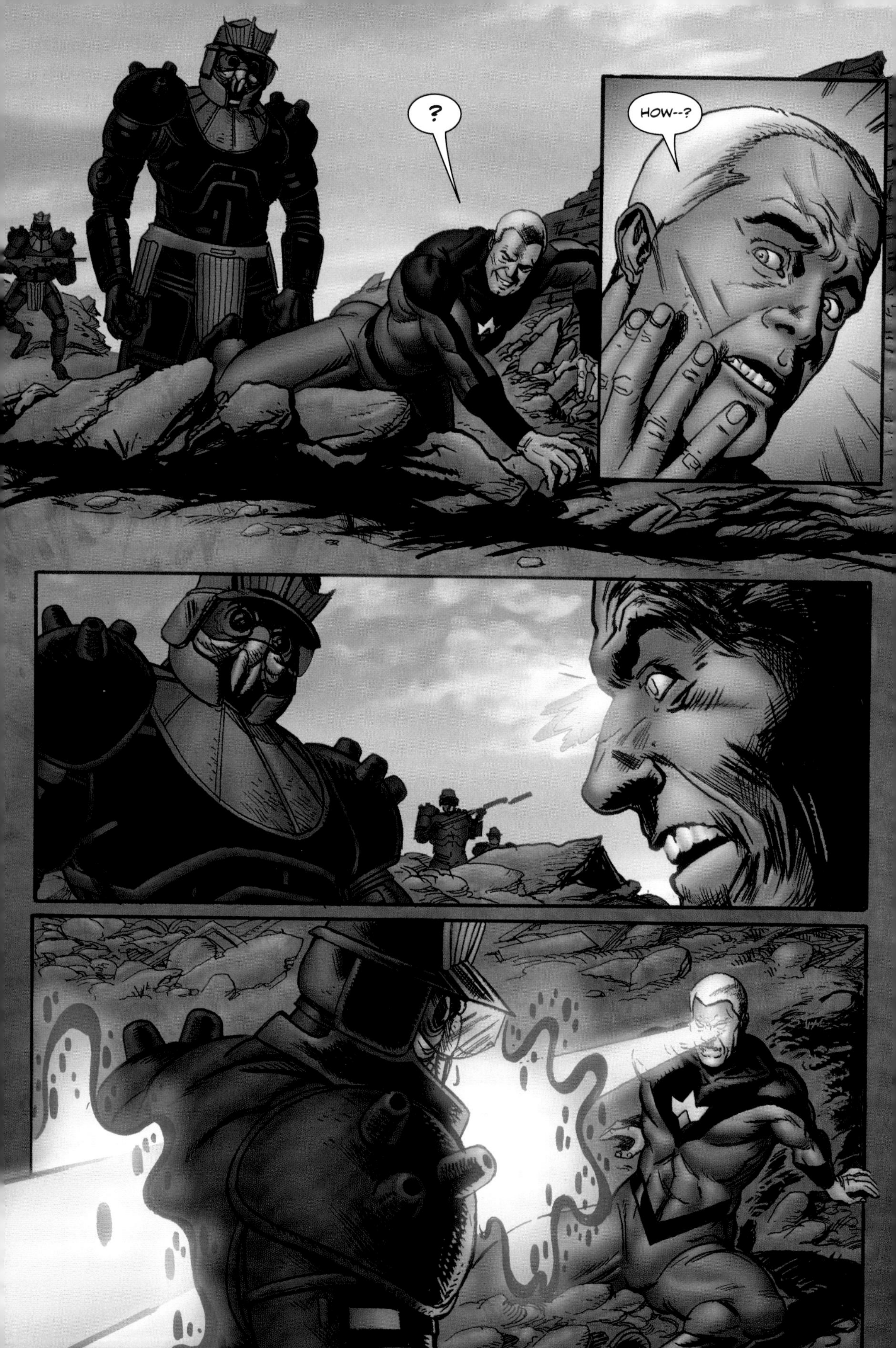
?
HOW--?

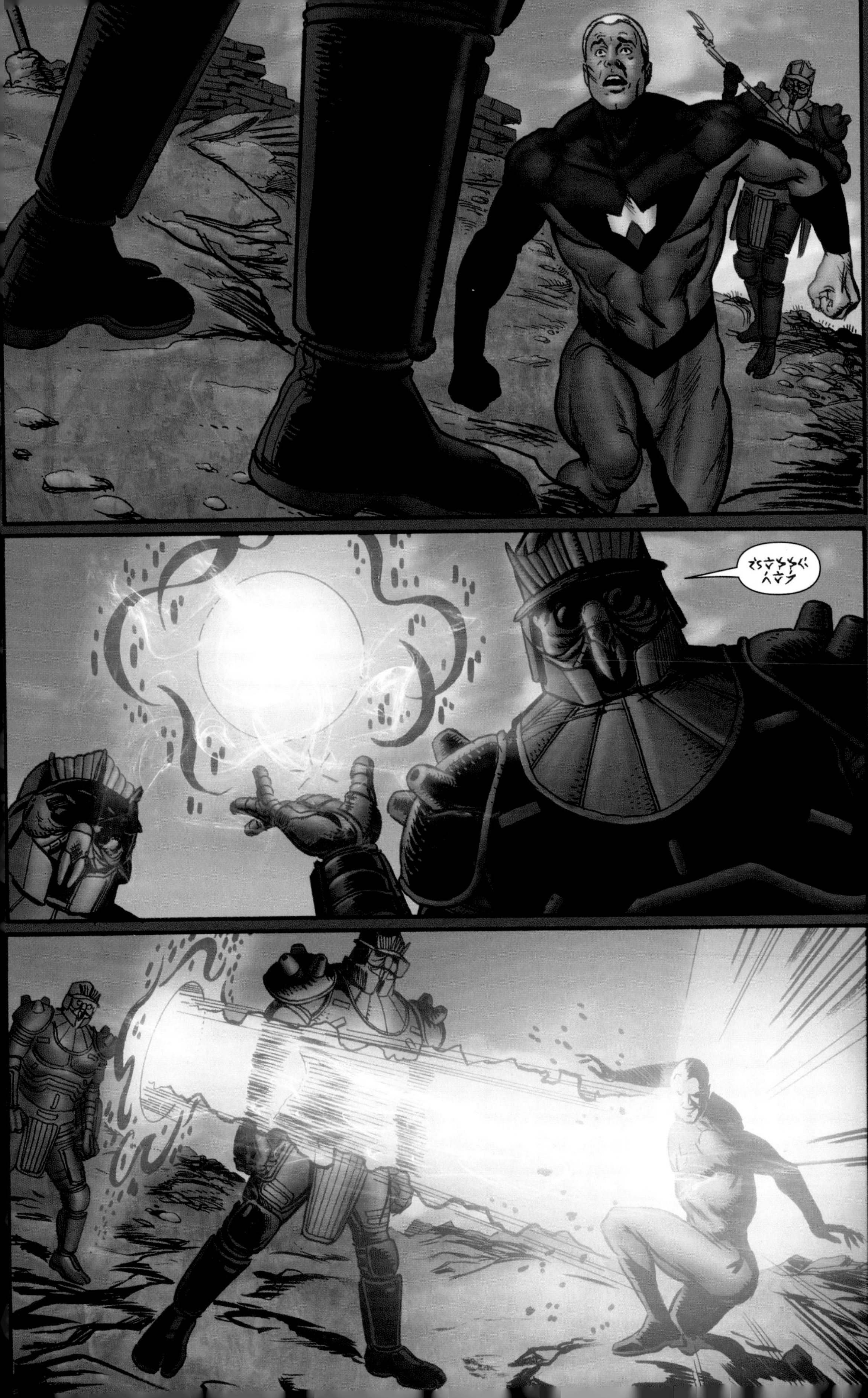

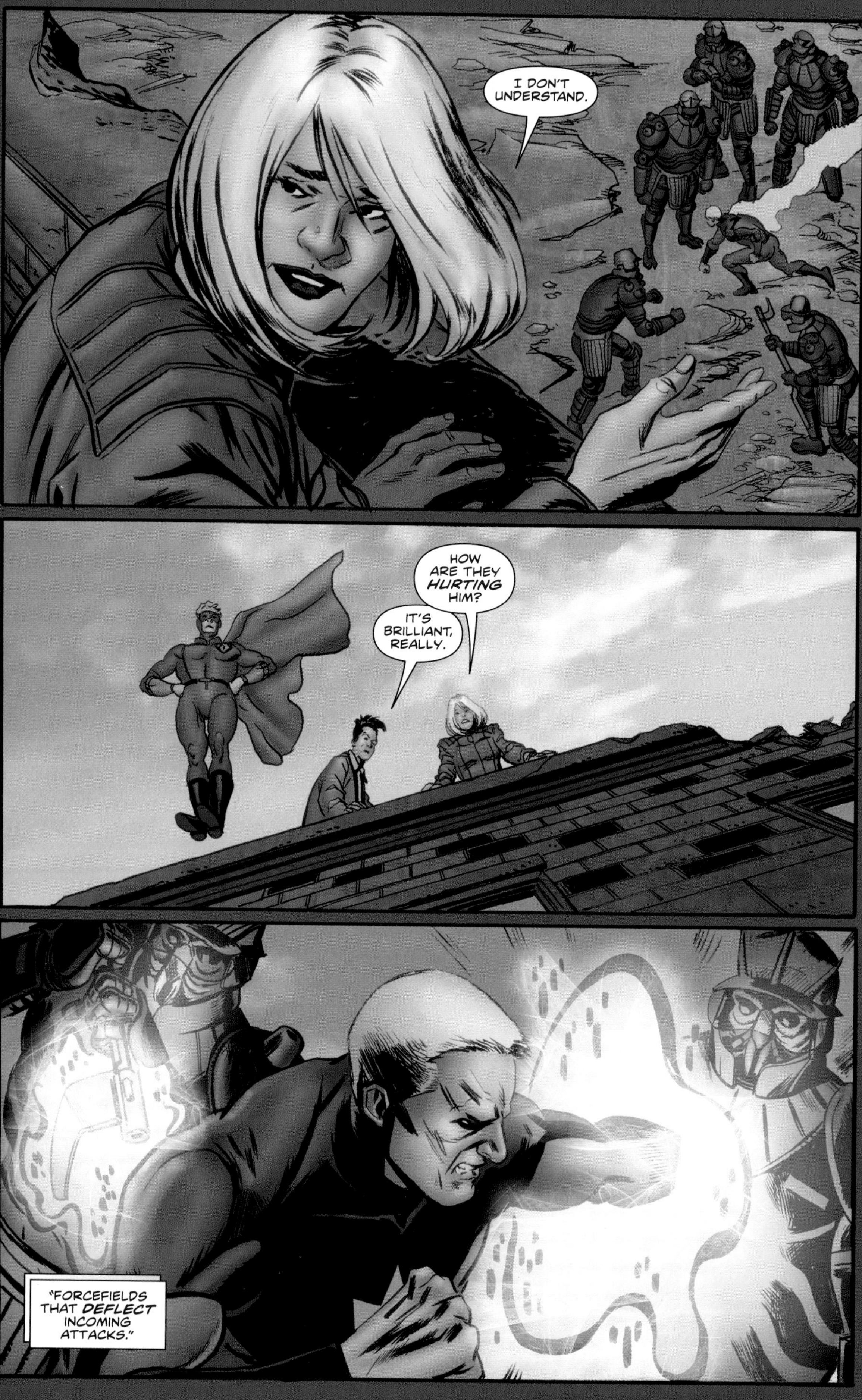
I DON'T UNDERSTAND.
HOW ARE THEY HURTING HIM?
IT'S BRILLIANT, REALLY.
"FORCEFIELDS THAT DEFLECT INCOMING ATTACKS."

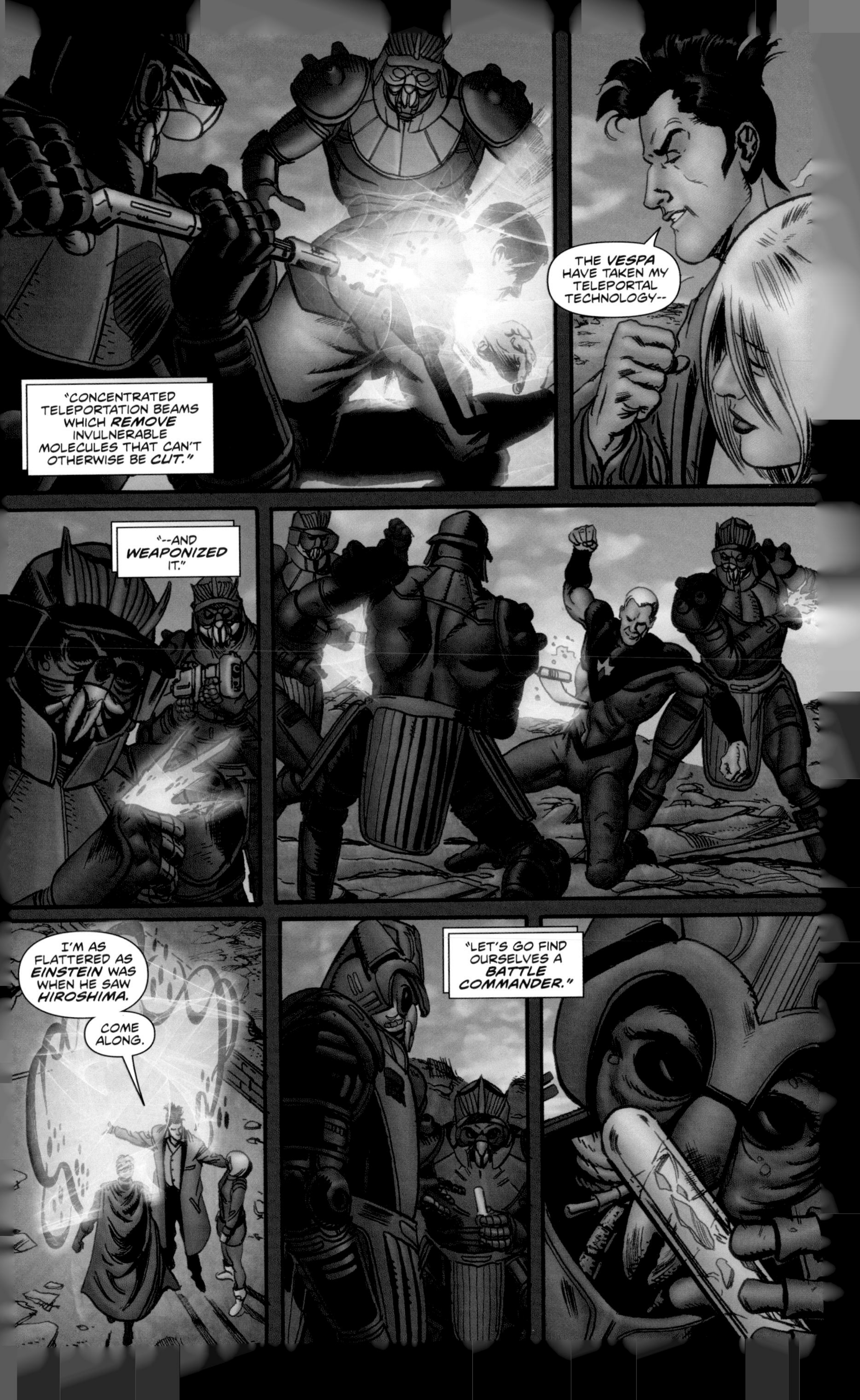
"CONCENTRATED TELEPORTATION BEAMS WHICH REMOVE INVULNERABLE MOLECULES THAT CAN'T OTHERWISE BE CUT."
THE VESPA HAVE TAKEN MY TELEPORTAL TECHNOLOGY--
"--AND WEAPONIZED IT."
I'M AS FLATTERED AS EINSTEIN WAS WHEN HE SAW HIROSHIMA.
COME ALONG.
"LET'S GO FIND OURSELVES A BATTLE COMMANDER."

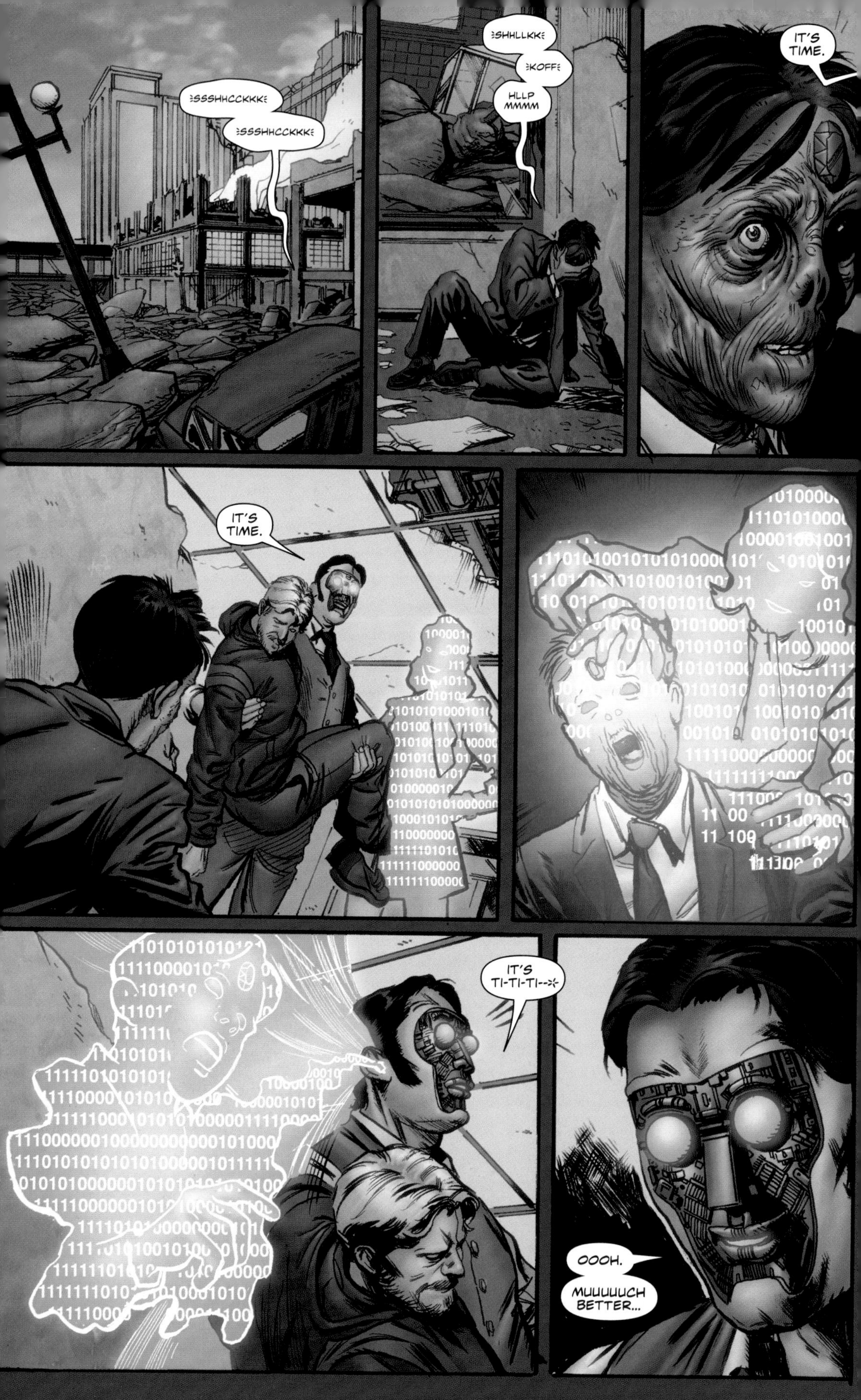
SSSHHCCKKK
SSSHHCCKKK
SHHLLKK
KOFF
HLLP MMMM
IT'S TIME.
IT'S TIME.
IT'S TI-TI-TI--
OOOH.
MUUUUUCH BETTER...

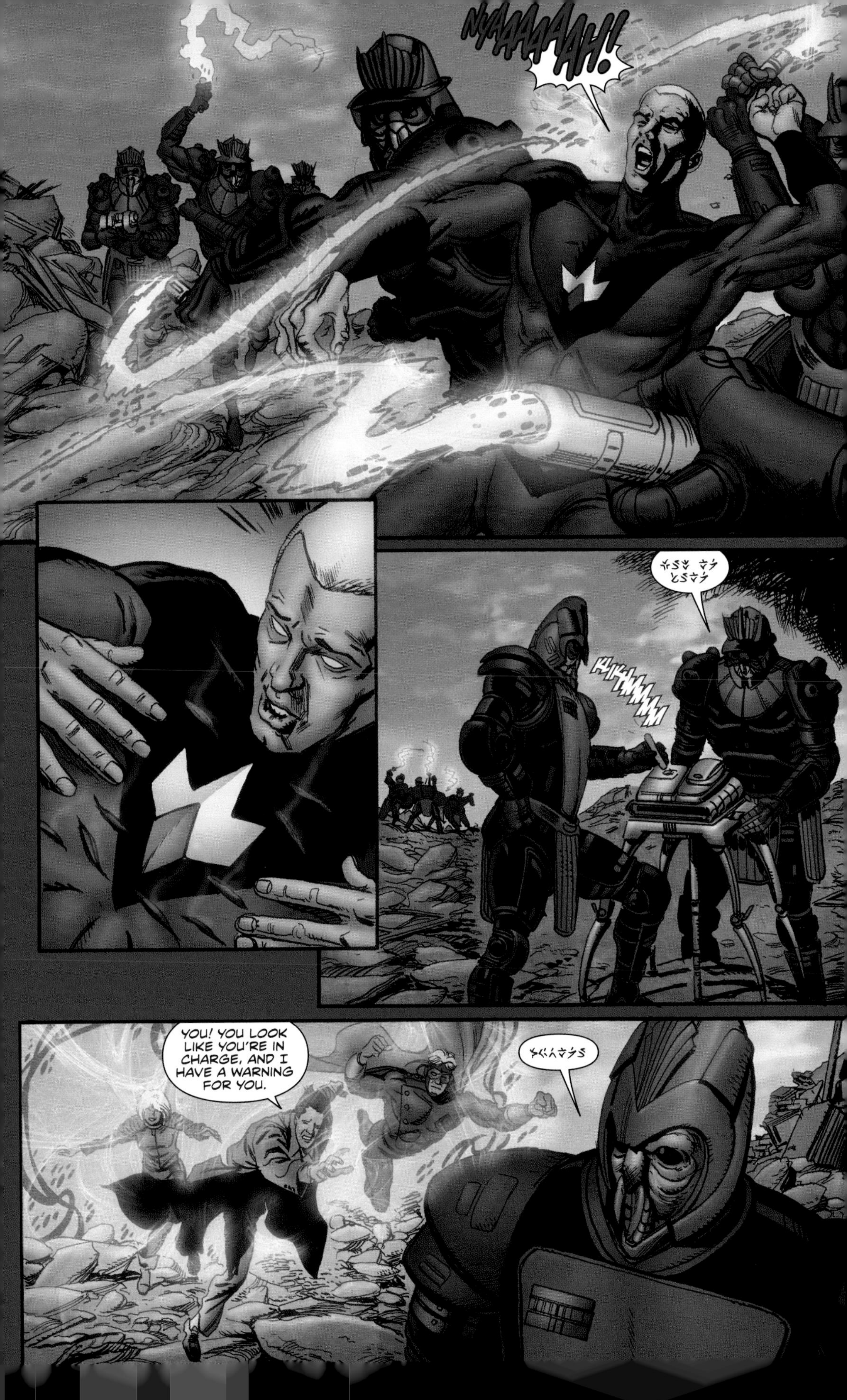
NYAAAAAAH!!
KLIKHMMMM
YOU! YOU LOOK LIKE YOU'RE IN CHARGE, AND I HAVE A WARNING FOR YOU.

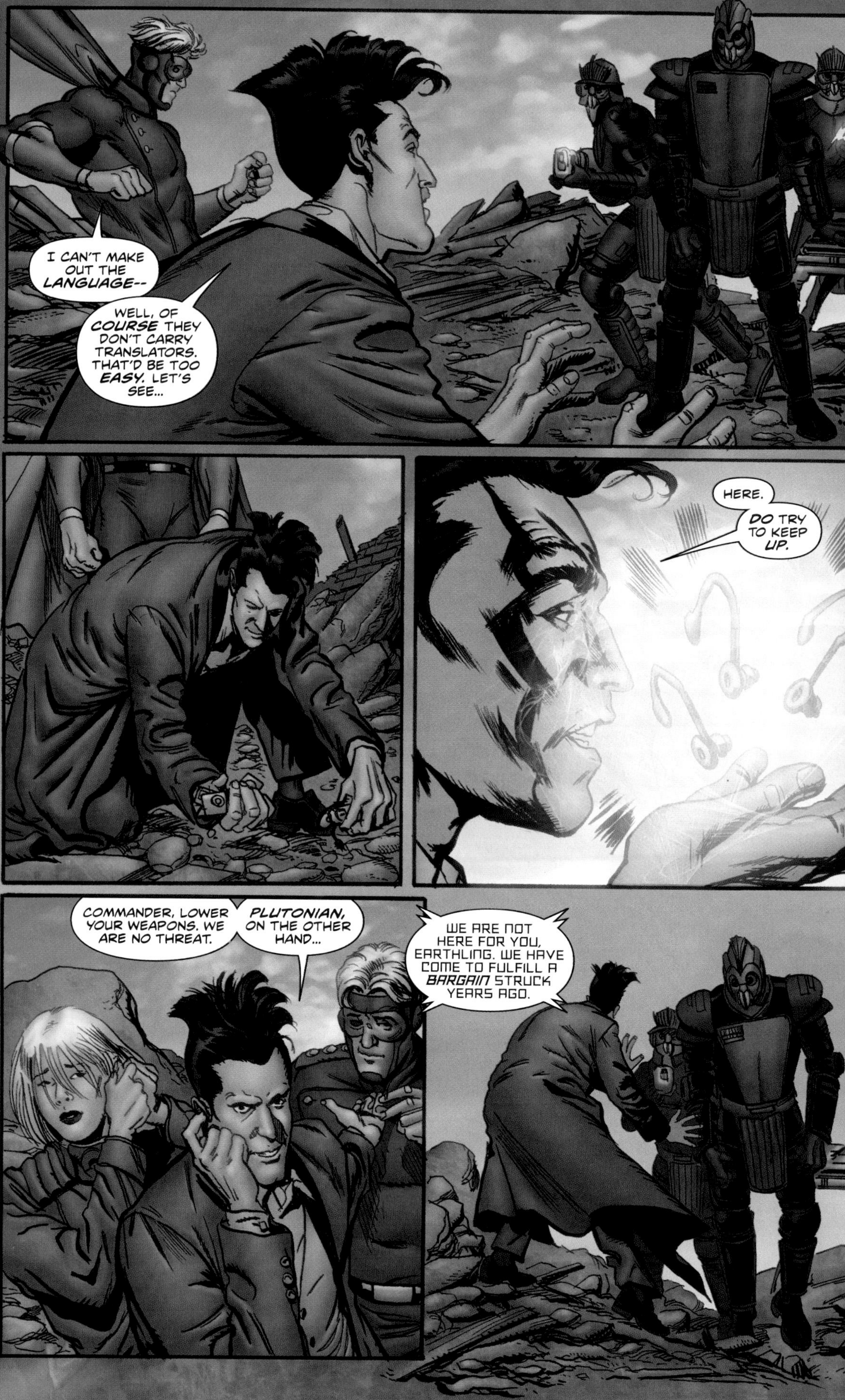

I CAN'T MAKE OUT THE LANGUAGE--
WELL, OF COURSE THEY DON'T CARRY TRANSLATORS. THAT'D BE TOO EASY. LET'S SEE...
HERE.
DO TRY TO KEEP UP.
COMMANDER, LOWER YOUR WEAPONS. WE ARE NO THREAT.
PLUTONIAN, ON THE OTHER HAND...
WE ARE NOT HERE FOR YOU, EARTHLING. WE HAVE COME TO FULFILL A BARGAIN STRUCK YEARS AGO.

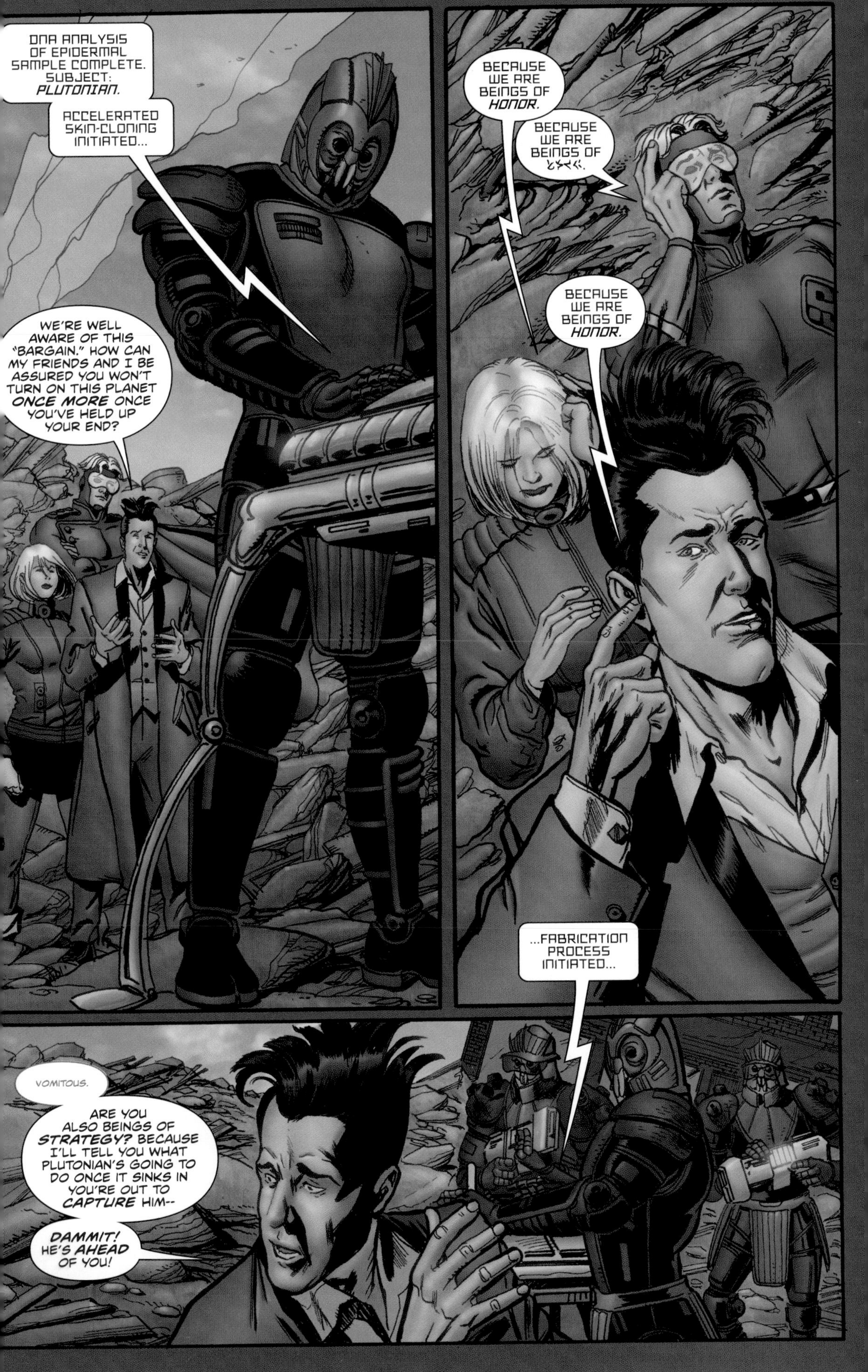
DNA ANALYSIS OF EPIDERMAL SAMPLE COMPLETE. SUBJECT: *PLUTONIAN*.
ACCELERATED SKIN-CLONING INITIATED...
WE'RE WELL AWARE OF THIS "BARGAIN." HOW CAN MY FRIENDS AND I BE ASSURED YOU WON'T TURN ON THIS PLANET **ONCE MORE** ONCE YOU'VE HELD UP YOUR END?
BECAUSE WE ARE BEINGS OF *HONOR*.
BECAUSE WE ARE BEINGS OF
BECAUSE WE ARE BEINGS OF *HONOR*.
...FABRICATION PROCESS INITIATED...
VOMITOUS.
ARE YOU ALSO BEINGS OF ***STRATEGY?*** BECAUSE I'LL TELL YOU WHAT PLUTONIAN'S GOING TO DO ONCE IT SINKS IN YOU'RE OUT TO ***CAPTURE*** HIM--
DAMMIT! HE'S ***AHEAD*** OF YOU!

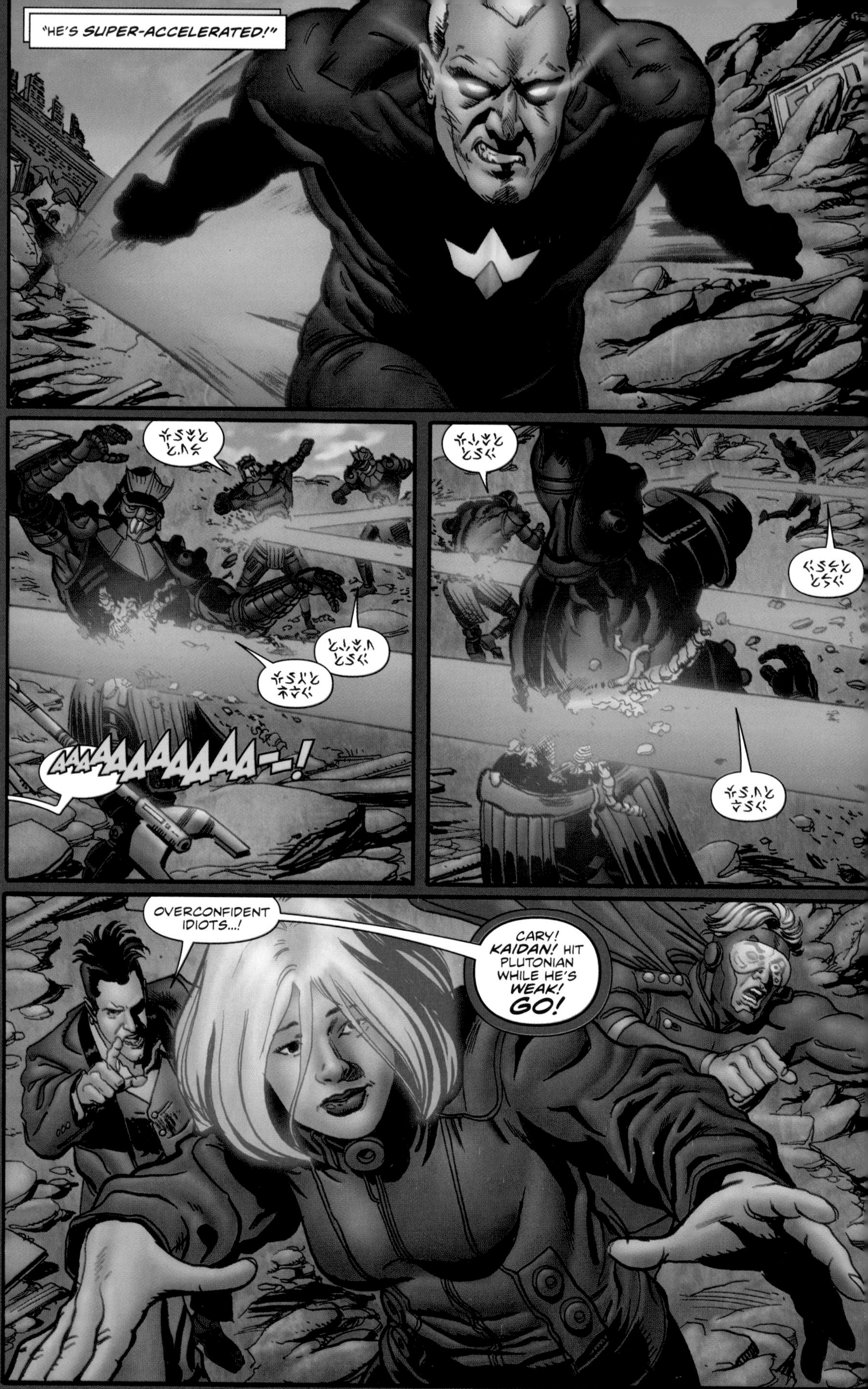
"HE'S SUPER-ACCELERATED!"
AAAAAAAAAA--!
OVERCONFIDENT IDIOTS...!
CARY! KAIDAN! HIT PLUTONIAN WHILE HE'S WEAK! GO!

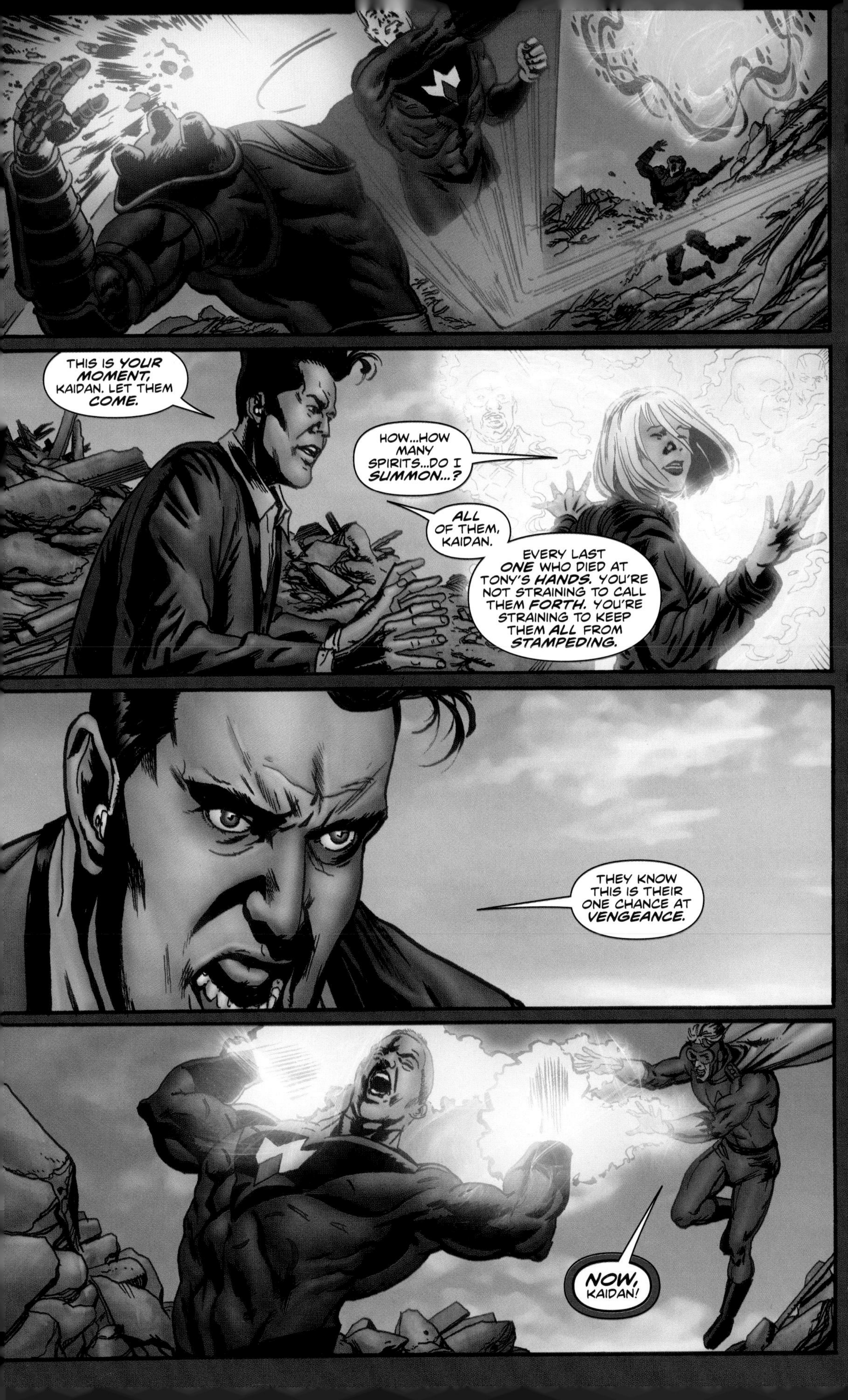
THIS IS YOUR MOMENT, KAIDAN. LET THEM COME.
HOW...HOW MANY SPIRITS...DO I SUMMON...?
ALL OF THEM, KAIDAN.
EVERY LAST ONE WHO DIED AT TONY'S HANDS. YOU'RE NOT STRAINING TO CALL THEM FORTH. YOU'RE STRAINING TO KEEP THEM ALL FROM STAMPEDING.
THEY KNOW THIS IS THEIR ONE CHANCE AT VENGEANCE.
NOW, KAIDAN!

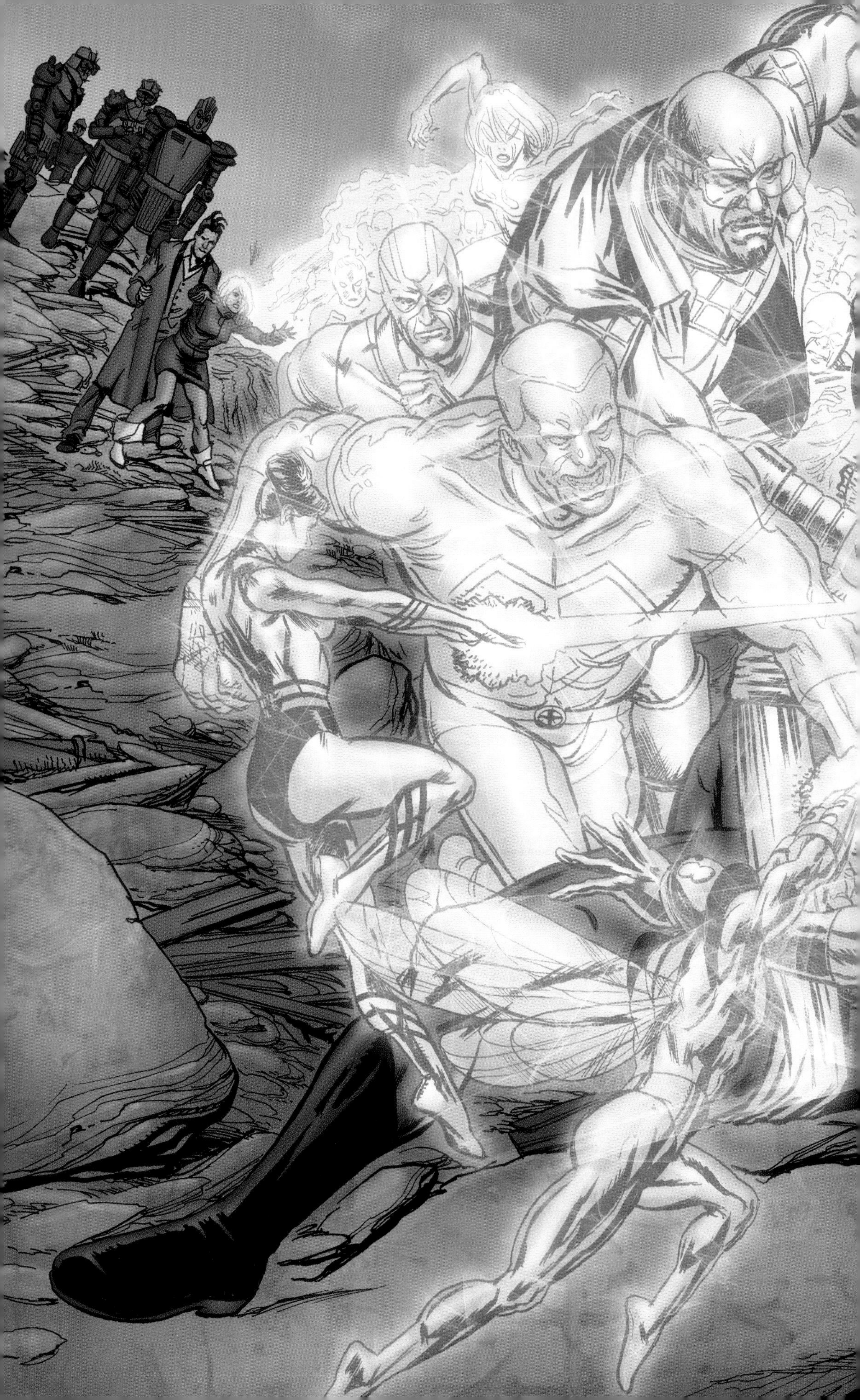

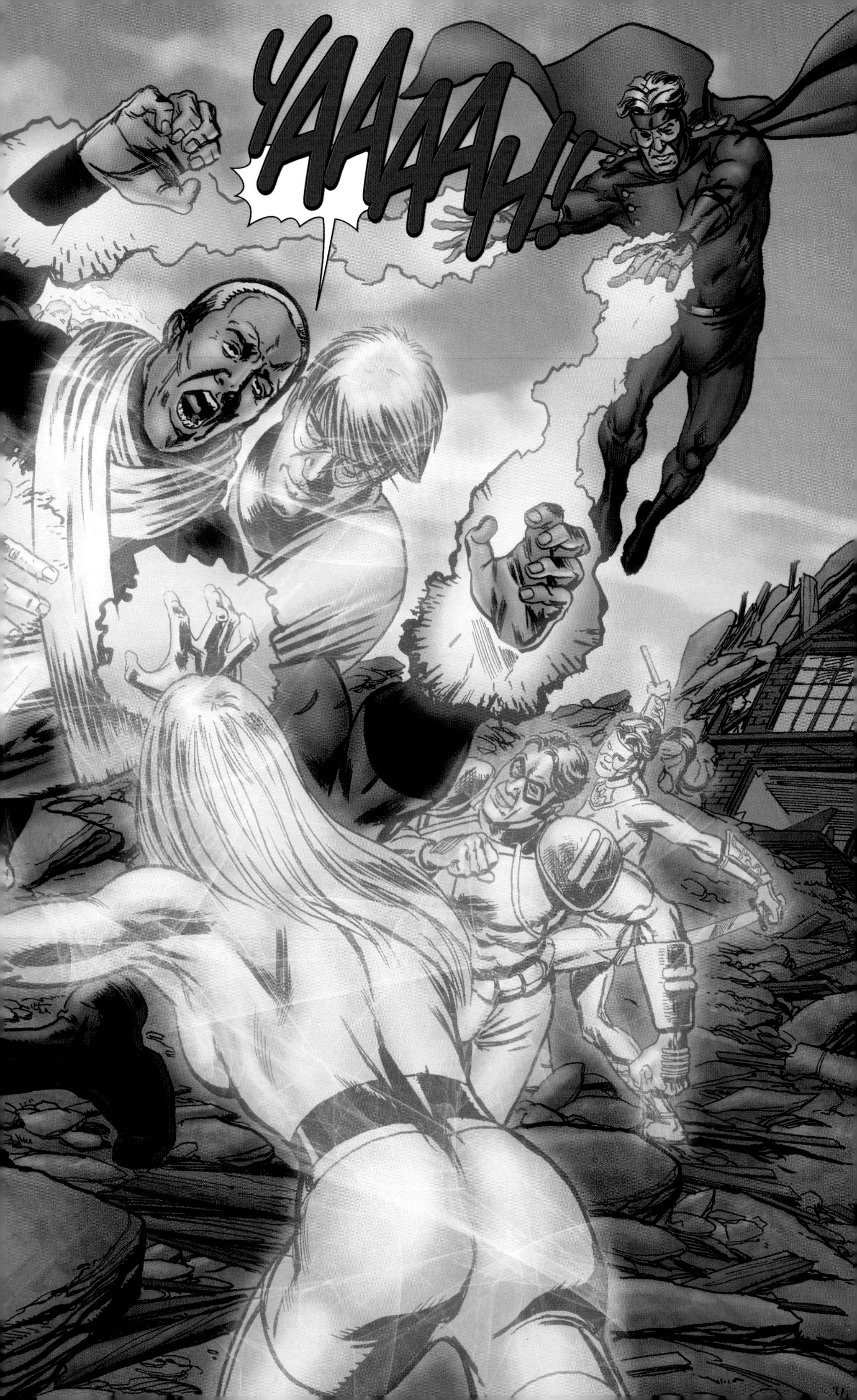
YAAAAH!

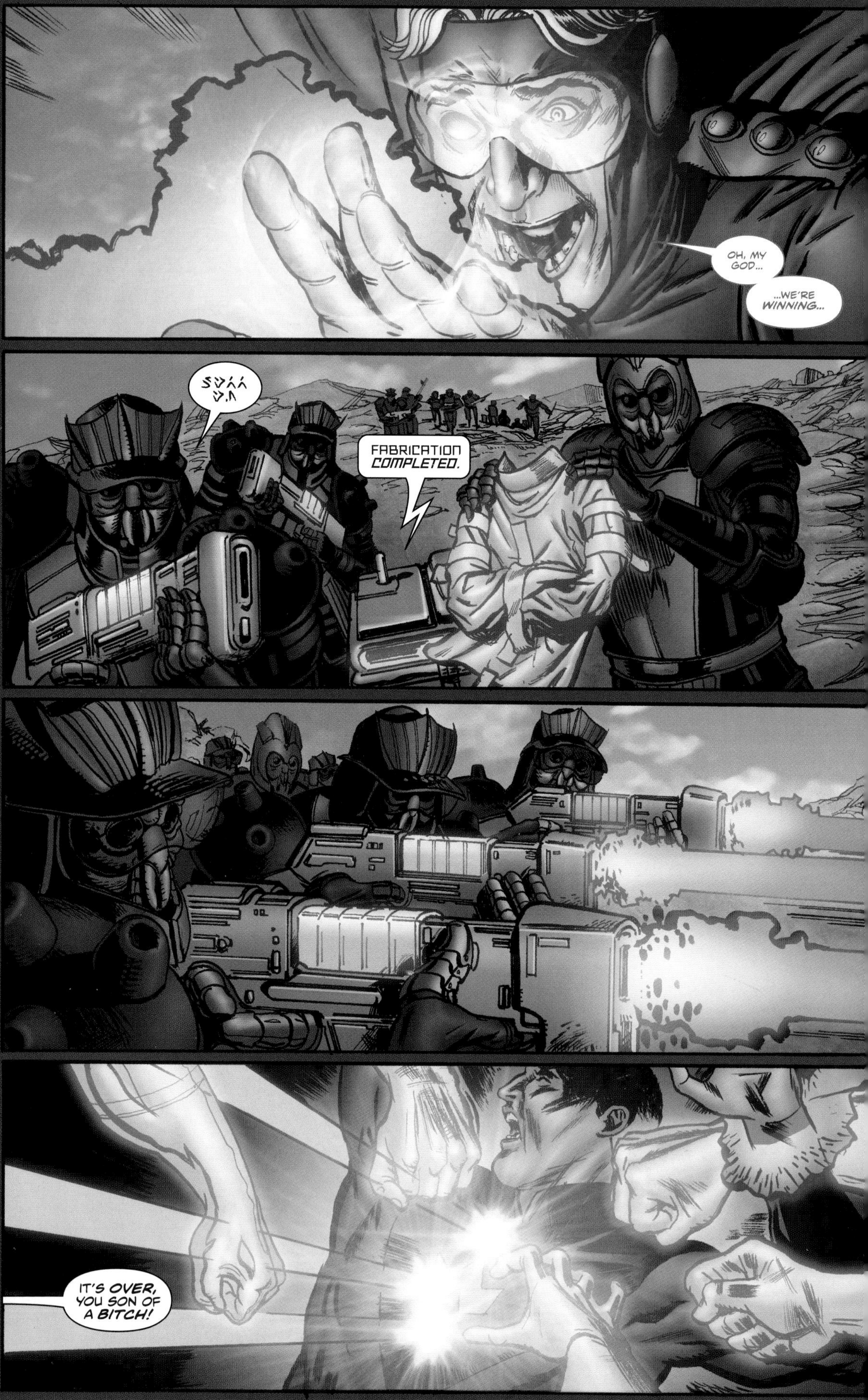
OH, MY GOD...
...WE'RE WINNING...
FABRICATION COMPLETED.
IT'S OVER, YOU SON OF A BITCH!

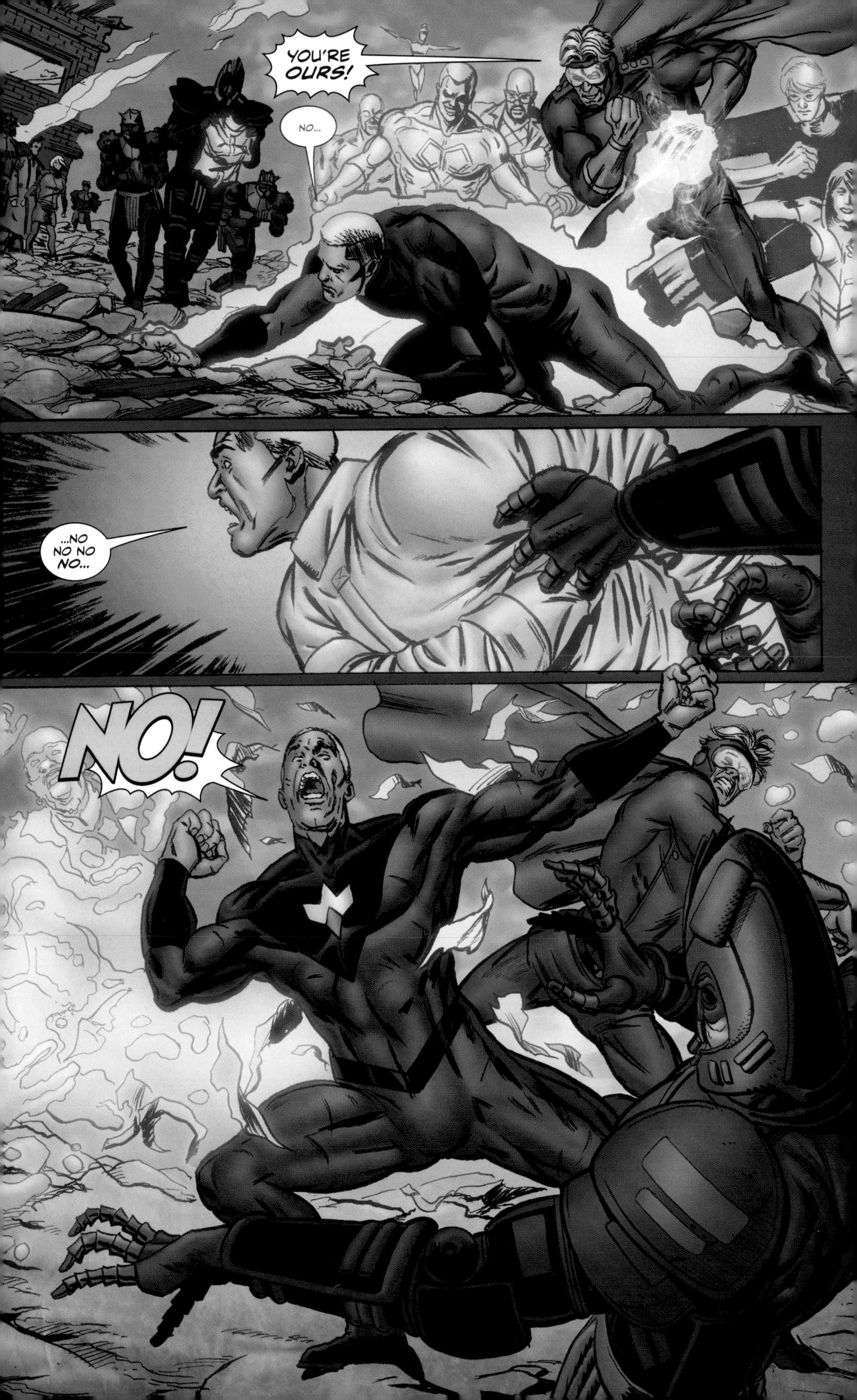
YOU'RE OURS!
NO...
...NO NO NO NO...
NO!

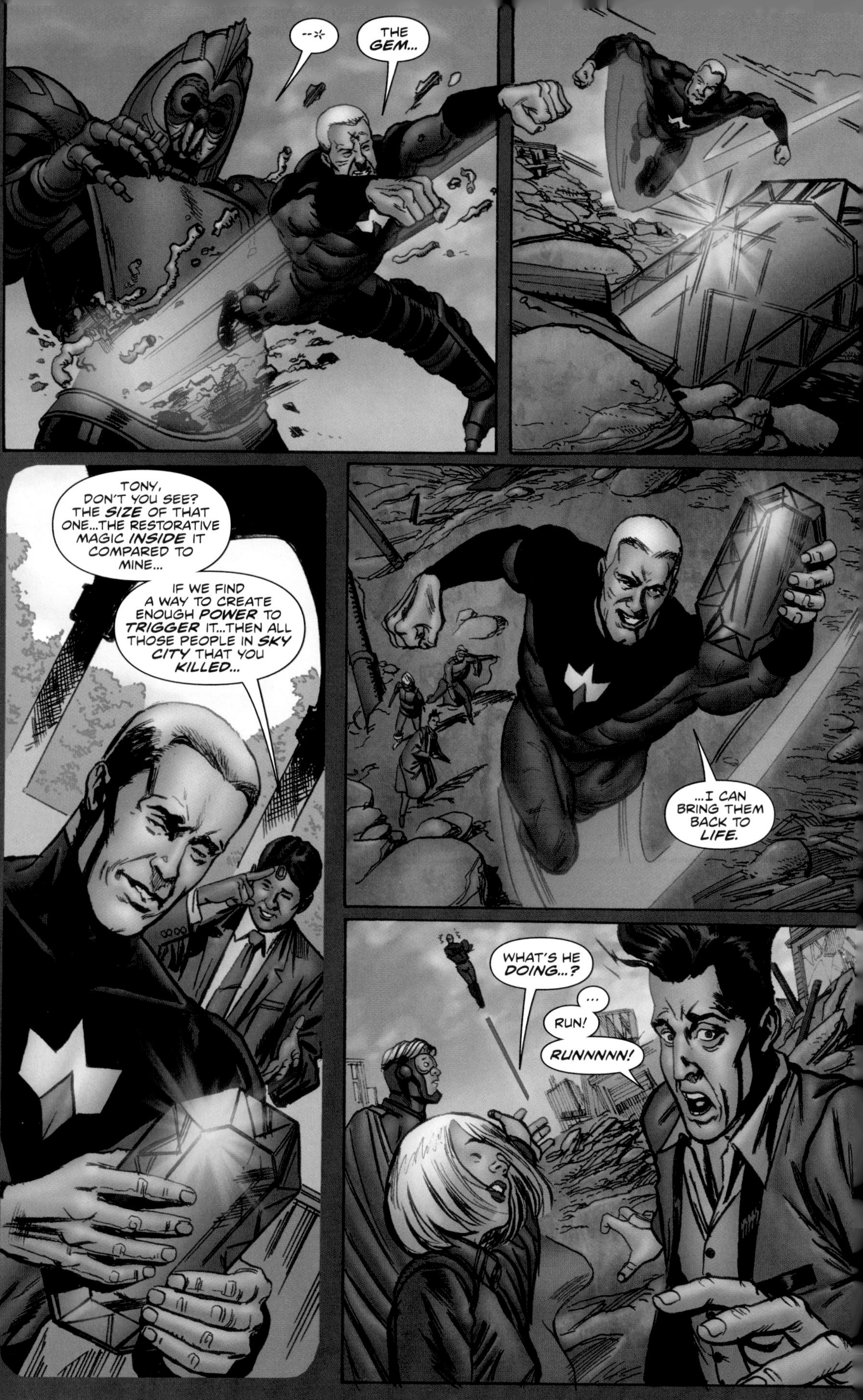
--*
THE GEM...
TONY, DON'T YOU SEE? THE SIZE OF THAT ONE...THE RESTORATIVE MAGIC INSIDE IT COMPARED TO MINE...
IF WE FIND A WAY TO CREATE ENOUGH POWER TO TRIGGER IT...THEN ALL THOSE PEOPLE IN SKY CITY THAT YOU KILLED...
...I CAN BRING THEM BACK TO LIFE.
WHAT'S HE DOING...?
...
RUN!
RUNNNNN!

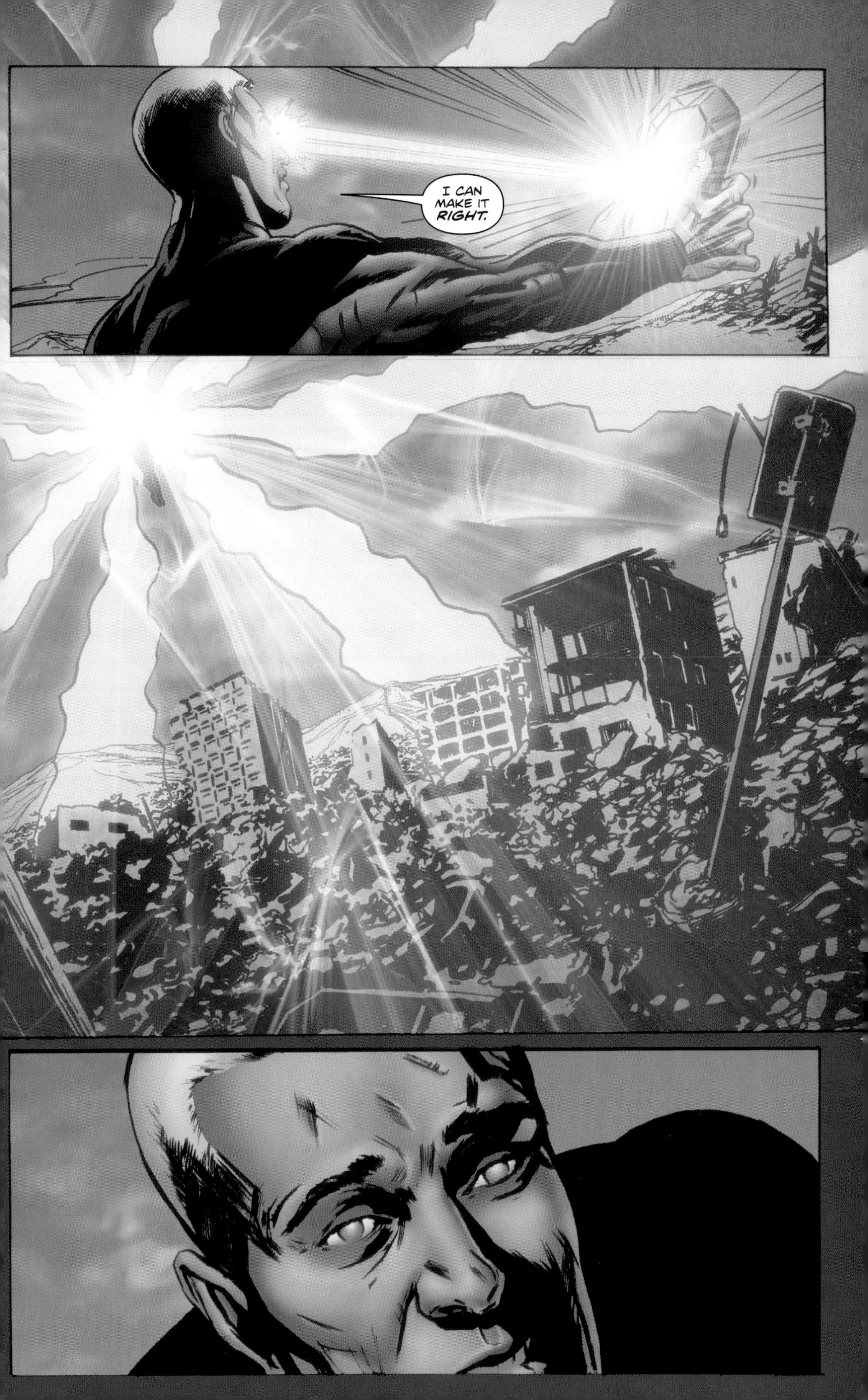
I CAN MAKE IT RIGHT.

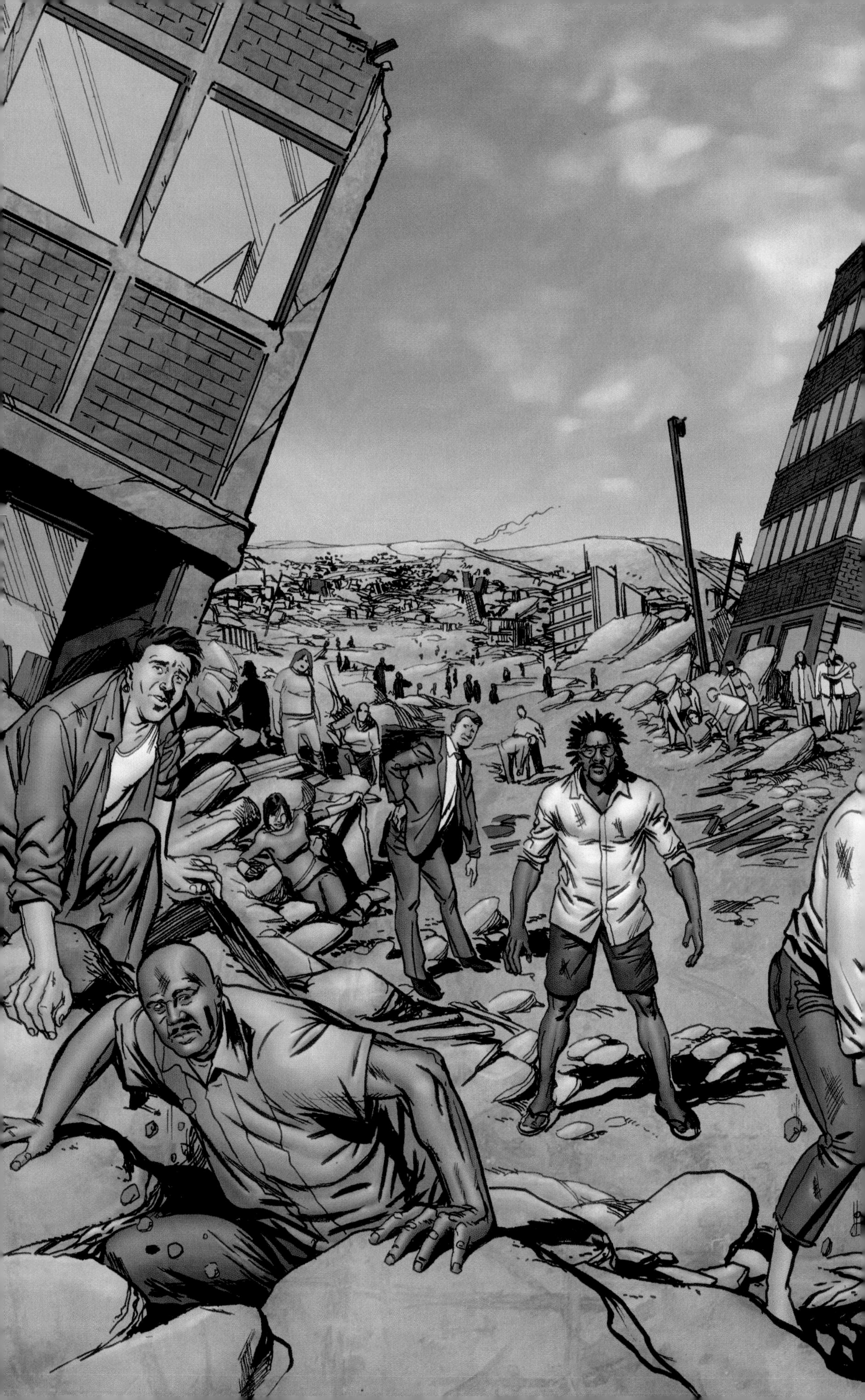

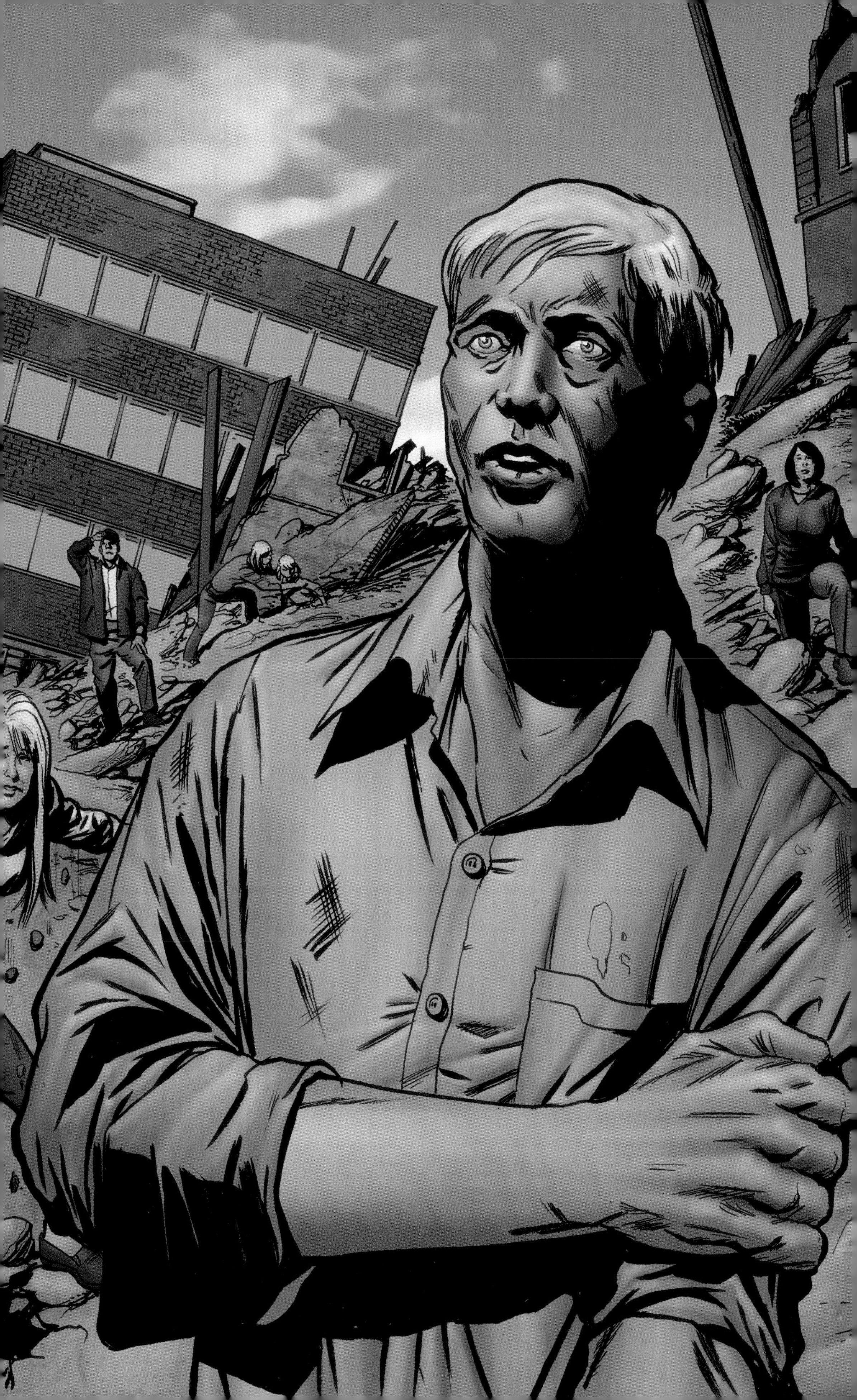

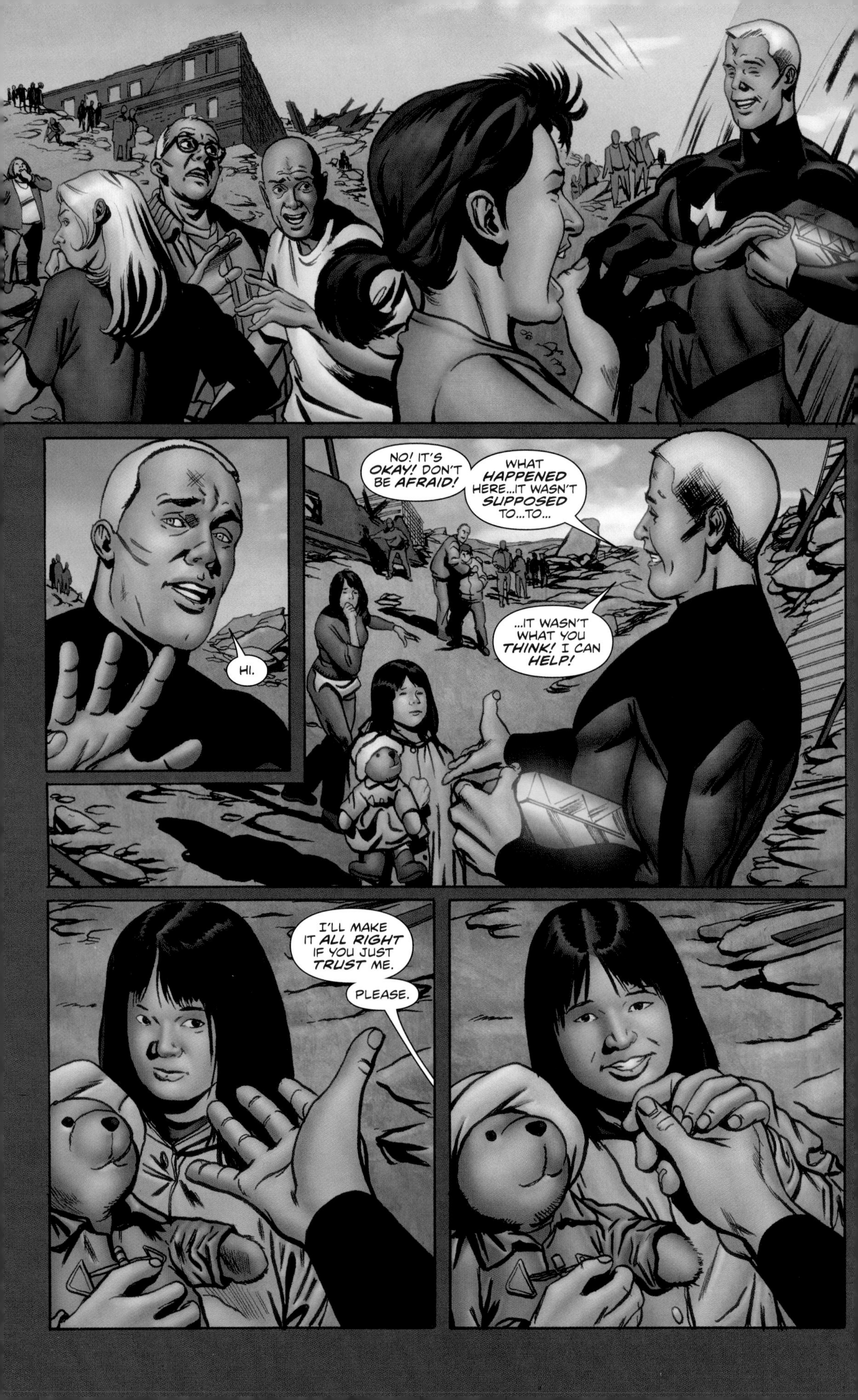
HI.
NO! IT'S OKAY! DON'T BE AFRAID!
WHAT HAPPENED HERE...IT WASN'T SUPPOSED TO...TO...
...IT WASN'T WHAT YOU THINK! I CAN HELP!
I'LL MAKE IT ALL RIGHT IF YOU JUST TRUST ME.
PLEASE.

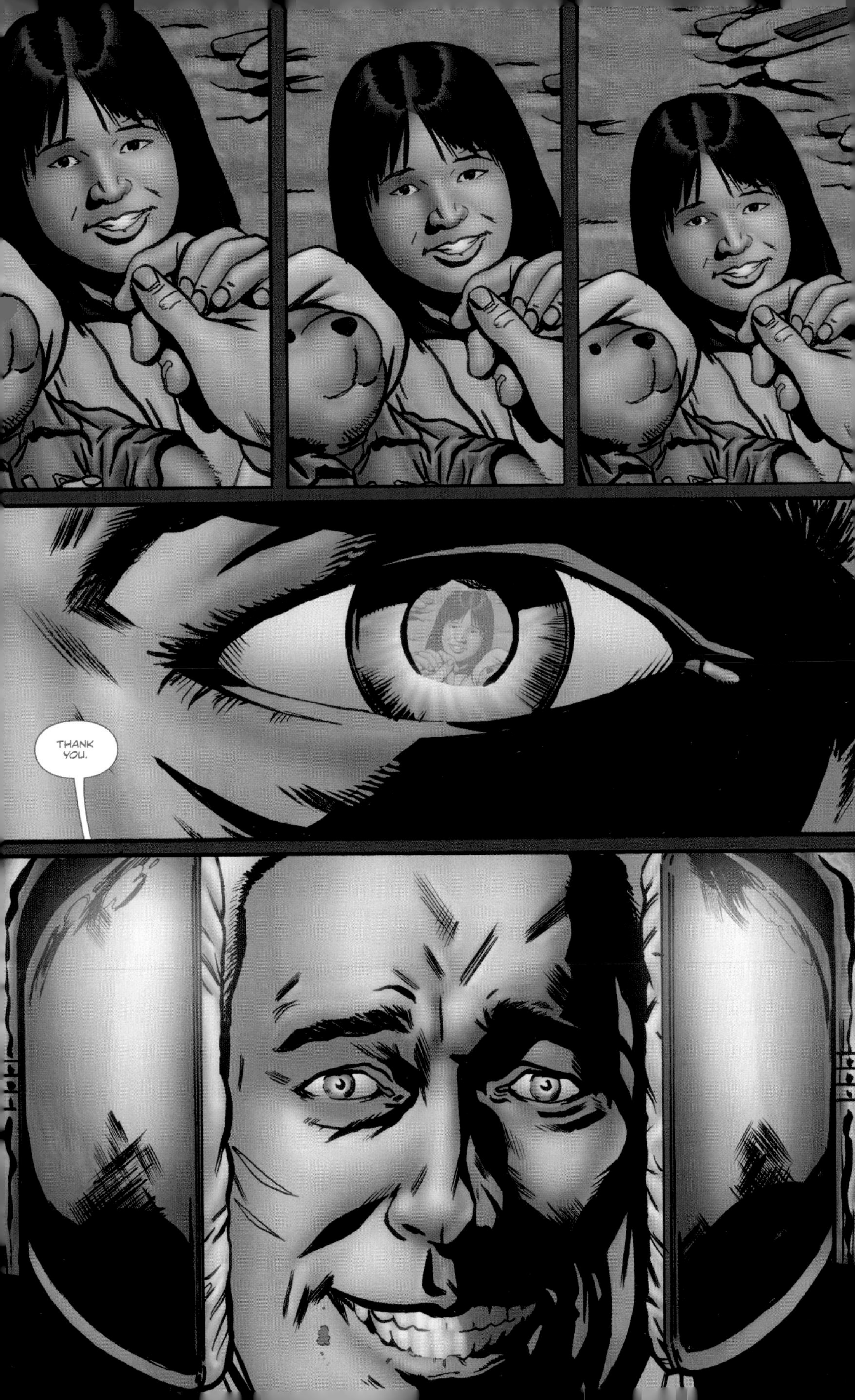
THANK YOU.

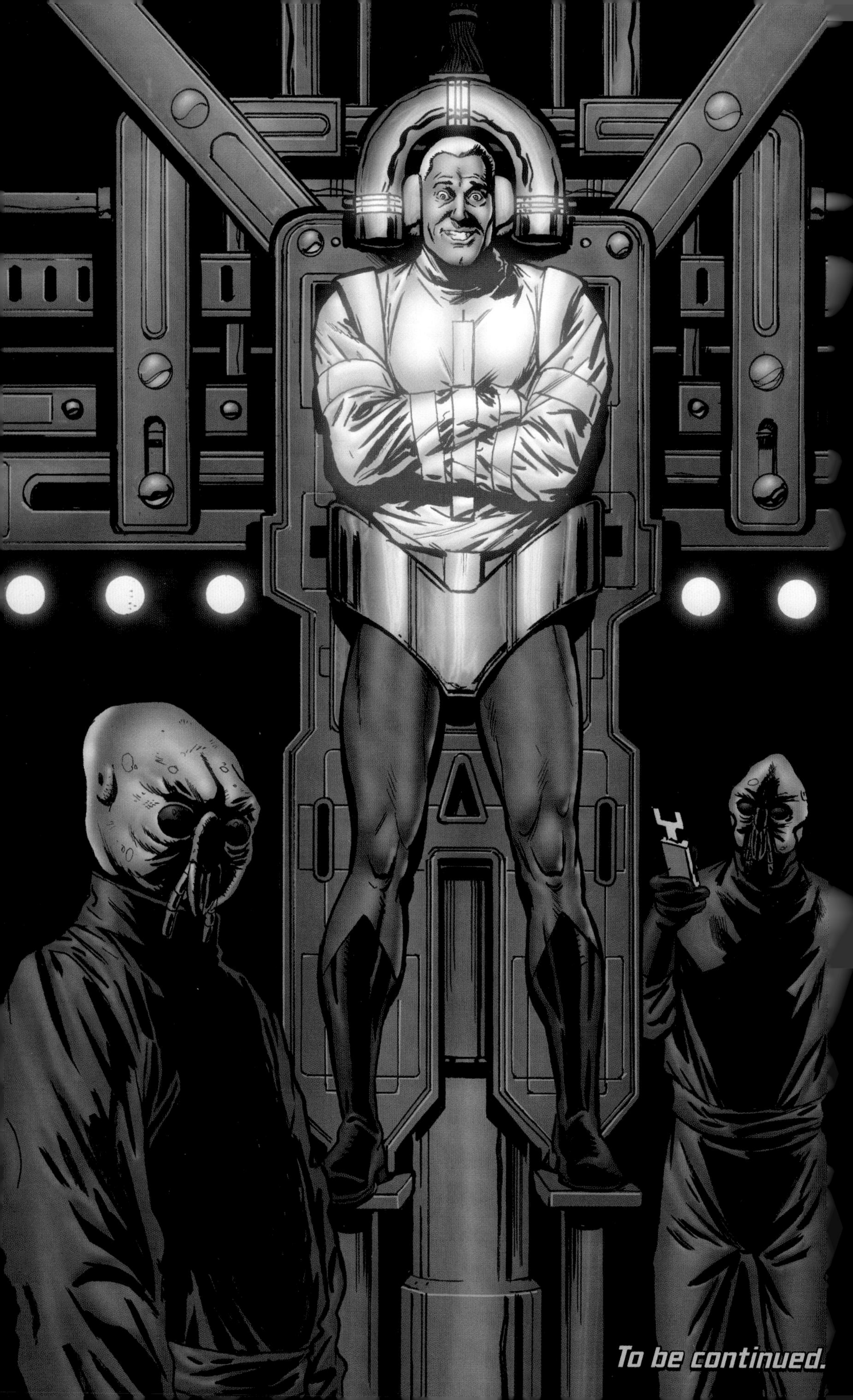

To be continued.

COVER GALLERY

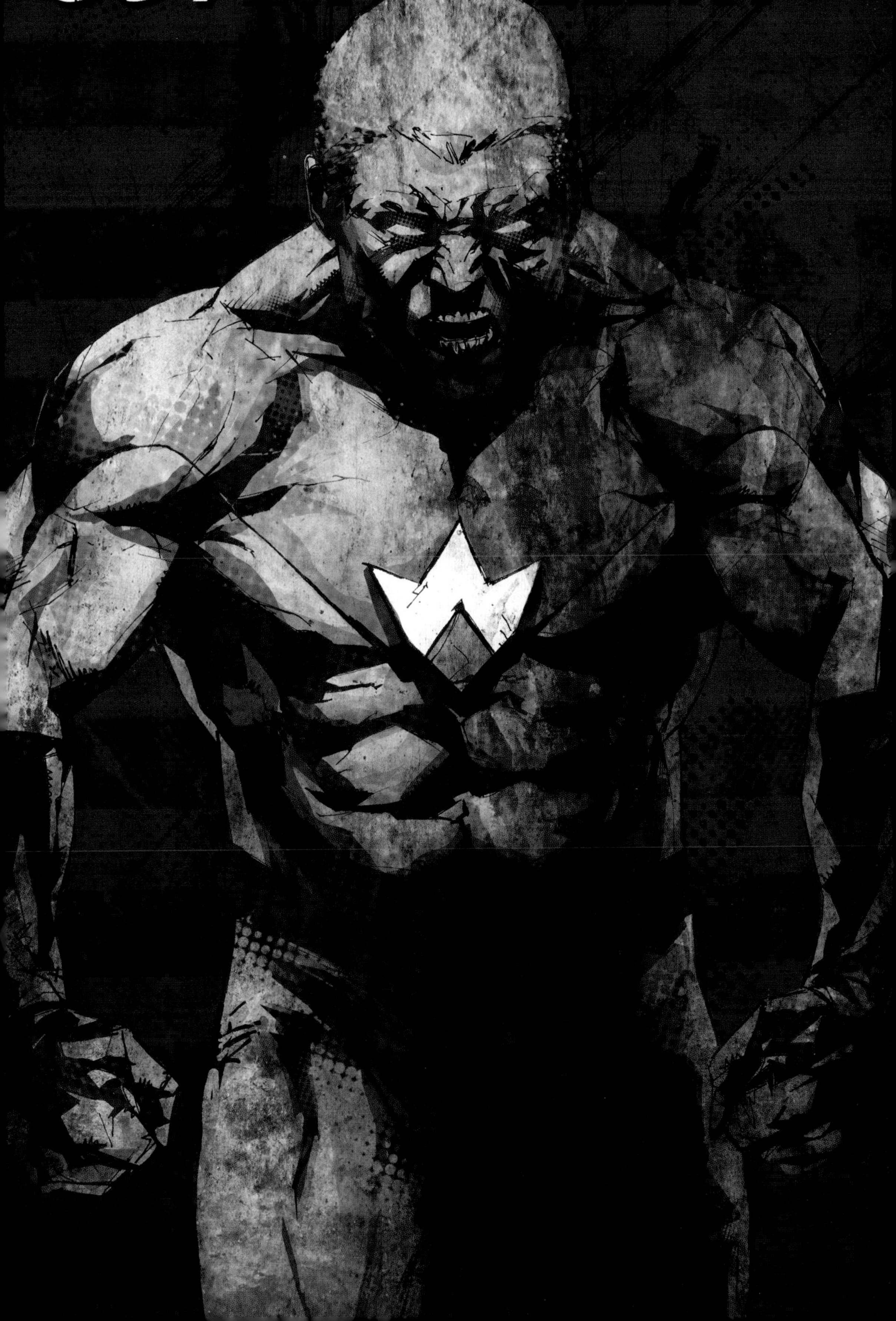

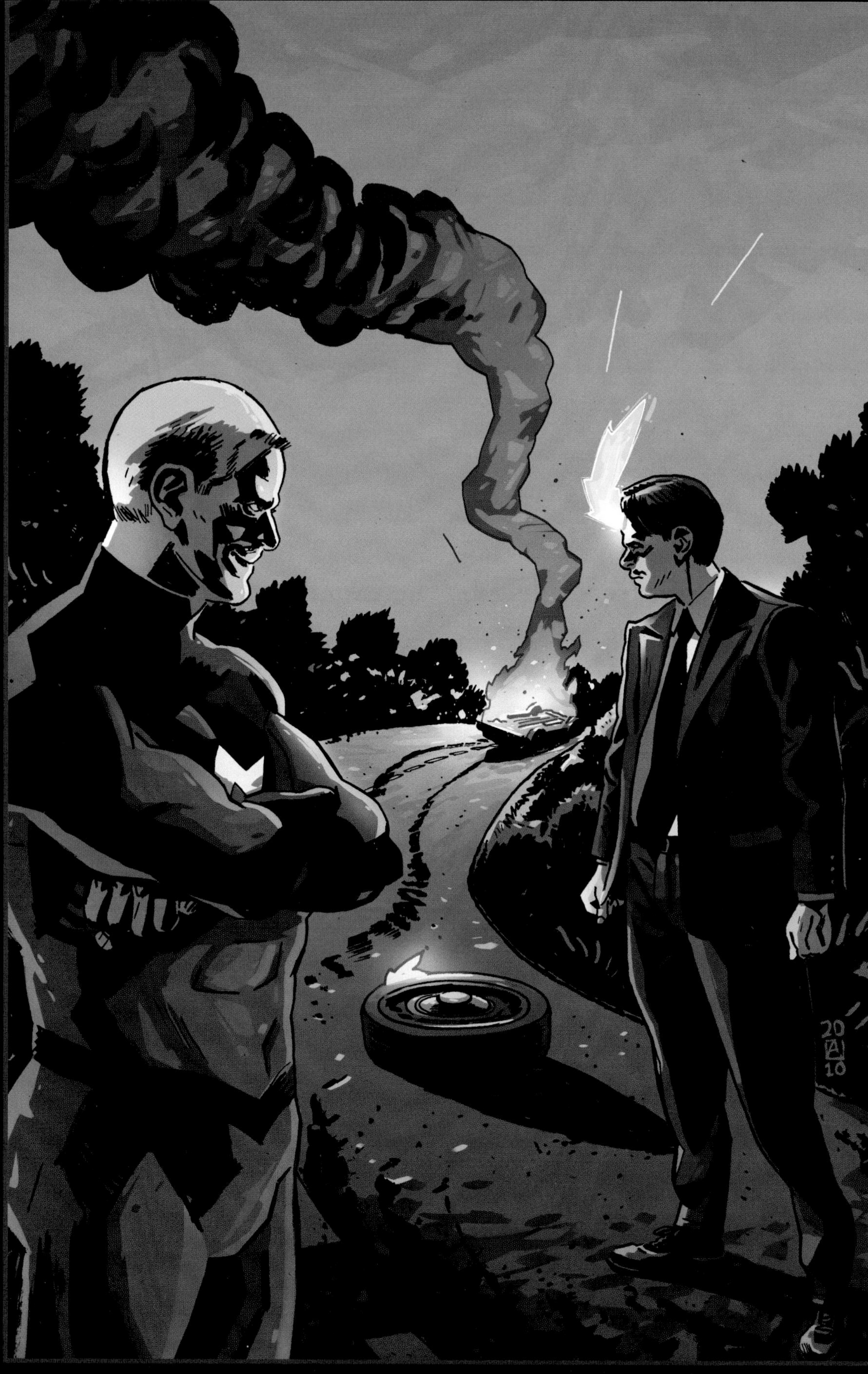
20
A
10

COVER 16A: PAUL AZACETA

COLORS: JUAN MANUEL TUMBURÚS

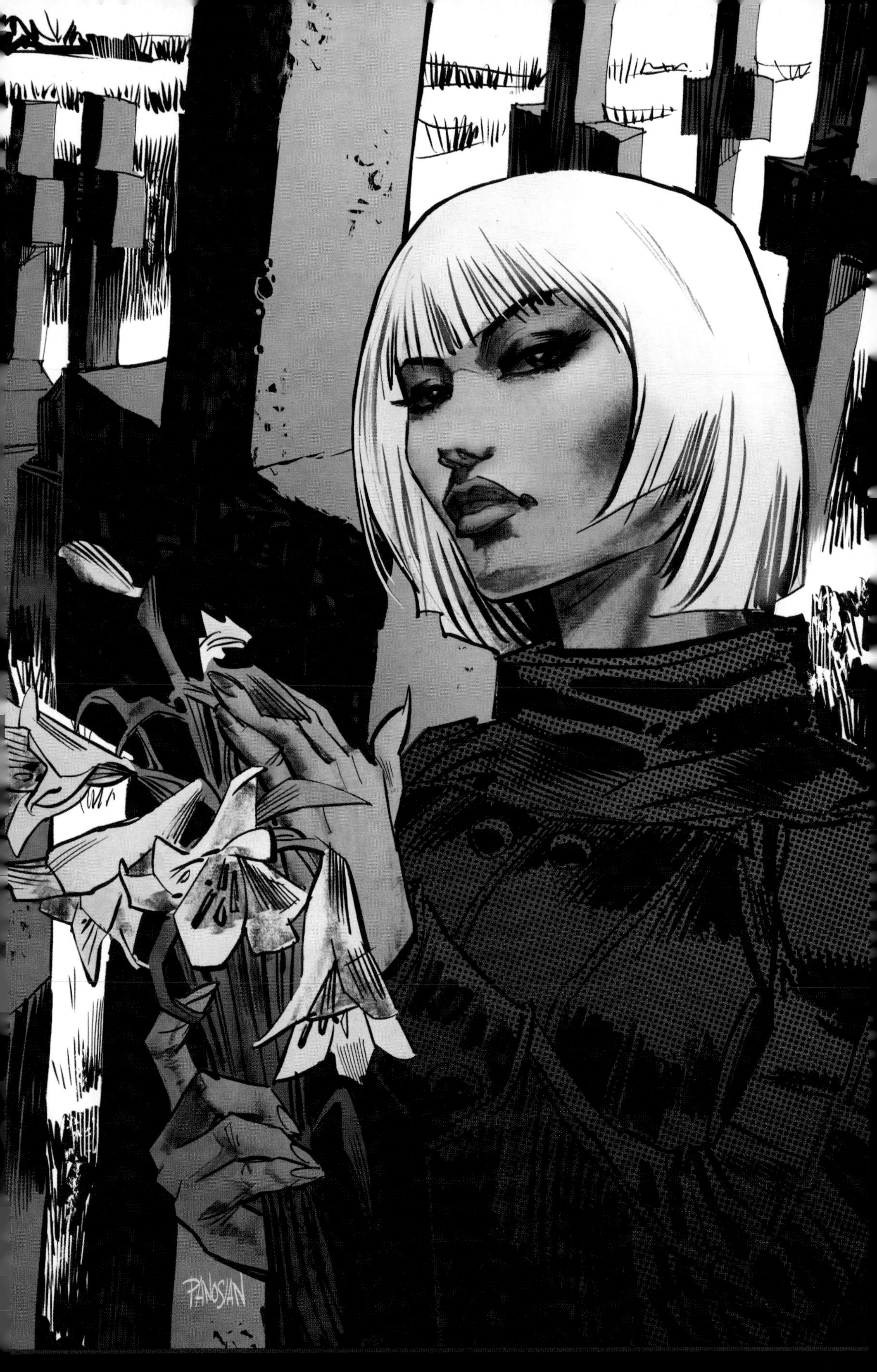
PANOSIAN
COVER 16B: DAN PANOSIAN

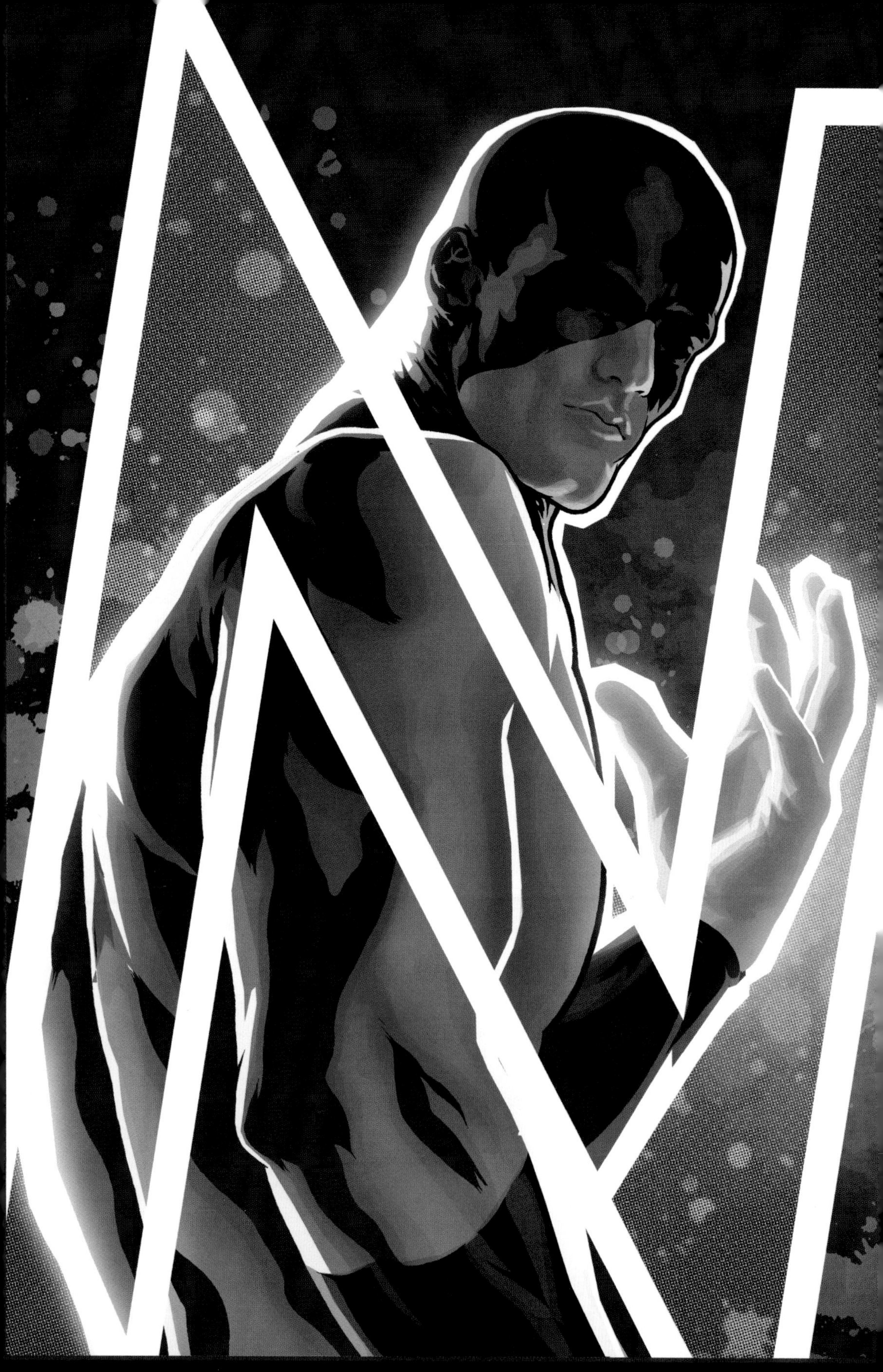

COVER 16C: JEFFREY SPOKES

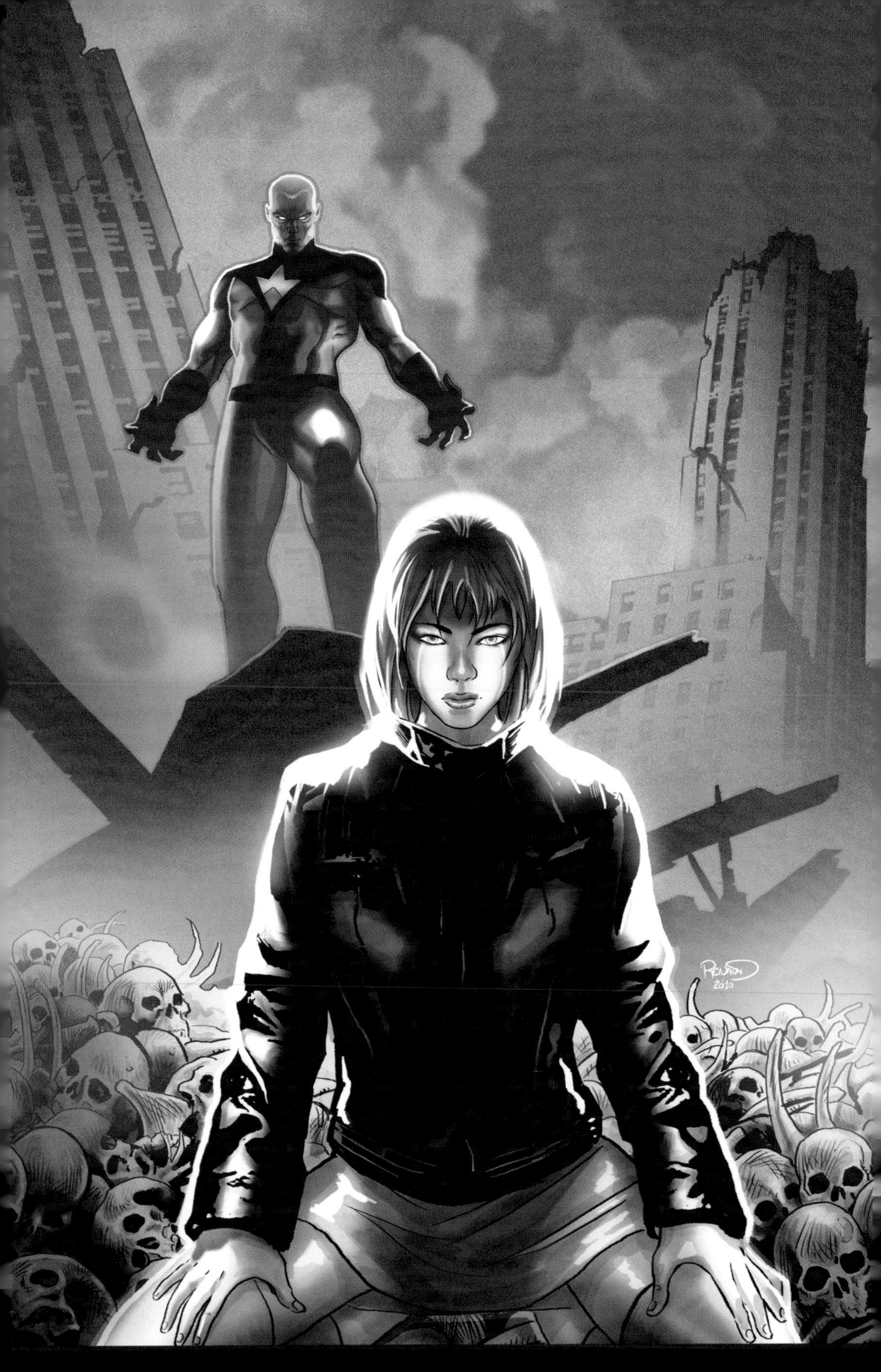
RENAUD
2010

COVER 17A: PAUL RENAUD

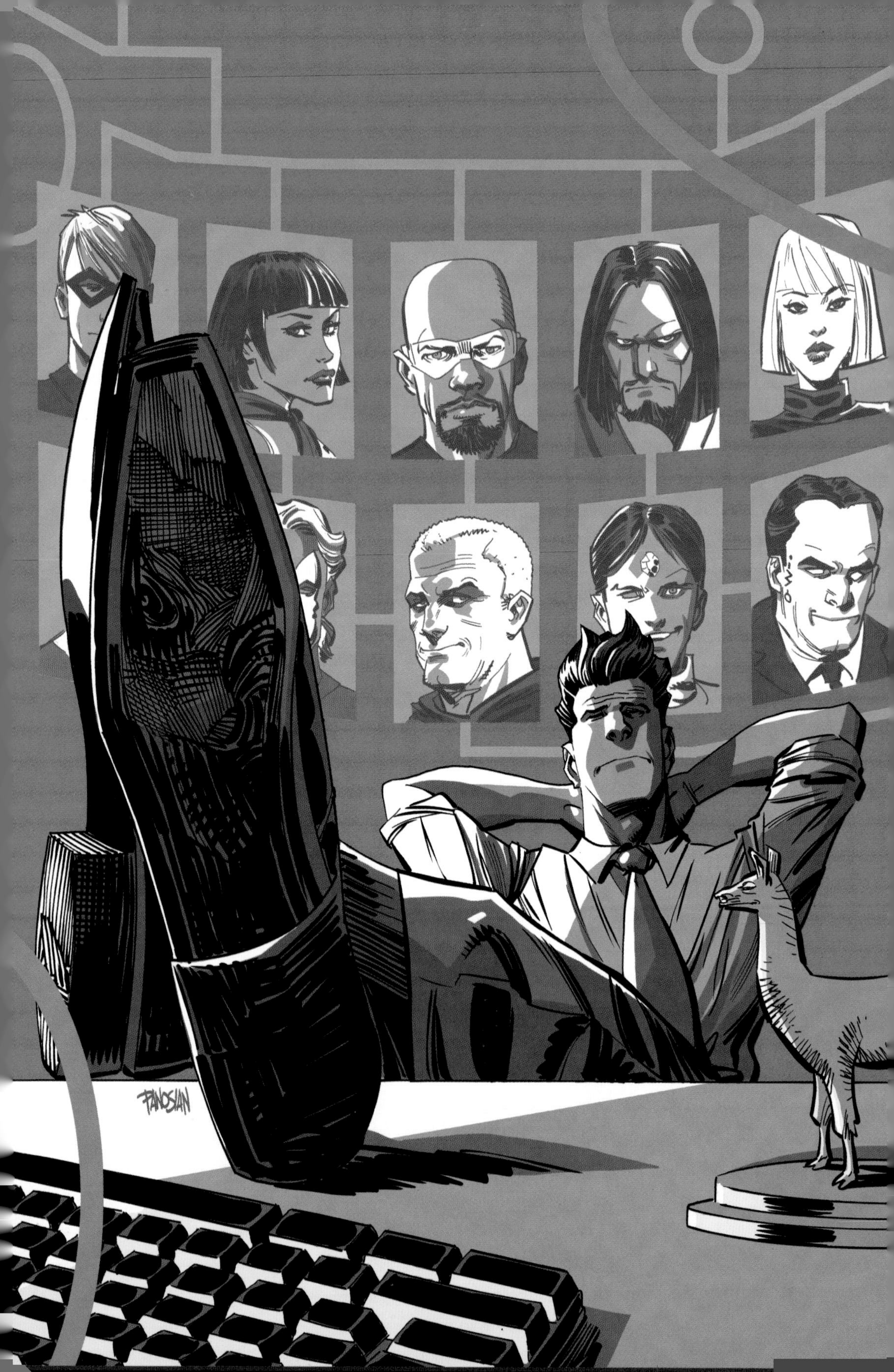
PANOSIAN

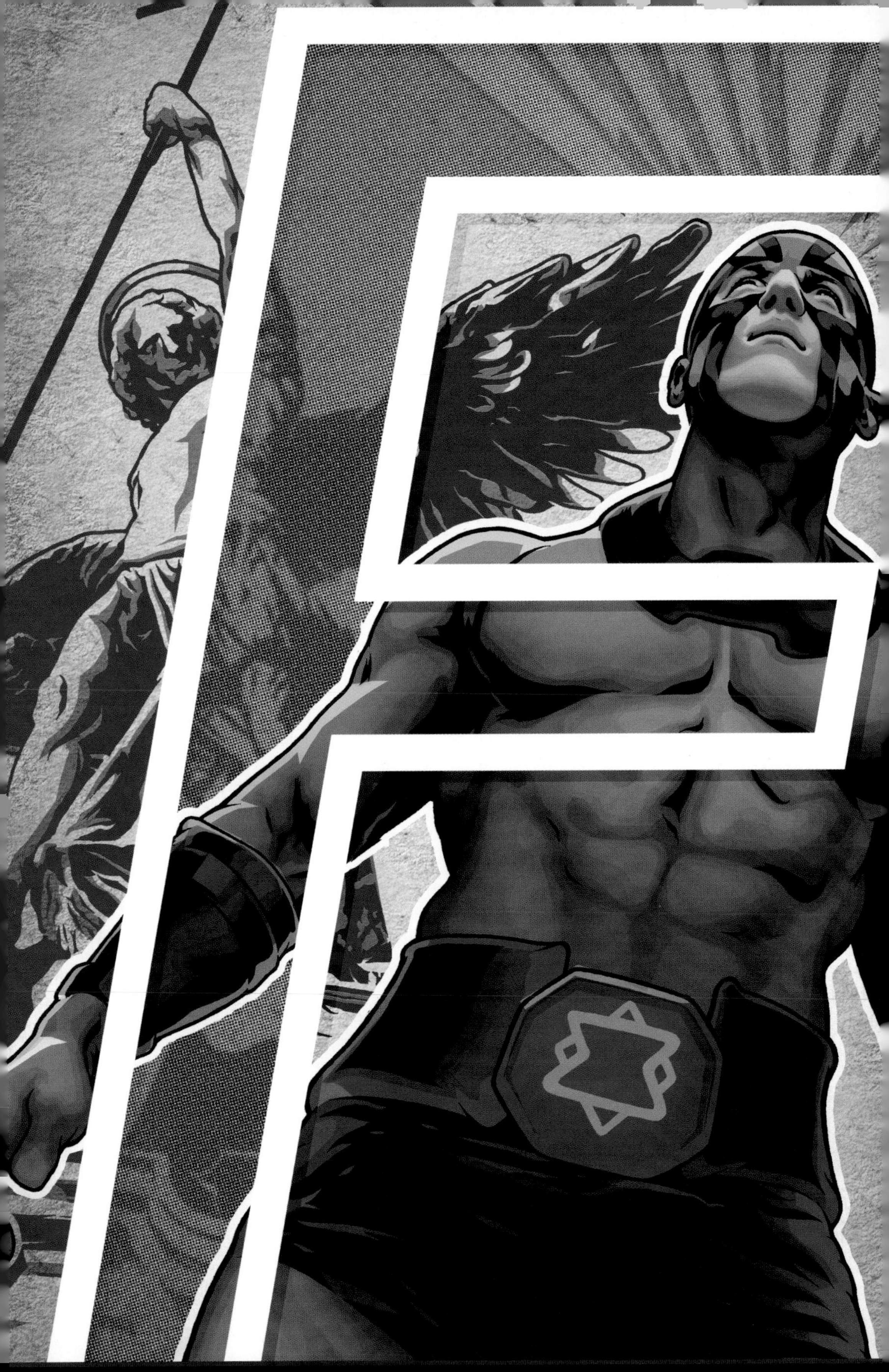

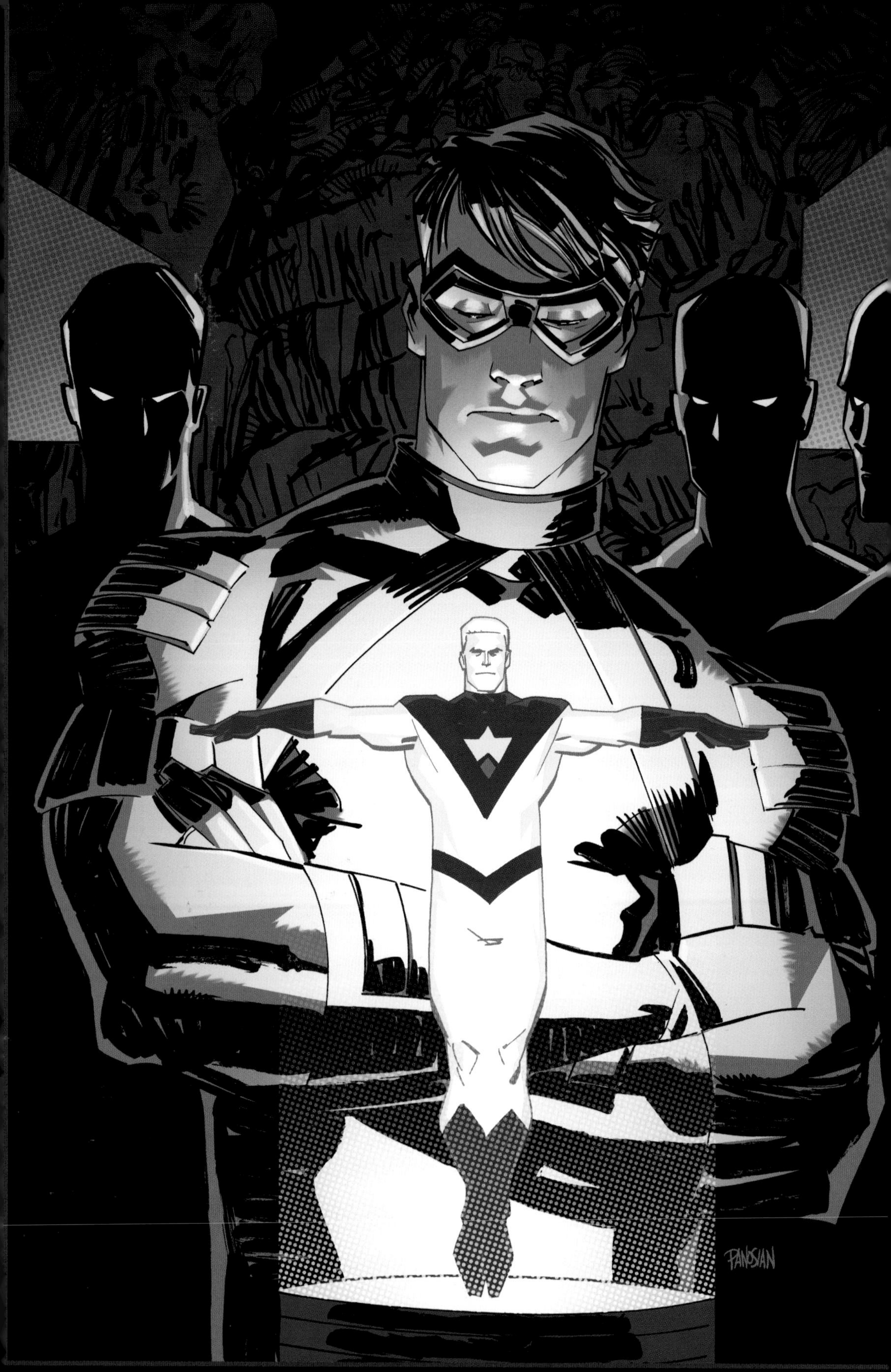
PANOSIAN

COVER 18A: DAN PANOSIAN

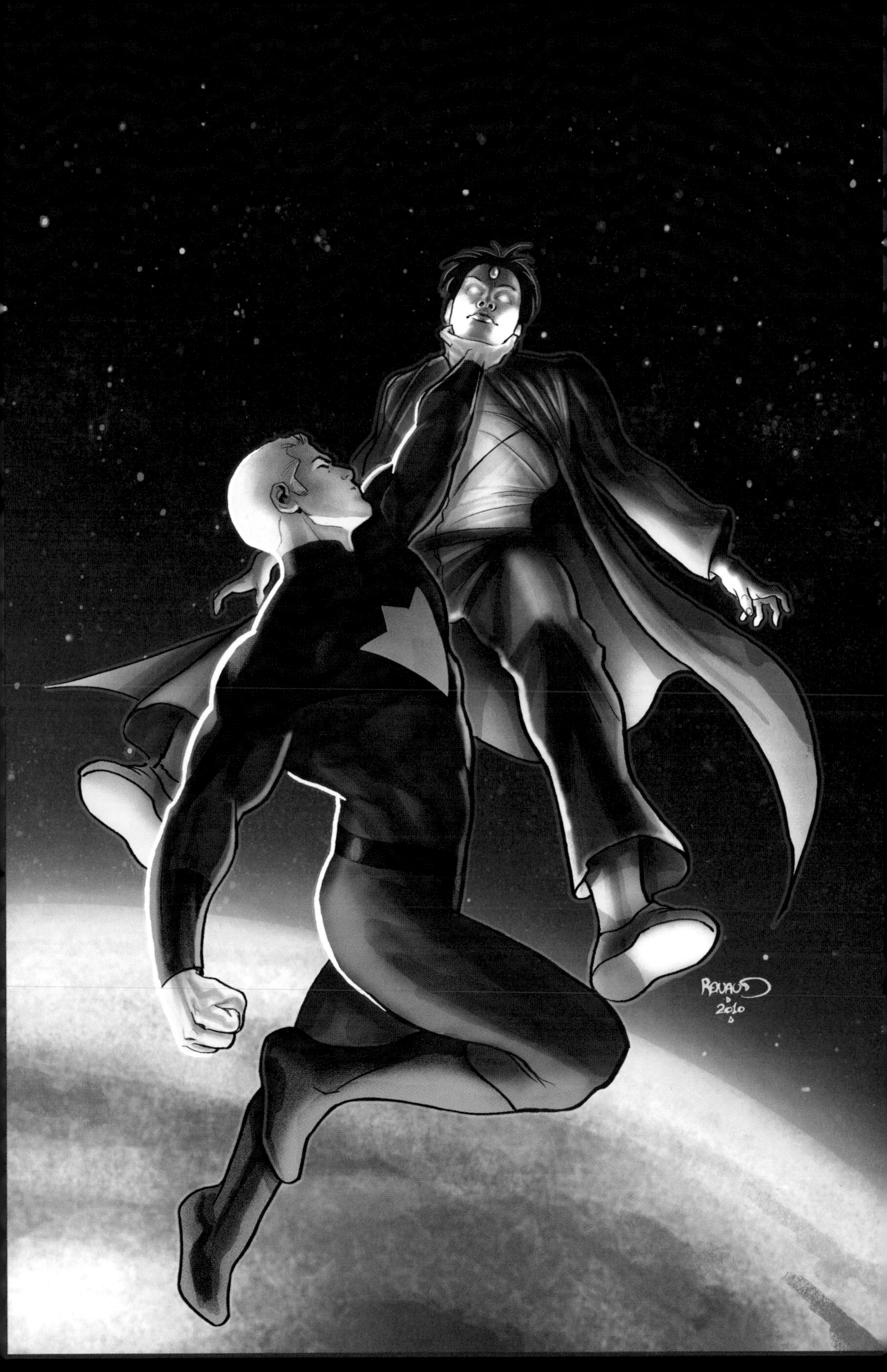

COVER 18B: PAUL RENAUD

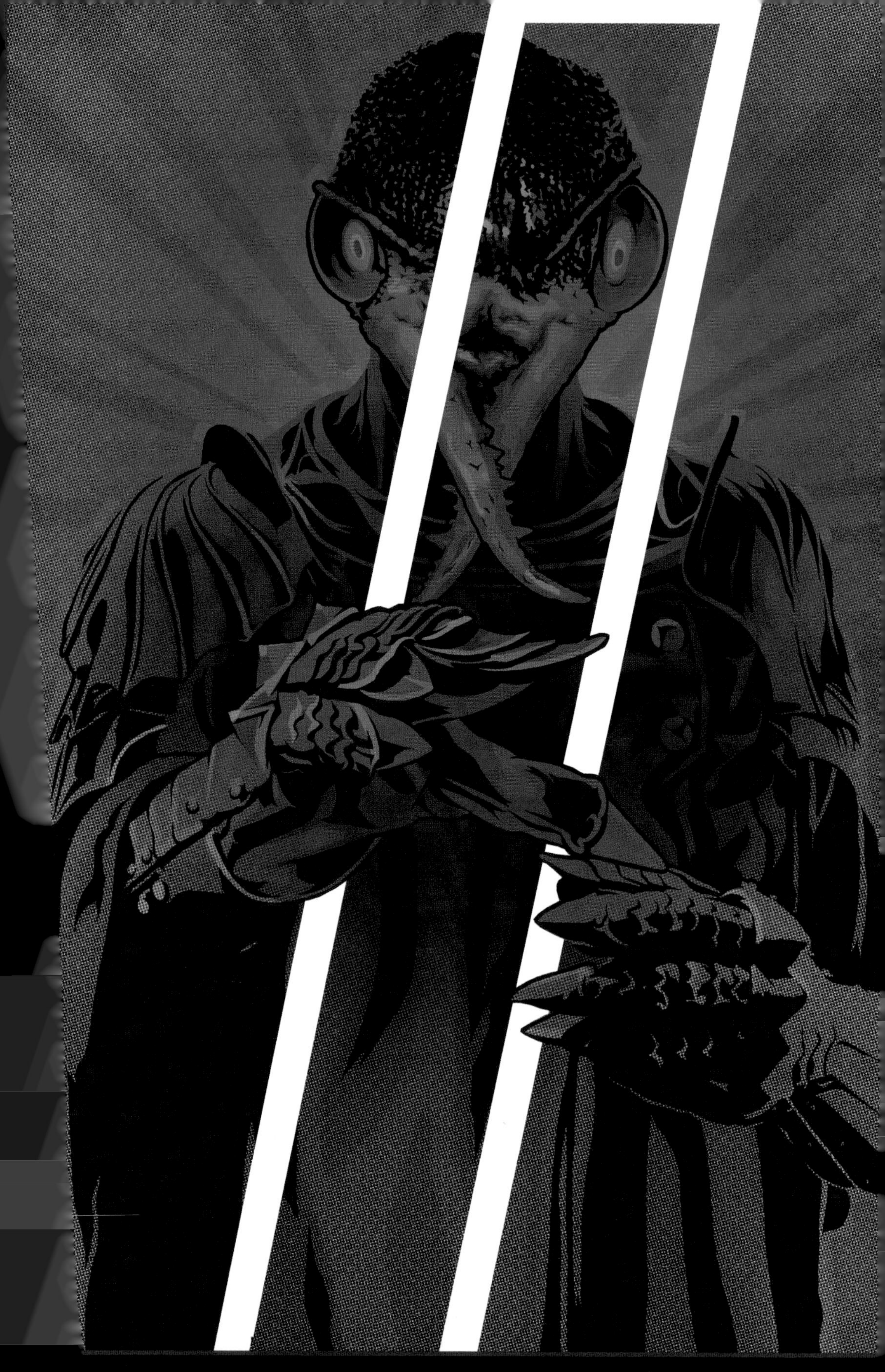

18C: JEFFREY SPOKES

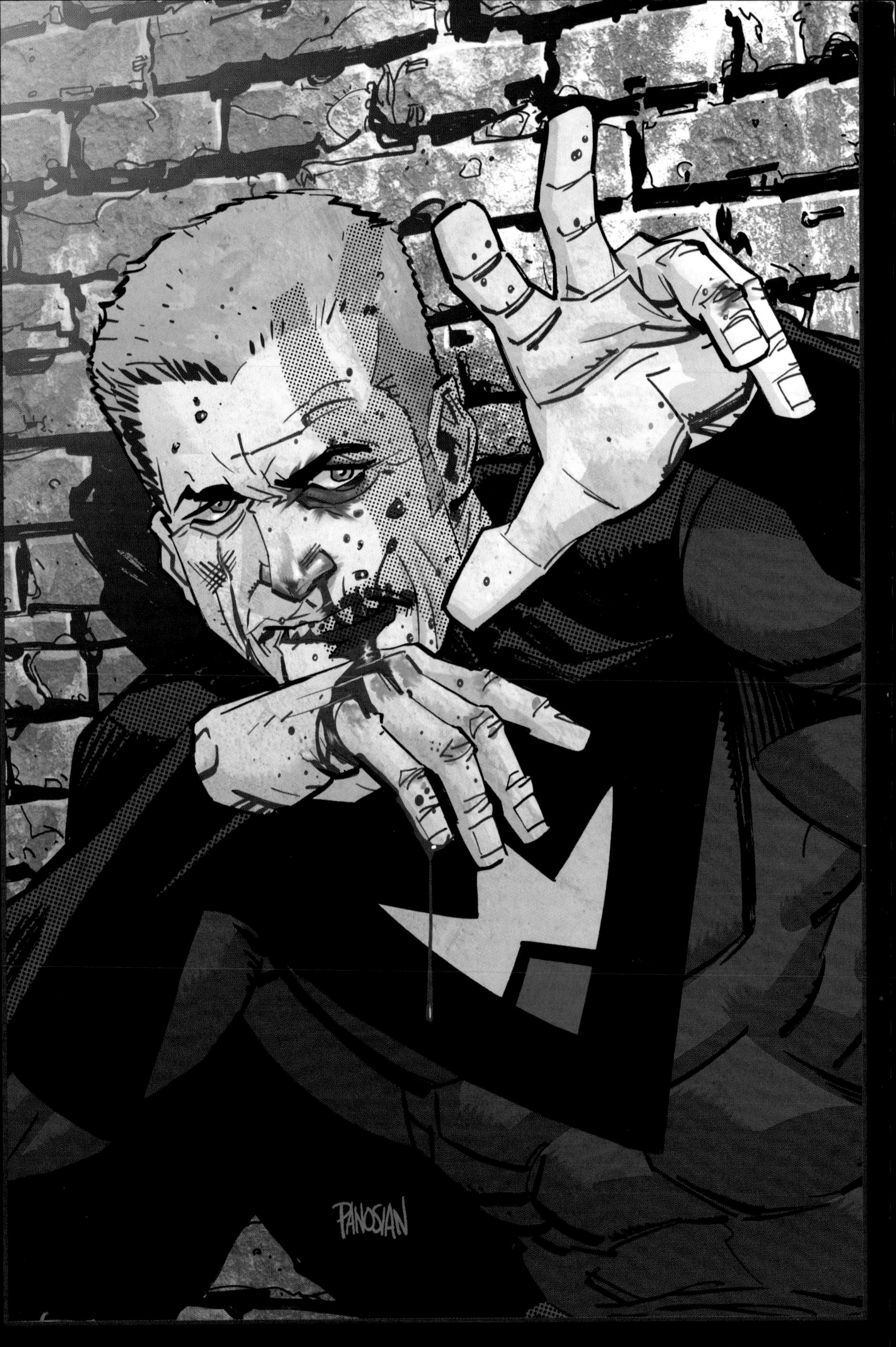
PANOSIAN

COVER 19A: DAN PANOSIAN

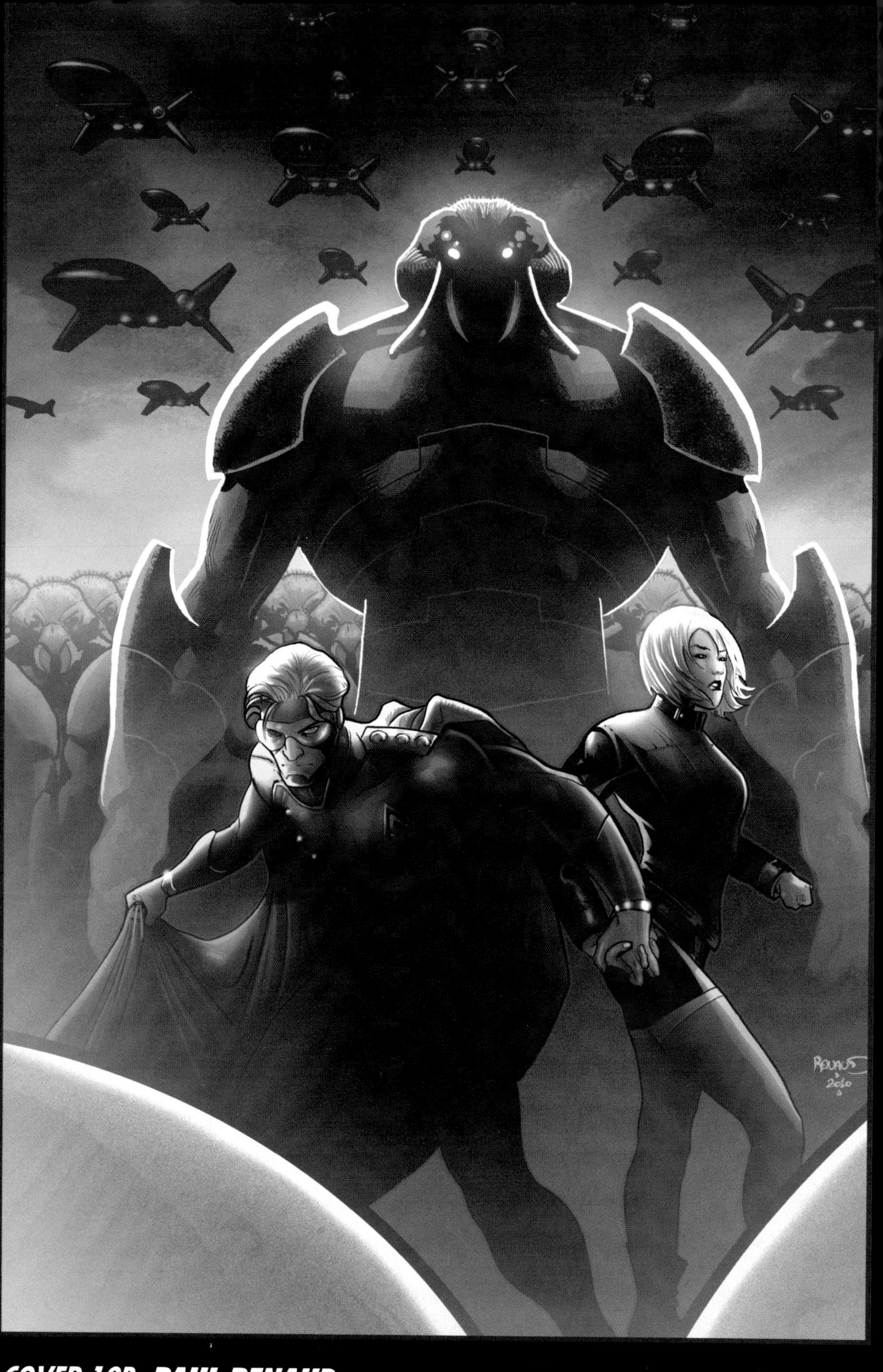

COVER 19B: PAUL RENAUD

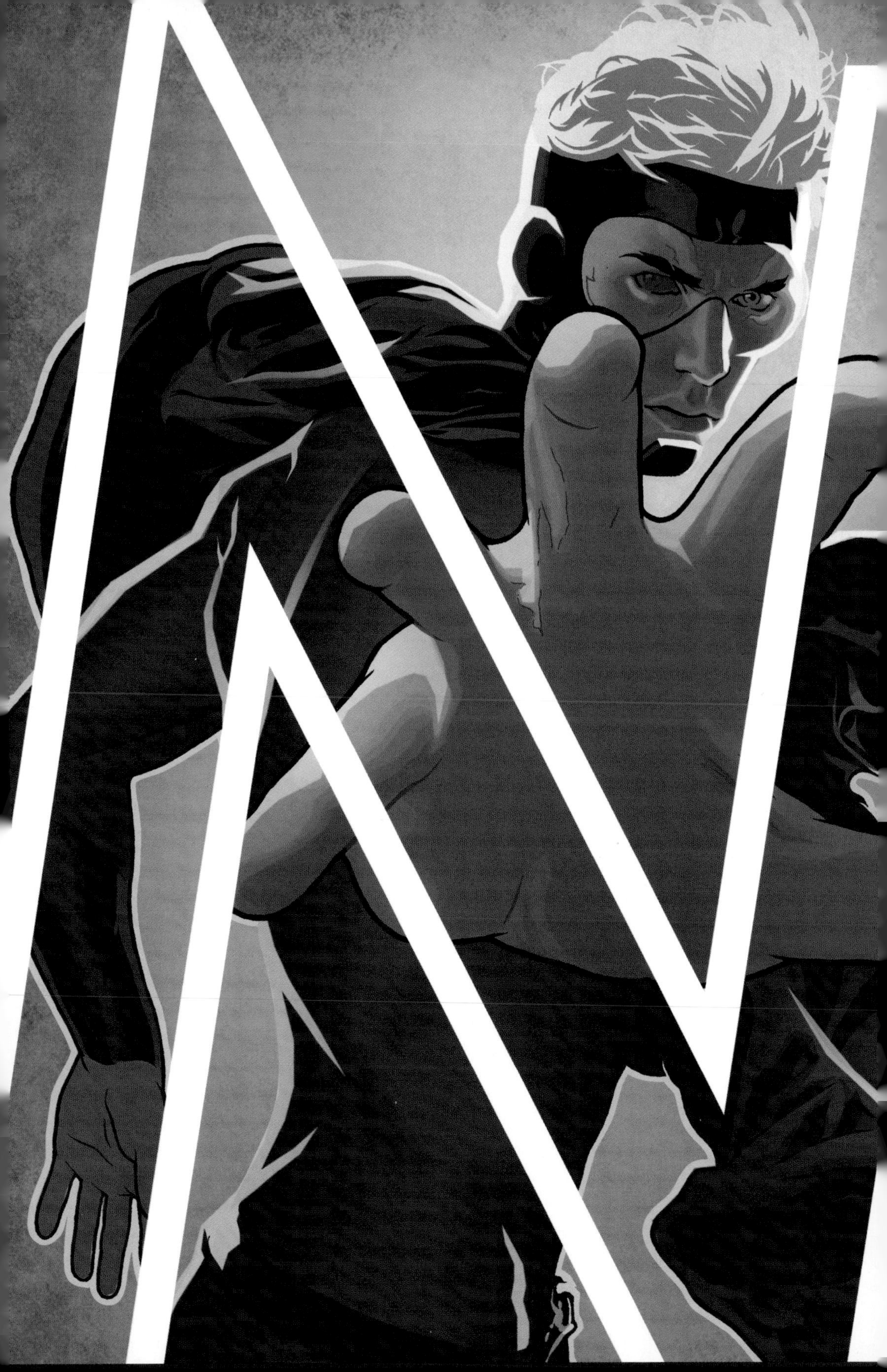

COVER 19C: JEFFREY SPOKES

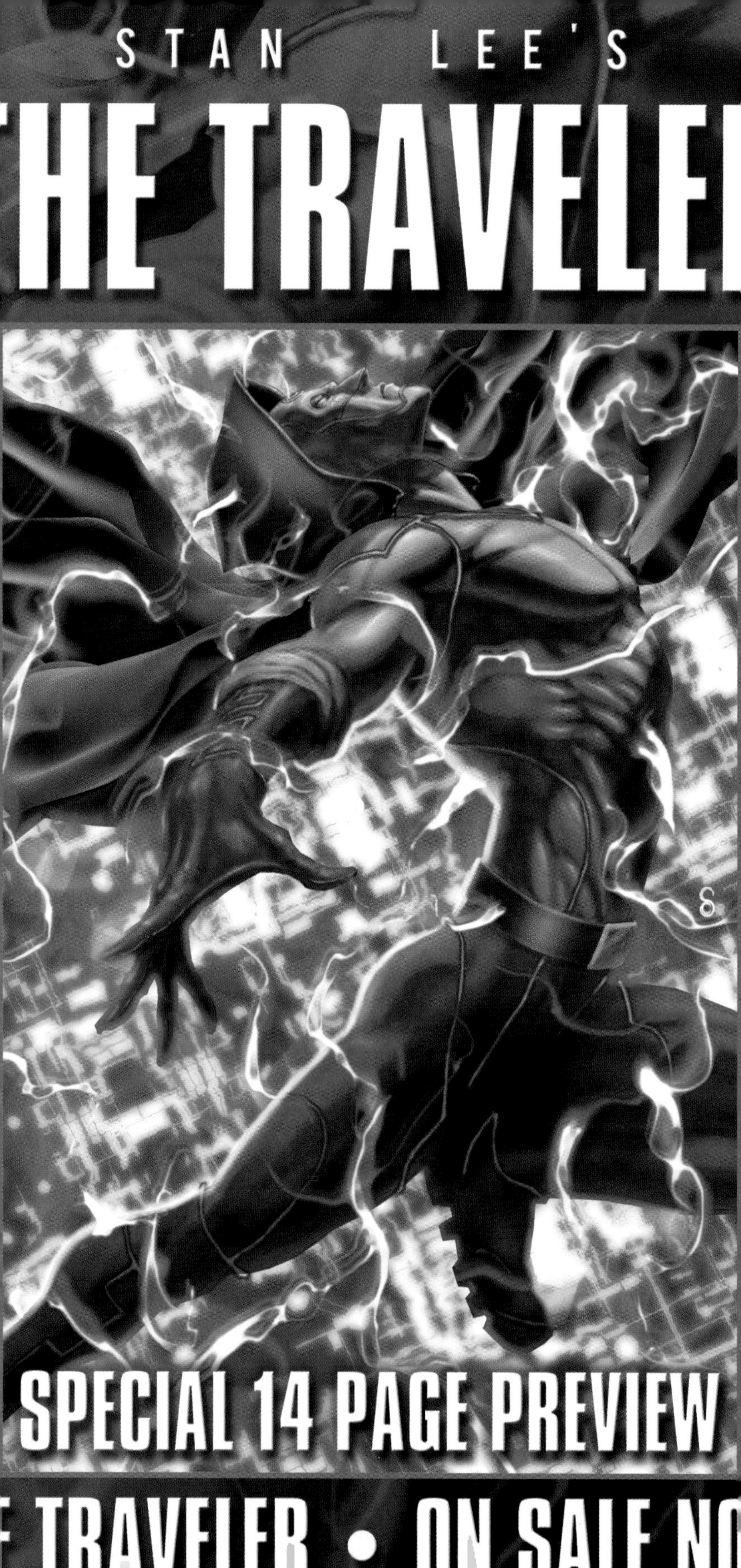
STAN LEE'S
HE TRAVELE
SPECIAL 14 PAGE PREVIEW
TRAVELER • ON SALE N

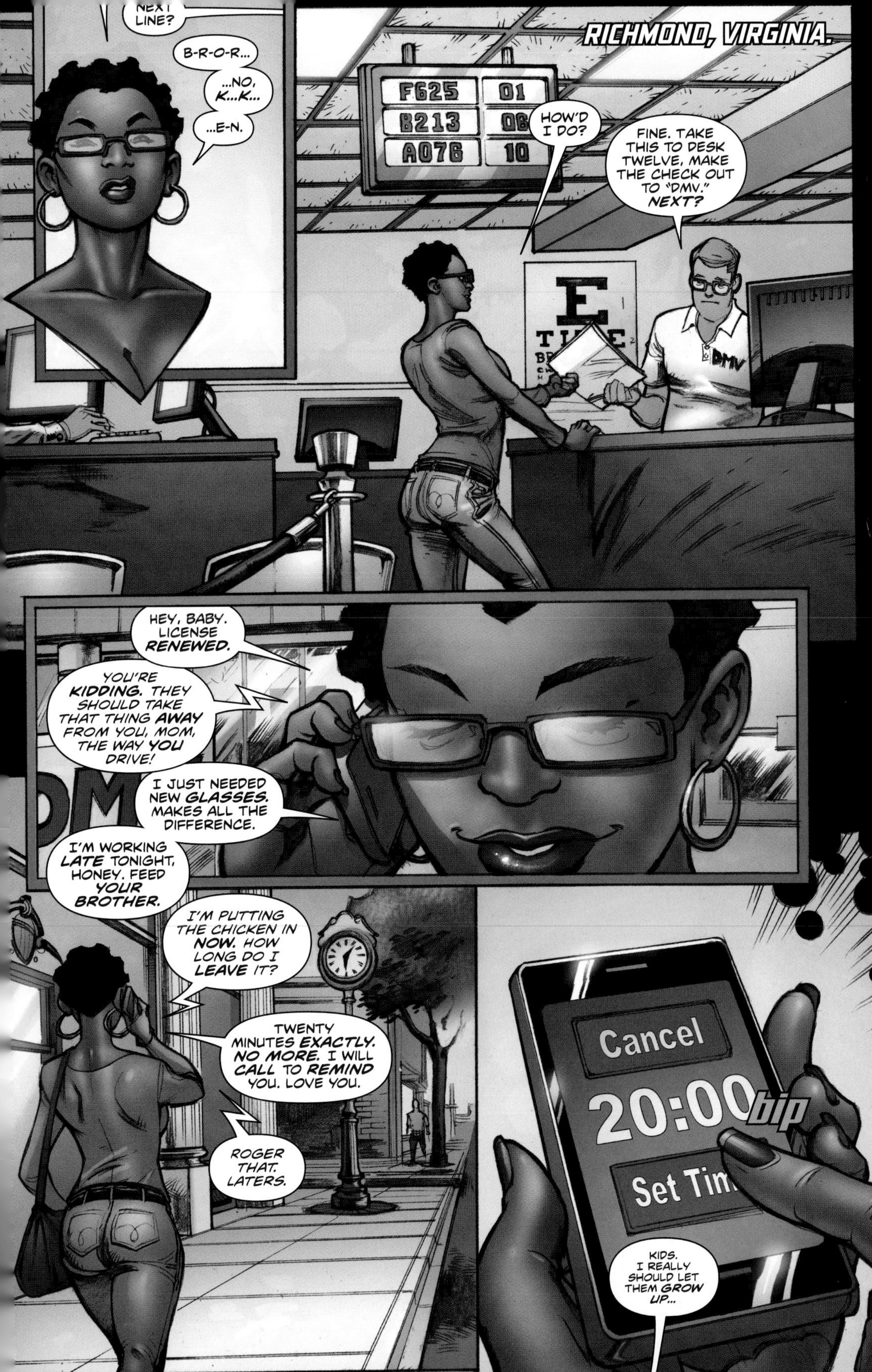
NEXT LINE?
B-R-O-R...
...NO, K...K...
...E-N.
RICHMOND, VIRGINIA.
F625 01
B213 06
A076 10
HOW'D I DO?
FINE. TAKE THIS TO DESK TWELVE, MAKE THE CHECK OUT TO "DMV." NEXT?
DMV
HEY, BABY. LICENSE RENEWED.
YOU'RE KIDDING. THEY SHOULD TAKE THAT THING AWAY FROM YOU, MOM, THE WAY YOU DRIVE!
I JUST NEEDED NEW GLASSES. MAKES ALL THE DIFFERENCE.
I'M WORKING LATE TONIGHT, HONEY. FEED YOUR BROTHER.
I'M PUTTING THE CHICKEN IN NOW. HOW LONG DO I LEAVE IT?
TWENTY MINUTES EXACTLY. NO MORE. I WILL CALL TO REMIND YOU. LOVE YOU.
ROGER THAT. LATERS.
Cancel
20:00
bip
Set Tim
KIDS. I REALLY SHOULD LET THEM GROW UP...

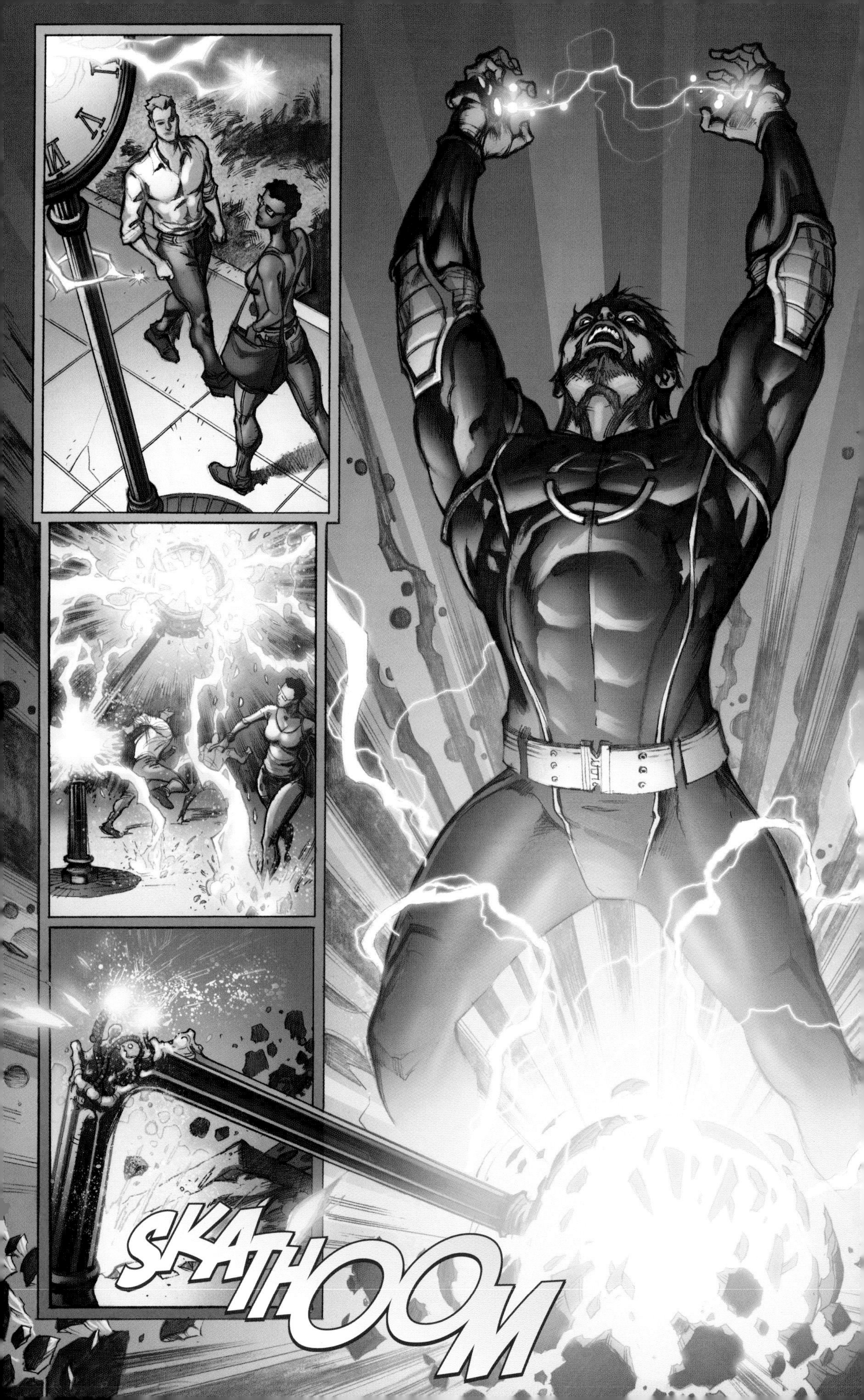
SKATHOOM

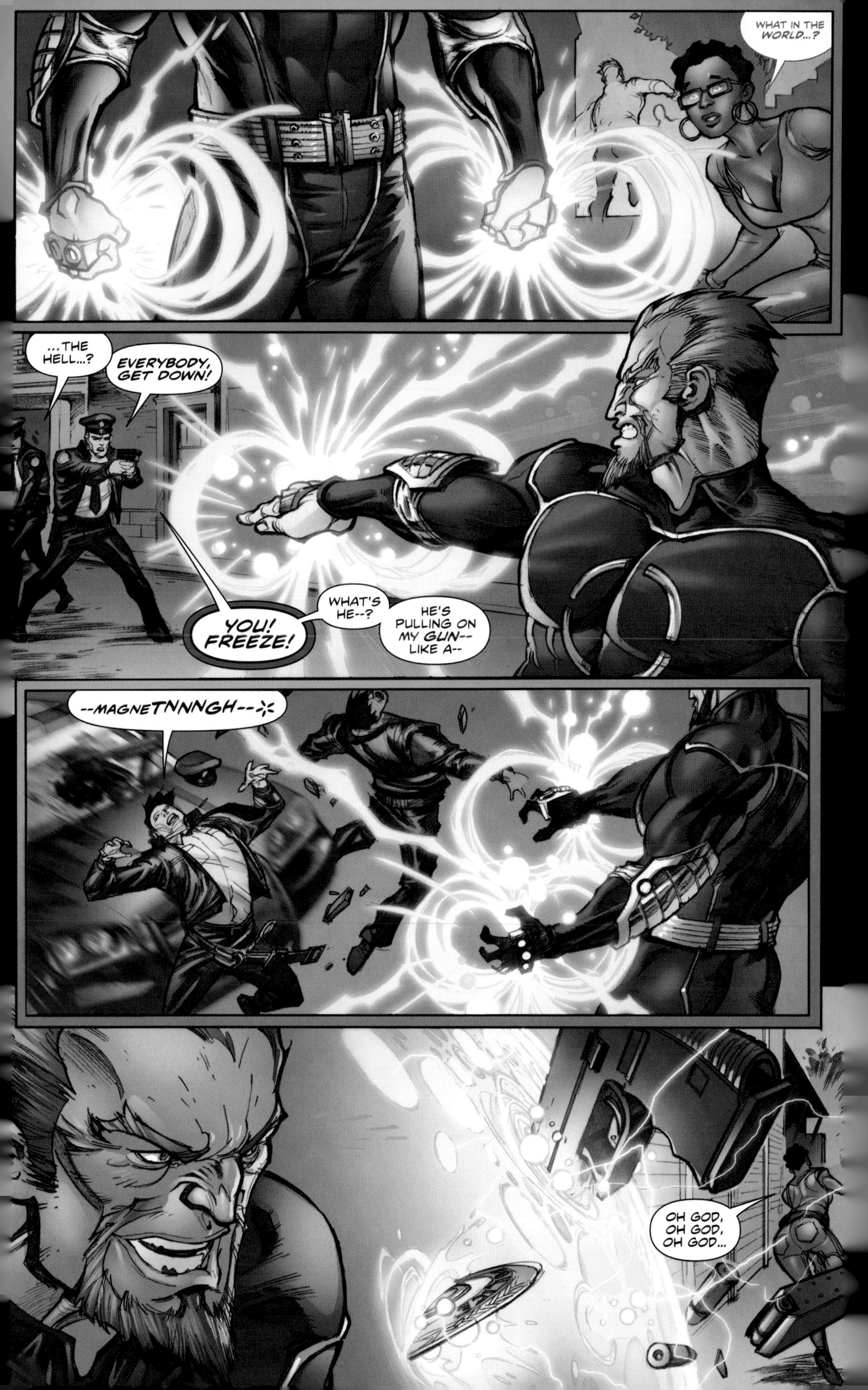
WHAT IN THE WORLD...?
...THE HELL...?
EVERYBODY, GET DOWN!
YOU! FREEZE!
WHAT'S HE--?
HE'S PULLING ON MY GUN-- LIKE A--
--MAGNETNNNGH--
OH GOD, OH GOD, OH GOD...

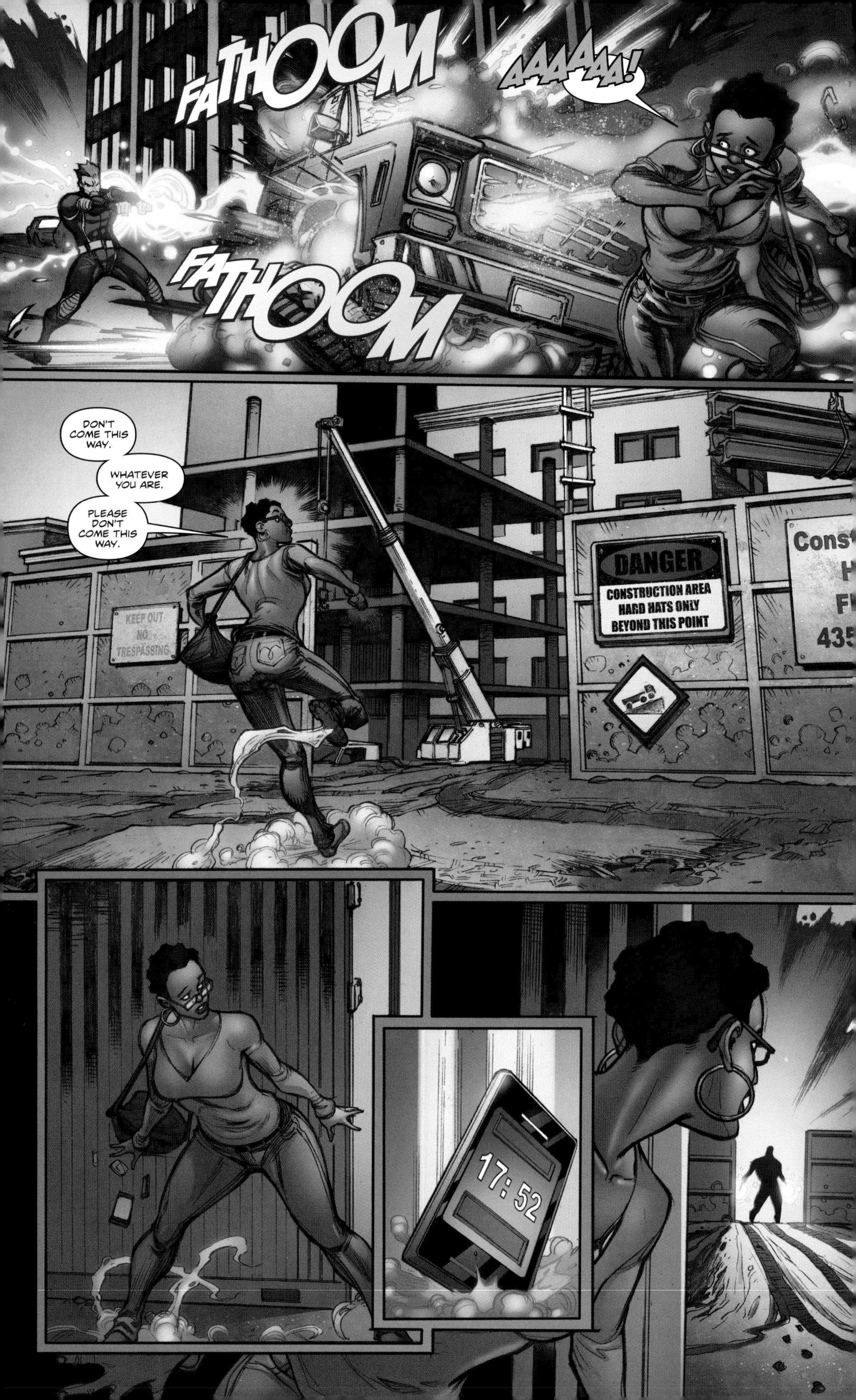
FATHOOM
AAAAAA!
FATHOOM
DON'T COME THIS WAY.
WHATEVER YOU ARE.
PLEASE DON'T COME THIS WAY.
KEEP OUT NO TRESPASSING
DANGER
CONSTRUCTION AREA HARD HATS ONLY BEYOND THIS POINT
17:52

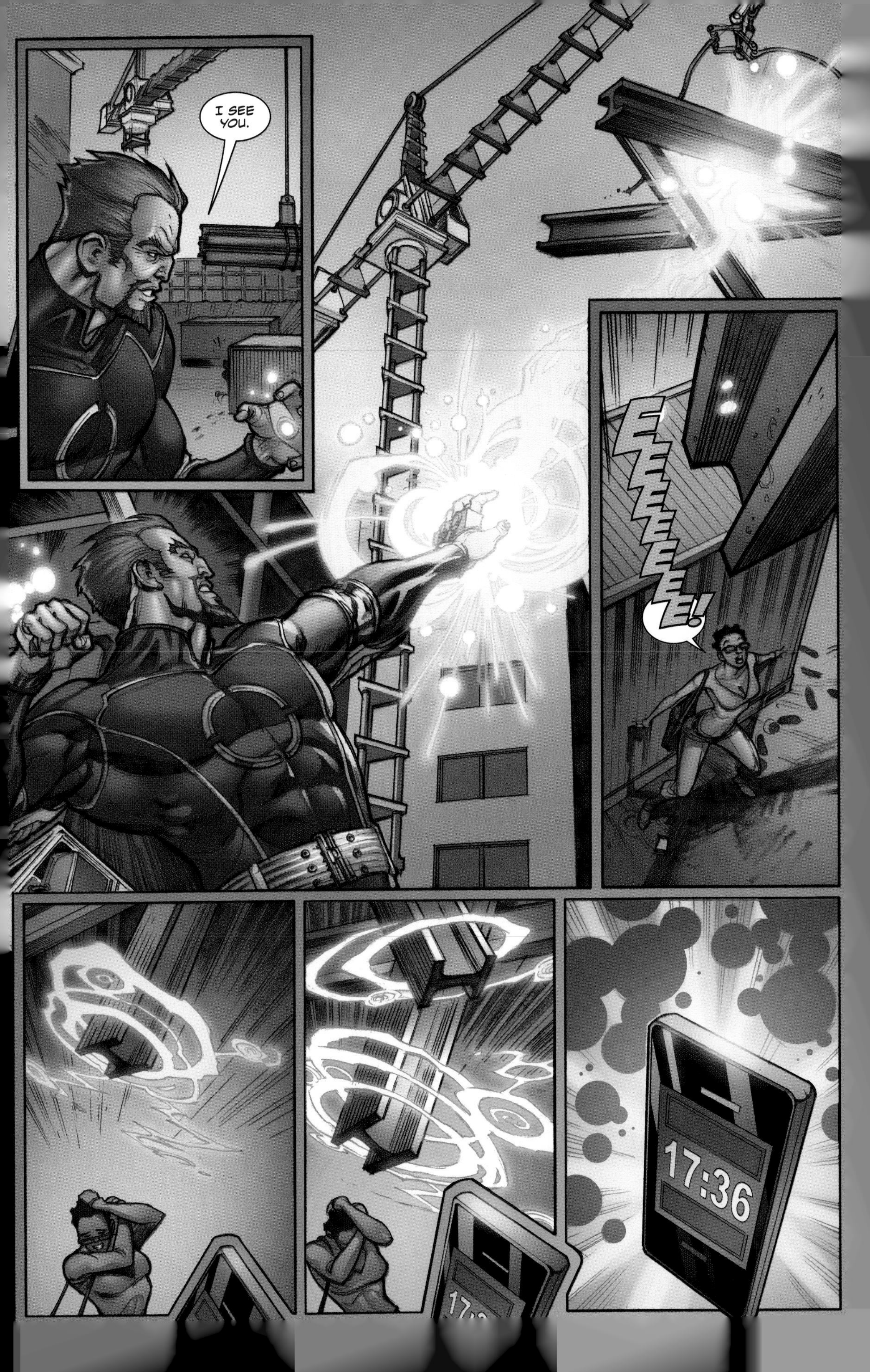
I SEE YOU.
EEEEEEE!
17:36

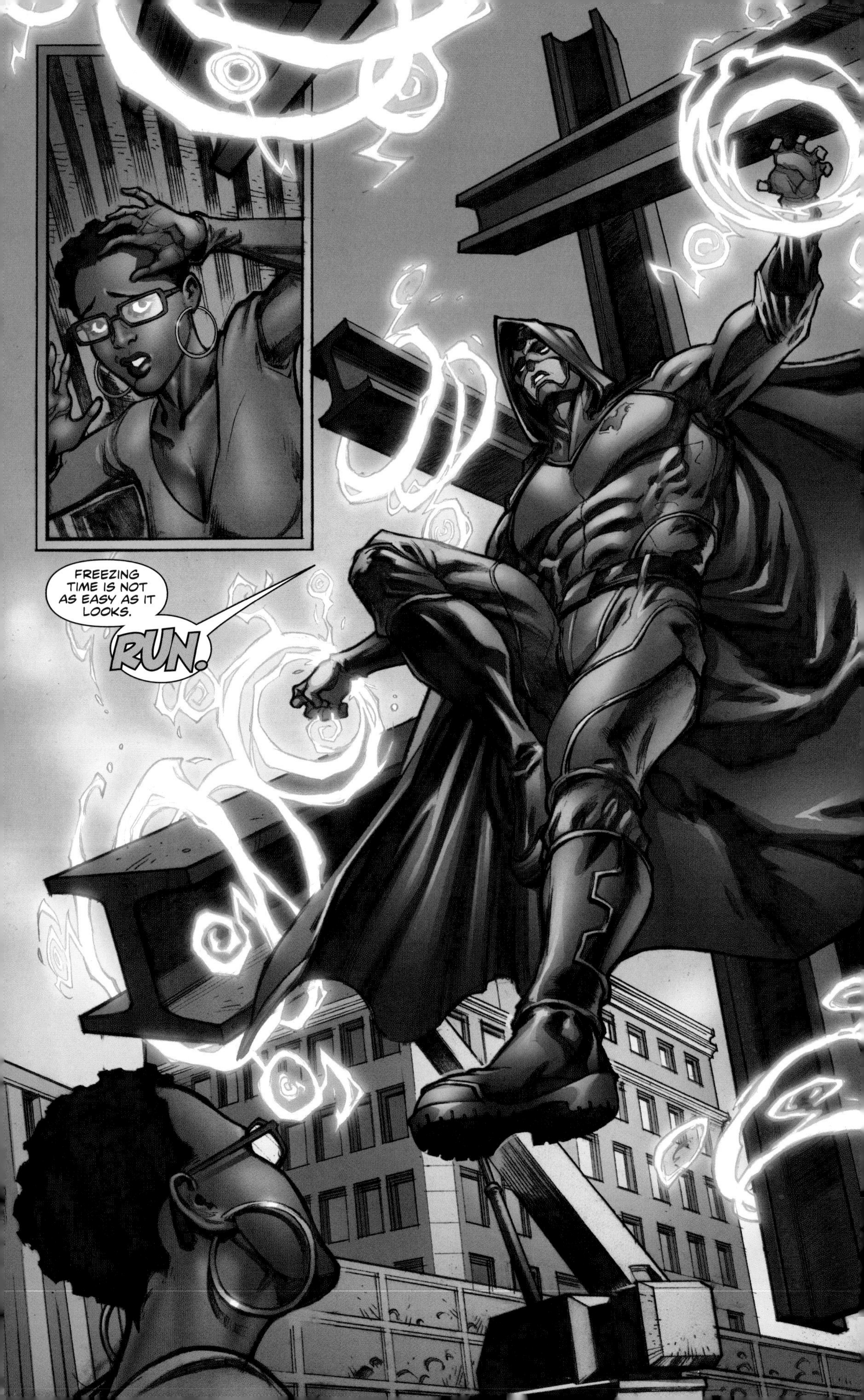
FREEZING TIME IS NOT AS EASY AS IT LOOKS.
RUN.

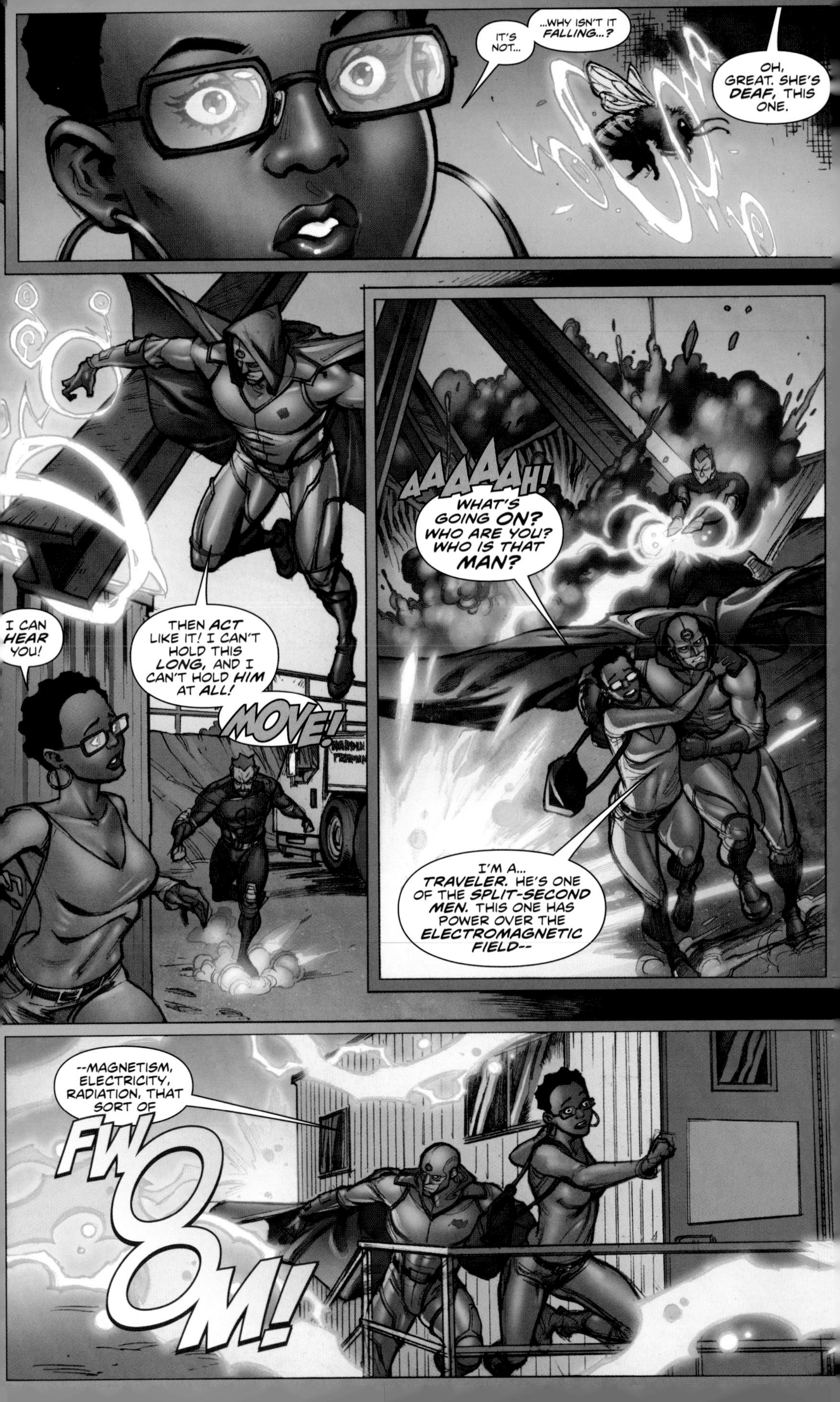
IT'S NOT...
...WHY ISN'T IT FALLING...?
OH, GREAT. SHE'S DEAF, THIS ONE.
I CAN HEAR YOU!
THEN ACT LIKE IT! I CAN'T HOLD THIS LONG, AND I CAN'T HOLD HIM AT ALL!
MOVE!
AAAAAH!
WHAT'S GOING ON? WHO ARE YOU? WHO IS THAT MAN?
I'M A... TRAVELER. HE'S ONE OF THE SPLIT-SECOND MEN. THIS ONE HAS POWER OVER THE ELECTROMAGNETIC FIELD--
--MAGNETISM, ELECTRICITY, RADIATION, THAT SORT OF
FWOOM!

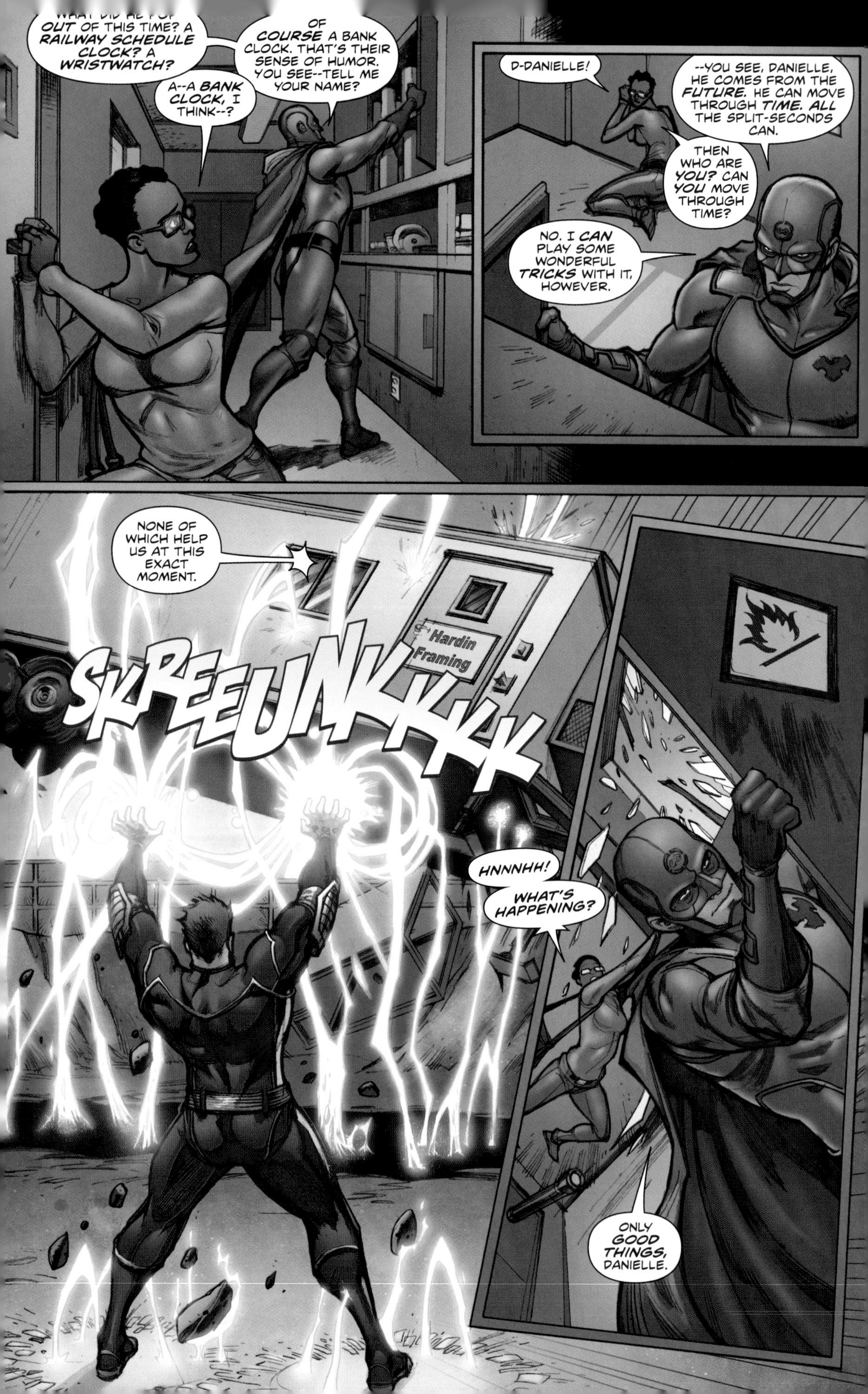
OUT OF THIS TIME? A RAILWAY SCHEDULE CLOCK? A WRISTWATCH?
OF COURSE A BANK CLOCK. THAT'S THEIR SENSE OF HUMOR. YOU SEE--TELL ME YOUR NAME?
A--A BANK CLOCK, I THINK--?
D-DANIELLE!
--YOU SEE, DANIELLE, HE COMES FROM THE FUTURE. HE CAN MOVE THROUGH TIME. ALL THE SPLIT-SECONDS CAN.
THEN WHO ARE YOU? CAN YOU MOVE THROUGH TIME?
NO. I CAN PLAY SOME WONDERFUL TRICKS WITH IT, HOWEVER.
NONE OF WHICH HELP US AT THIS EXACT MOMENT.
Hardin Framing
SKREEUNKKKK
HNNNHH!
WHAT'S HAPPENING?
ONLY GOOD THINGS, DANIELLE.

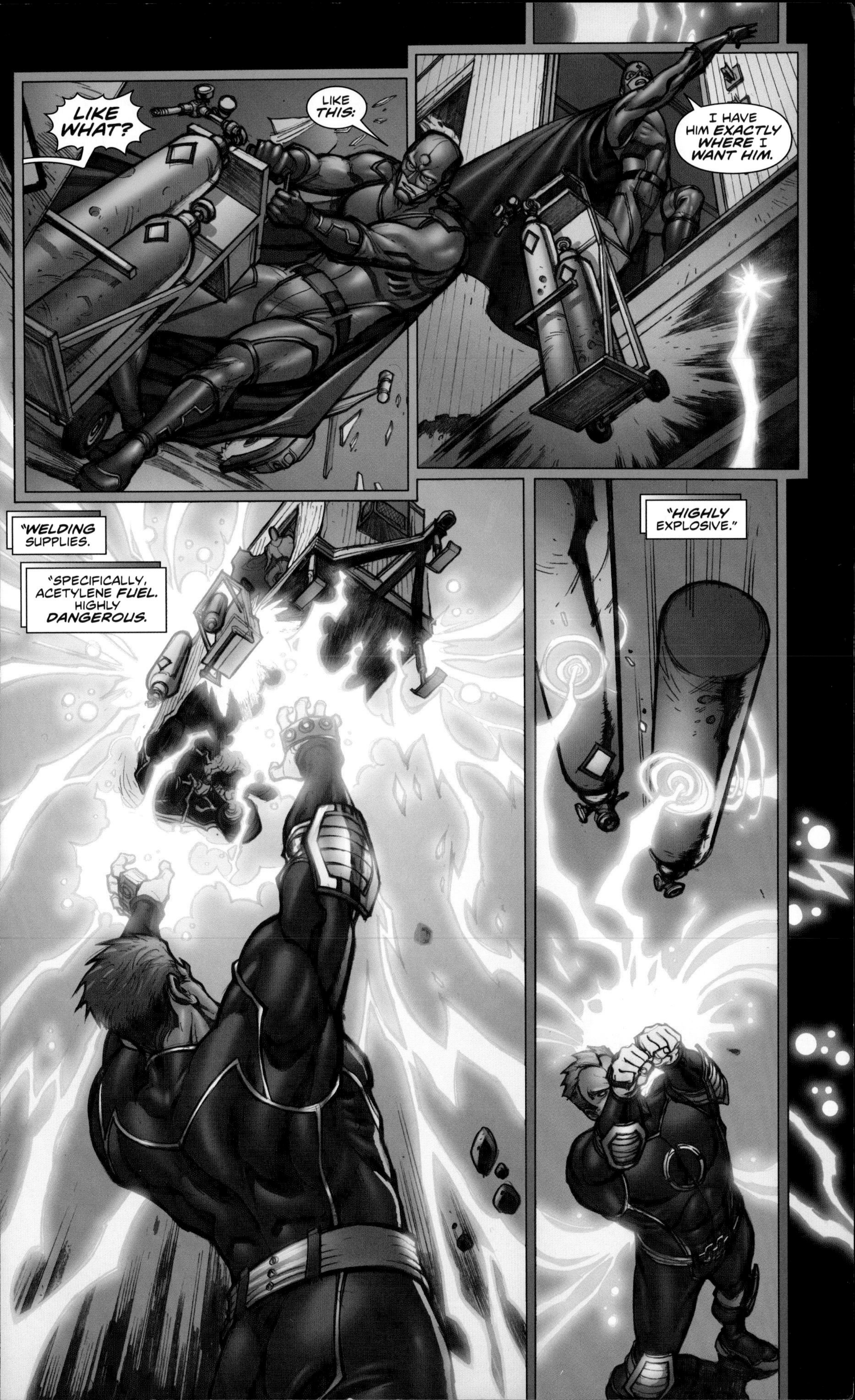
LIKE WHAT?
LIKE THIS:
I HAVE HIM EXACTLY WHERE I WANT HIM.
"WELDING SUPPLIES.
"SPECIFICALLY, ACETYLENE FUEL. HIGHLY DANGEROUS.
"HIGHLY EXPLOSIVE."

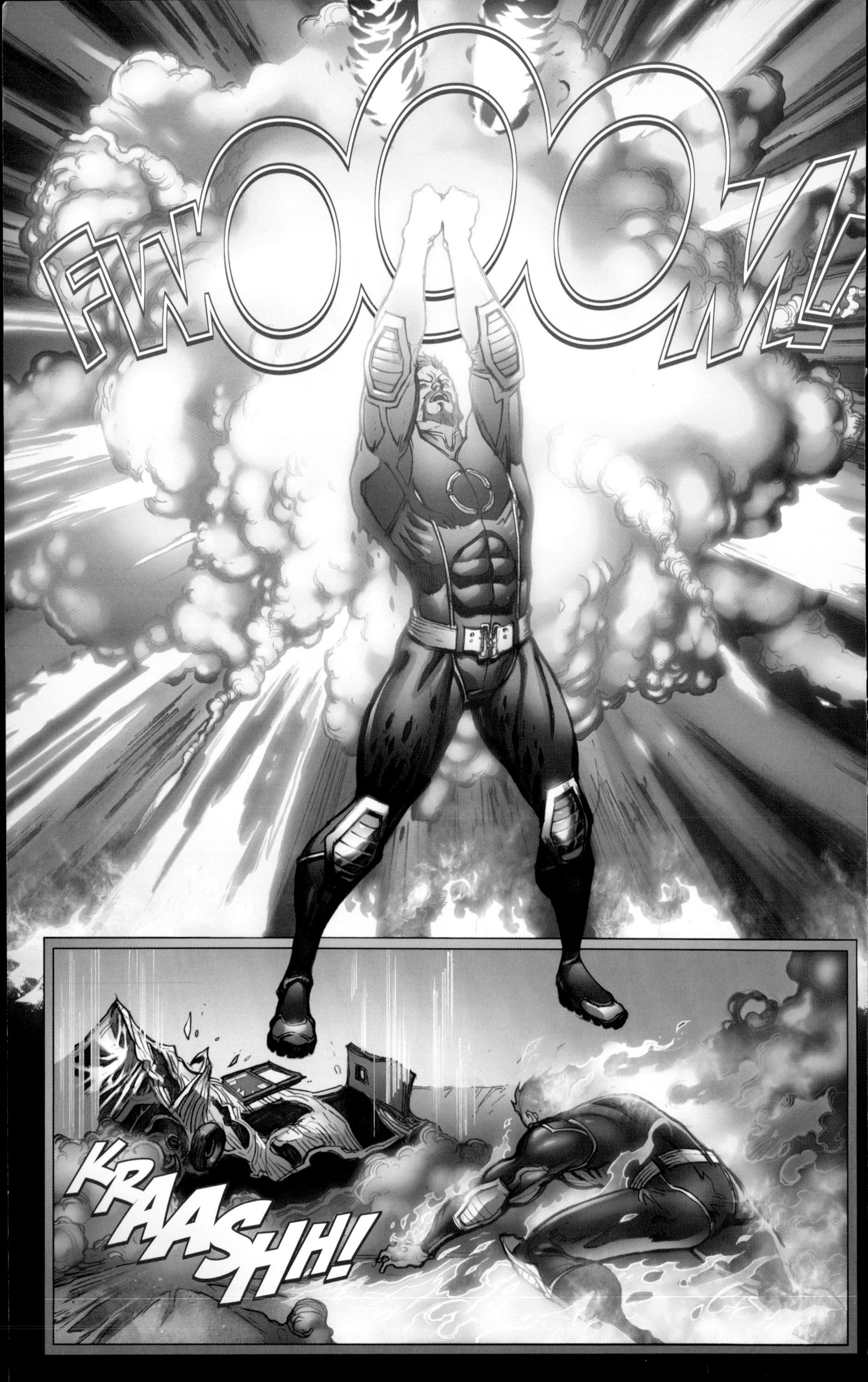
FWOOOM!!
KRAASHH!

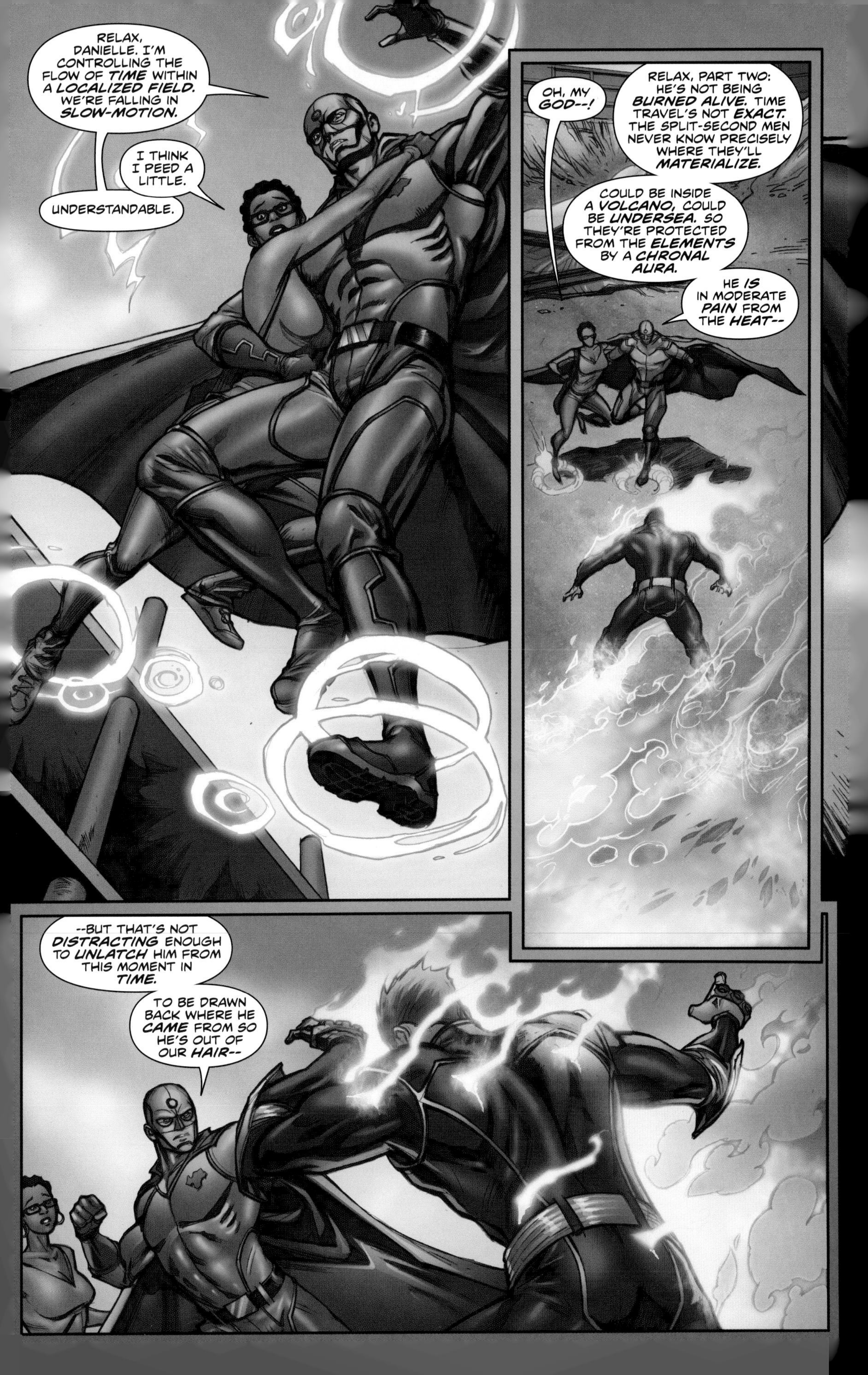
RELAX, DANIELLE. I'M CONTROLLING THE FLOW OF TIME WITHIN A LOCALIZED FIELD. WE'RE FALLING IN SLOW-MOTION.
I THINK I PEED A LITTLE.
UNDERSTANDABLE.
OH, MY GOD--!
RELAX, PART TWO: HE'S NOT BEING BURNED ALIVE. TIME TRAVEL'S NOT EXACT. THE SPLIT-SECOND MEN NEVER KNOW PRECISELY WHERE THEY'LL MATERIALIZE.
COULD BE INSIDE A VOLCANO, COULD BE UNDERSEA. SO THEY'RE PROTECTED FROM THE ELEMENTS BY A CHRONAL AURA.
HE IS IN MODERATE PAIN FROM THE HEAT--
--BUT THAT'S NOT DISTRACTING ENOUGH TO UNLATCH HIM FROM THIS MOMENT IN TIME.
TO BE DRAWN BACK WHERE HE CAME FROM SO HE'S OUT OF OUR HAIR--

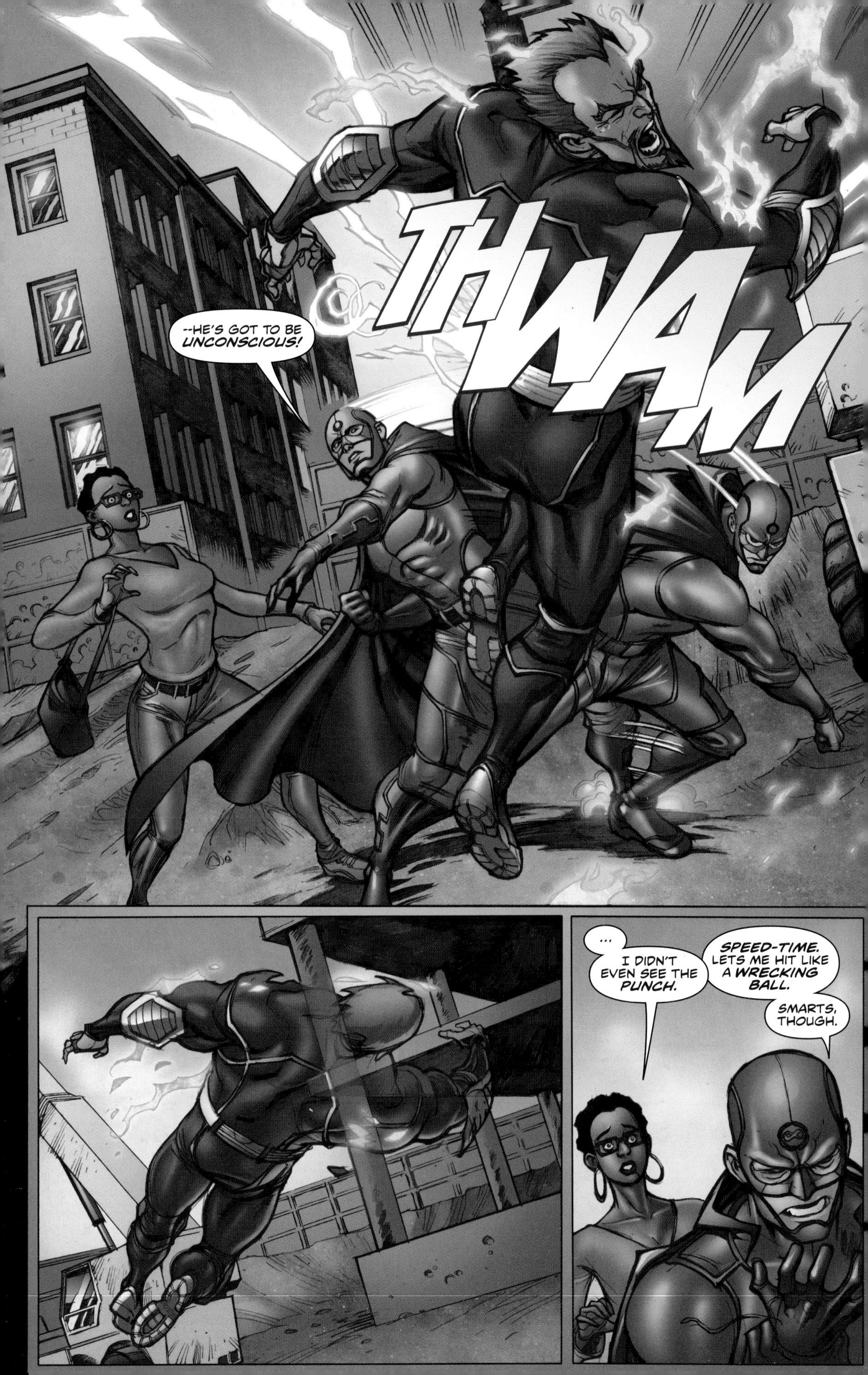
--HE'S GOT TO BE UNCONSCIOUS!
THWAM
...
I DIDN'T EVEN SEE THE PUNCH.
SPEED-TIME. LETS ME HIT LIKE A WRECKING BALL.
SMARTS, THOUGH.

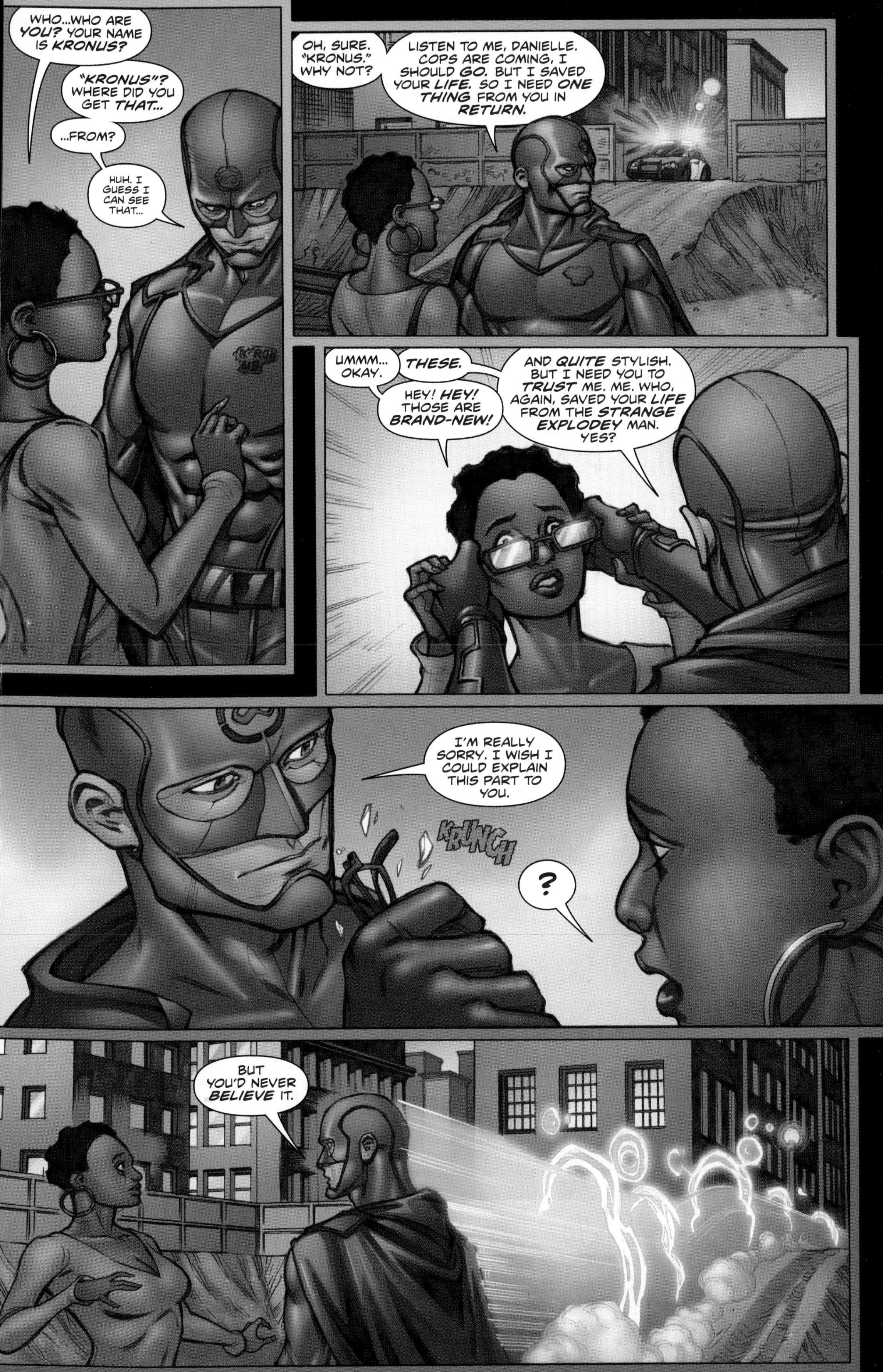
WHO...WHO ARE YOU? YOUR NAME IS KRONUS?
"KRONUS"? WHERE DID YOU GET THAT...
...FROM?
HUH. I GUESS I CAN SEE THAT...
OH, SURE. "KRONUS." WHY NOT?
LISTEN TO ME, DANIELLE. COPS ARE COMING, I SHOULD GO. BUT I SAVED YOUR LIFE. SO I NEED ONE THING FROM YOU IN RETURN.
UMMM... OKAY.
THESE.
HEY! HEY! THOSE ARE BRAND-NEW!
AND QUITE STYLISH. BUT I NEED YOU TO TRUST ME. ME. WHO, AGAIN, SAVED YOUR LIFE FROM THE STRANGE EXPLODEY MAN. YES?
I'M REALLY SORRY. I WISH I COULD EXPLAIN THIS PART TO YOU.
KRUNCH
?
BUT YOU'D NEVER BELIEVE IT.

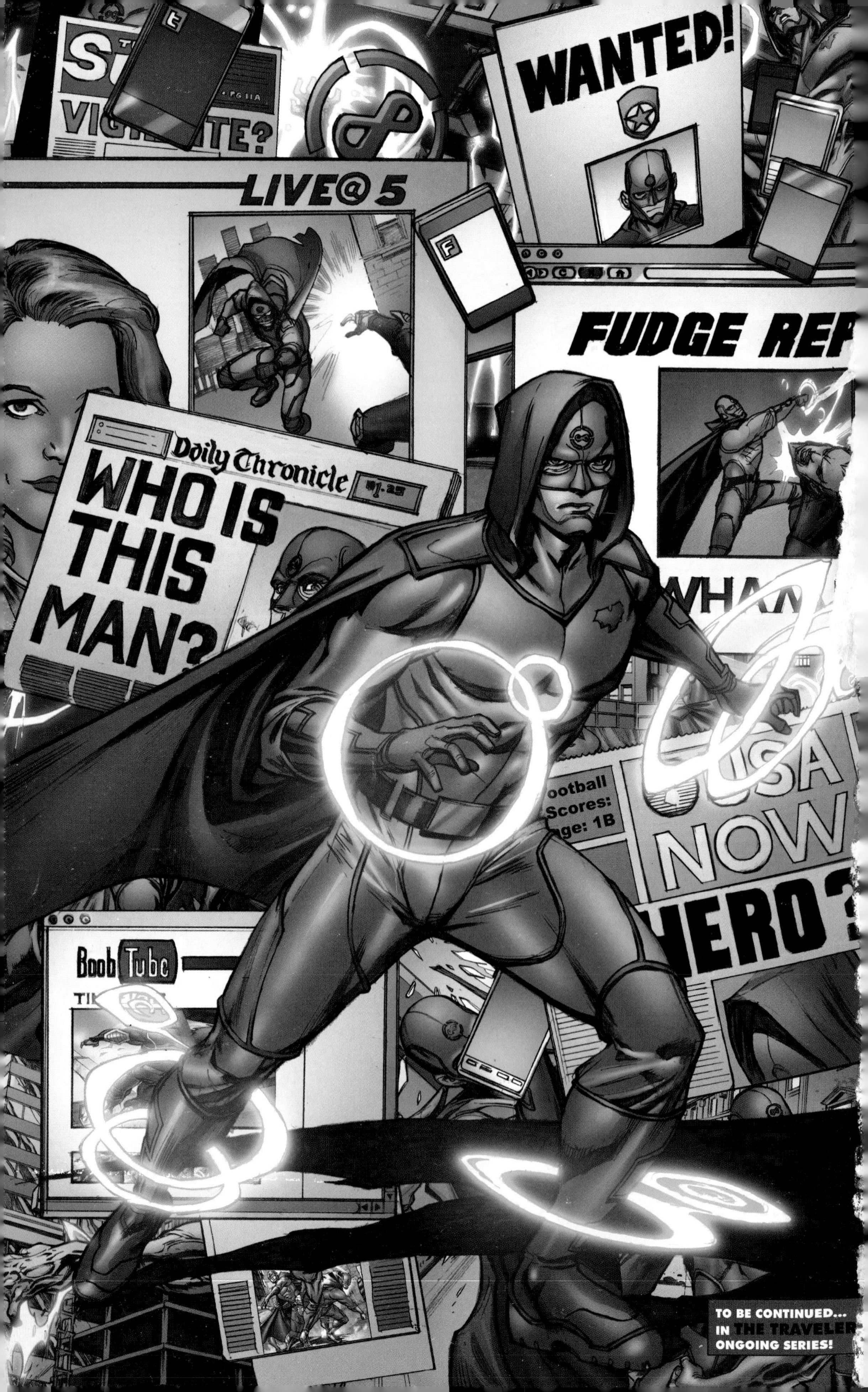
WANTED!
LIVE@5
FUDGE REP
Daily Chronicle
$1.25
WHO IS THIS MAN?
ootball
Scores:
ge: 1B
USA NOW
HERO?
Boob Tube
TO BE CONTINUED...
IN THE TRAVELER
ONGOING SERIES!